ELEMENTS OF DESIGN

Donald M. Anderson, *University of Wisconsin*

Holt, Rinehart and Winston

New York · Chicago · San Francisco · Toronto · London

acknowledgments

Thanks go to my colleagues of the Department of Art and Art Education of the University of Wisconsin for furnishing both classroom projects and stimulating suggestions. From sister laboratories over the country many other teachers offered student projects and useful comment on subjects to be covered. A few of the many to whom I am indebted are such creative teachers as Neil Welliver, Josephine Ainsworth, Hannes Beckman, H. Douglas Pickering, Misch Kohn, Helen Patton, Norman Gorbaty, and David Pease.

Friends in the University of Wisconsin community, distinguished in their fields of research, helped with leads to stimulating pictorial material, translations, and special knowledge. Among these were Hugh Iltis, Milton Barnett, John Kienitz, Paul MacKendrick, Julian Harris, Lemuel Fraser, Emma Fisk, and Karl Smith. Among the many library and collection specialists who helped on difficult questions of source were Felix Pollak, Curator of Rare Books; Helen Northrup and staff in reference; Helen Crawford, Medical Librarian; and Iconography Curator Paul Vanderbilt of the State Historical Society. And a deep bow to the staff of the Photographic Laboratory, where skill was exceeded only by patience.

Special thanks go to officials of these institutions: Forest Products Laboratory, Madison; The Metropolitan Museum of Art, New York; Eastman Kodak Company, Rochester; the American Museum of Natural History, New York; Bibliothèque Nationale, Paris; Hermitage Museum, Leningrad; South African Museum, Capetown; and the Museum of Modern Art, New York, with Willard Tangen of its Photographic Services deserving special mention.

The very many business institutions in the United States who provided service gratis are too numerous to mention. Many, of course, are sponsors of our best efforts in the fields of design and education. Scores of publishing firms in the United States and Europe offered visual material and valuable information.

Thanks go to such busy designers as Herb Lubalin, Joseph Low, Bradbury Thompson, Gene Federico, Ralph Coburn, J. Alcorn, and Paul Rand. These and many others working in areas of design for printing contributed fine pieces.

Among the many contemporary art figures who graciously contributed examples of work are Vin Giuliani, Peter Takal, Stanley William Hayter, Robert Gwathmey, Max Ernst, Gregorio Prestopino, Barbara Ellison Fumagalli, Ben Shahn, and Michael Ponce de Leon. Distinguished photographers Walker Evans, Aaron Siskind, and Val Telberg lent their talent.

Perhaps the person helping most was Marjorie Elizabeth Anderson, who seemed not to tire.

preface

The material in this book is arranged to help an instructor prepare a foundation college-level course in two-dimensional graphic representation and to help a student understand it. We now realize that all concepts of the design course, no matter how they may differ, preclude the idea of design as ornamentation, or arrangement, or the expression of modern technology. The foundation course in design is in reality concerned with the structure of effective communication in world art and with the structure of our environment, the ultimate source of form. With the field thus broadly defined, our problem is in selection and reduction. In this task *Elements of Design* seeks to initiate those studio and study experiences which will prepare students for advanced work in a number of areas: painting, graphics, commercial design, and so on. The course structure of today's college reflects the spectrum of career opportunities somewhat more completely than it once did, and has rather broadened our concept of the foundation design course.

As we know, students may be motivated through pictorial material. *Elements of Design* seeks to practice in book form what instructors preach on this subject, and it makes a special effort to relate classroom experiences to those of the students' backgrounds. An ever increasing number of students enrolling in foundation design courses are from other areas of the college. These students may not have developed skills or a sophisticated understanding of art structure, yet their understanding of structure in such fields as physics, zoology, and botany may be quite sophisticated indeed. The pictorial matter in this text is designed to suggest ways in which students with special interests may contribute to the cooperative classroom effort and to suggest to the high school art specialist that structure is a somewhat broader subject than he may have suspected.

In general plan this text proceeds gradually from easy to difficult. Thus Line is toward the beginning, Simplification of Form in the middle, and Images Out of Order, encompassing surrealist imagery, is at the end of the book. Since there are no absolutes in a foundation course, natural sequences are broken up to provide variety in reading.

The first section on Motivation in Design provides background material. It is a natural depository for a number of personal opinions, and as such should encourage the instructor to supply supplementary readings which might well counter these printed views. Specialists in the fields of esthetics, psychology, sociology, anthropology, and art history might be asked to lecture on ways in which the several disciplines seek to find the reasons behind art production.

In Perception and Space Illusion our manner of receiving environmental information is related to the manners of art production, that is, illusion. While perception is technically difficult and obscure at the cell level, the illusion of environmental form as expressed in two dimensions is based on a few principles which can be taught and understood. A few studio projects should be devised to identify the monocular clues necessarily used by all artists and to take the mystery out of the subject. Specialists in physics and psychology may provide provocative material on the subtleties.

Projects which might be arranged in a sequence begin with suggestions at the end of Perception and Space Illusion and proceed with Sections 4, Line; 6, The Shape of Things; 8, The Simplification of Form; and 10, The Function of Texture. These sections begin with form built up by points, develop line (the point in motion), shape (defined by line with value added), define the role of the plane (the line moving), and end with a discussion of the place of surface variation. Our basic tools are provided here.

The "source" sections are interspersed to suggest the gradual inclusion of environmental material into studio projects. By themselves they provide the basis for a systematic collection of visual material showing the typical and significant environmental forms which have inspired creative people. Design source materials are to be found in Sections 3, Sources of Design: the Natural Environment; 5, Sources of Design: Man-Made; 7, Sources of Design: World History; 9, Symbol: the Cultural Source; and 13, Expression in Word Form.

Instructors may well choose to spend a considerable time exploring materials and techniques. Thus Section 12 is designed to indicate the scope of this kind of project and at the same time suggest to the student possible final areas of specialization. Studio tours might be encouraged here, since few students have opportunities for seeing the activity in advanced classes until they are enrolled in them.

Somewhat more sophisticated ideas are outlined in Sections 11, The Point of View; 15, Transparency; 17, Motion; and 19, Images Out of Order. While pointing out the special reasons why the modern art movement and modern technology are uniquely involved in these subjects, historical precedent for these ideas is pointed out in the visual material and in the discussion. Here we seek to dispel notions that the modern art movement is odd or unrelated to the logical representation of ideas. All of these ideas are easily assimilated in theory and, as student projects demonstrate, are subject to the rewarding breakthrough in practice.

Color sections may be taken in order: 14, Fundamentals of Color; 16, Symbolism of Color; and 18, Color in Action. Or they may be introduced as the instructor thinks best. Section 14 could be used after the discussion on texture, reviewing the fundamental projects but with color added. Section 9, Symbol: the Cultural Source, might be coupled with Section 16, Symbolism of Color, to provide a unit of study.

While providing a general sequence in order of difficulty, this text seeks a flexible approach to the organization of a foundation course in graphic representation. *Elements of Design* seeks to provide the student with a guide in the form of discussion and motivating pictorial material which bears on our main concerns with continuity, not rigidity.

D. M. A.

Madison, Wis.
May 2, 1961

iv

contents

MAXIMIANVS

1 *motivation in design*

While the term "artist" is popularly used in two ways—painter and brilliant public performer—it is also used to designate especially skilled performers in a wide variety of endeavors. A golfer may be described as an artist with the putter, and a fine chef frequently achieves this designation. Perhaps this latter usage is especially interesting because we may discern in it the seeds of a meaningful definition of artist. An artist is one who, manipulating a set of such raw materials as clay, wire, pigment, data, sounds, words, numbers . . . , transforms them into cohesive structures on a higher level of significance. Thus if an individual who uses mud to fashion a Venus is an artist, so too is the political figure who implements a plan which results in transforming arid land to the green of life. When seen in this light, art has rather broad connotations. This is properly so, since painters, sculptors, pianists, and novelists are not the sole contributors to that distance put between the human creature and the inferior beasts. And while our discussion here will center on the visual arts, the student will find fruitful parallels between his own creative work and that of his friends in many fields of study.

When design is searched, a complex of diverse parts emerges. Below is a partial listing of categories under design in the Manhattan telephone book, here used as a source of current usage of the kind not found in dictionaries.

· metal works
· tool and machine
· jewelry
· rugs and linoleum
· interiors
· product styling
· trademark, poster and package
· men's clothing
· furniture
· containers
· gowns
· merchandising displays
· textiles
· wallpaper
· drapery
· lighting equipment
· lingerie
· automatic machinery
· optical, mechanical and electronic
· booklets
· business and industry

Now the common factor in the association of design with these various endeavors is not immediately apparent. Rugs and linoleum are given forms and colors which provide a pleasing visual stimulus, but most people do not require this quality in automatic machinery. A poster consists of thin pigment films bonded to a thin paper carrier and is essentially two-dimensional, while tools, possessing length, width, and thickness, are three-dimensional entities. One can scarcely think of objects more utilitarian than optical instruments nor objects less so than jewelry. It is apparent, then, that design has not exclusively to do with whether the end product is two- or three-dimensional nor is it fundamentally associated with utility or visual elegance.

Design is associated with the creation of a knife, a theatrical costume, a poster, a bridge, the Brink's robbery, a golf course, a jet liner, a political campaign, a national highway system, the conquest of Poland, the United Na-

Frontispiece *Art reflects the dignity of man. Mosaic decoration representing the Emperor Justinian and his retinue, from San Vitale, Ravenna, Italy. Executed before 547. Courtesy Instituto Geographico de Augustini, Novara, publishers of Chiese di Ravenna, 1957, by Giuseppe Bovini. The mosaic technique is described briefly in Section 12.*

Fig. 1 *Tattooed man from the Marquesas Islands, as sketched by a member of a party of explorers led by the Russian Captain Krusenstern in 1803. The engraving appears in* Voyages and Travels, *by G. H. Von Langsdorff, 1813. The original motivation behind tattooing is obscured in time, but it is certain that only wealthy members of the group could afford a complete covering.*

tions, and the United States. All of these are preconceived ends and their common element is design. The idea—the definition of the problem—the thinking—the planning—the rejections—the correlation of parts: this is the process of creation called design. A political campaign is designed to elect a candidate as a knife is designed to cut bread.

Now it is clear that design and the public good may not be in perfect alignment. Language permits one to have designs on a lady or on her pocketbook, and an advertising campaign may be designed to increase the sale of harmful goods. The process of design is then pragmatic; methods effective in achieving the preconceived end are used. Occasionally designs stem from potentially harmful practices. The practice of tattooing is one of these, having produced some astonishing visual material (Fig. 1) at a cost of frequent infection and even death.

Design then is the process of accomplishing some end. It is widely used in endeavors other than visual. Other terms are occasionally used; for example, a person who writes music is said to *compose* it. The word also used to designate an end product, although most frequently the object has a name of its own: bridge, stage set, trumpet, and so on.

the two-dimensional conception

As we have seen, the activity called designing embraces work in both two and three dimensions. In this text our principal concern will be with two-dimensional work. We are in an age of specialization and we study special fields. The anthropologist E. R. Leach writes that in North Burma every male in a village is an expert in the construction of houses. In our society this activity becomes specialized in depth, with architect, contractor, carpenter, mason, electrician, and tinsmith collaborating. Each of these work areas has its particular training regimen. Professional schools have been organized which arrange courses of study for architects, city planners, and the several kinds of engineers. All take years to train. So too, those who intend to concentrate on two-dimensional design have their own curriculum to study and master.

There is, however, a decisive conceptual difference which divides those working in two- and three-dimensional fields and which provides the natural reason for specialized study. That conceptual difference concerns space. Workers in both areas possess in common the dimensionless function of the mind, but beyond this, space separates them. We experience a three-dimensional world—one in which objects are perceived in an inseparable flux of tallness, wideness, and deepness, not in the measured order of words on a page but as a whole and automatic effect like one's outer skin. And as in the case of one's skin, one is not especially concerned with spatial quality until something unusual happens to it. An individual may become acutely aware of space when there is too little of it, when there is too much of it under his feet, or when he cannot see. Designers of three-dimensional objects are sharply conscious of space in all that they do. Space impinges on materials, function, and cost. Architects learn to shape space and to put limits on it; sculptors learn to bend, mold, and lock it inseparably into their works. Those who design in two dimensions, on the other hand, must master the various devices used to *create the illusion of space.* The consistent application and control of these devices is of the greatest importance in designing on flat surfaces. Here we have no real dimension of depth. Depth is an illusion. It is faked.

Another ever-present factor for the three-dimensional designer is the force of gravity. Weight enters into his every calculation. Gravity determines the tensile strength of materials and thus distances of span. Gravitational forces are abrogated for the manipulator of illusions, and this gives him a certain freedom from physical logic. Creation of a form like that of the New Caledonian artists pictured in Figure 2 would present some difficulty to a sculptor.

Two- and three-dimensional works differ in another important respect—the way in which they are experienced. The impact of flat work is almost entirely communicated through a visual process—rarely a tactile one like touching the surface of a painting. Real forms, too, are experienced through visual processes, but they are also experienced by means of physical contact and, in architecture, through the quality of sound reacting with the structure. These factors in the esthetic of real forms find only distant echoes in the qualities of satisfaction found in works in the flat. Our course of study thus becomes more specifically pointed: *communication through visual processes.* In the world of our senses, that which we call the real world, a sense of space depends on objects in it. No objects—no space. We are not born with a completed ability to interpret objects and space. We gain our sense of space by an accumulated knowledge of the visual characteristics of familiar objects at varying distances from us. A thought experiment should verify this. Imagine you are living in a world identical to the one seen on looking up on a cloudless day. Everywhere you look it is the same. It would be impossible for you to receive any sensation of "far" or "near." Now as we have seen, two-dimensional work uses a substitute space and it follows that this illusion of space is made possible by the positioning and treatment of substitute objects. In other words,

Fig. 2 *Members of a New Caledonian community raise a steeple to the top of a house. These artists engrave bamboo; subjects are anything that suits their fancy, with the manner of presentation unhampered by laws of perspective or gravity. From* L'Art Néo-Calédonien, *by G. H. Luquet, a leading theorist on primitive art, Paris, 1926.*

3

whatever causes the sensation of space in a painting is not a real entity which can be felt or tasted.

dimensions and symbols In flat work the substitution of illusion for living space makes all such imagery symbolic. A symbol is something which stands for, represents, or denotes something else. Thus an ordinary stone may simply exist but a painting of that stone exists on a symbolic level. Illusionistic devices stand in place of real space. Freedom is gained upon understanding of the fact that reality and symbol image are two quite separate areas of experience. Since it is impossible in representing an apple to give the image the qualities of tactile appeal, aroma, and taste inherent in the nature object, one must see that the symbol image (no matter how faithful to the object in visual terms) is the weaker experience. Hence the symbolic object must be endowed with special visual characteristics that, in heightening visual impact, make up for qualities it cannot project. Recent critical arguments contend that we should not think of a painting as a substitute for anything, that it is properly to be considered a new original object as valid as a log. Even in nonimitative paintings, however, space illusions are created by use of a limited number of traditional devices. The weight of tradition also points to the fact that painting is something different from a found object—a leaf or a seashell. Painting has been rather more important as a commentary on experience than as experience itself—in short, it has been a symbolic expression.

Two-dimensional surfaces are the natural carrier of symbolic material, through convenience. It is easier to make a black mark on a surface than to carve that same mark. Such codified symbolic material as language, numbers, musical notation, score cards, and wiring diagrams are usually carried on flat surfaces. The designer has many of these coded systems at his disposal. Then too, there has developed over the centuries a rather intimate connection between the broad drawn symbol and language, a coded system. This tradition is especially useful in teaching and in advertising design, where a double and corroborating impact can be communicated through the images of word and pictorial symbol. There are thus good reasons for the student of two-dimensional design to be aware of the symbolic nature of his field and to interest himself in symbolic forms of communication wherever they appear.

nonutilitarian aspects of art

Man has been making marks on walls for over 50,000 years. And as he has crawled over the world since, he has kept busy forming, scratching, carving, and daubing every conceivable kind of material. In Figure 3 we see

Fig. 3 Some of the many areas in which man uses his design talents. a. 19th-century locomotive, courtesy Wisconsin State Historical Society. b. Contemporary jack of clubs, courtesy The United States Playing Card Company. c. Fish-net floats from The Decorative Art of British New Guinea, *by A. C. Haddon, Royal Irish Academy, 1894. d. Ceremonial garment in woodcut, appearing in the 19th-century Japanese volume* morokoshi meishō zue, *by Gyokuzan Okado. e. Detail from a 6th-century* B.C. *Greek krater, a vase for mixing wine and water. Courtesy of The Metropolitan Museum of Art, Fletcher Fund, 1931. f. 19th-century revolver from the collection of Professor J. H. Mathews, Madison, Wis. g. Blackfoot Indian ceremonial tepee. Courtesy The American Museum of Natural History.*

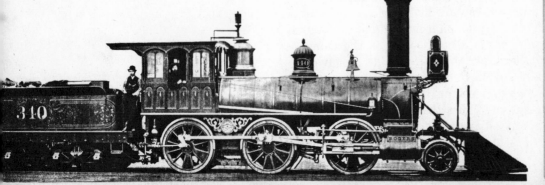

some of the multifarious objects on which he has placed his elaborations. These elaborations have appeared on weapons, tools, games, dwellings, garments, containers, means of transportation, and, as we observed in Figure 1, fellow human creatures. When one speculates on this output, seeking fundamental reasons for it, one is confronted with a real mystery. The factor which seems to make this mystery a dark one is the apparently superfluous nature of much of man's design activity. As we shall see, motivation can be assigned in specific instances, but on an over-all basis the direct connection between art and group survival would seem remote indeed. Art persists in areas where survival is a daily gamble, and it must be remembered that the artist is an economic drag on his group. While the artist is smearing pigment, he is not out hunting animals or gathering nuts or making wine. His companions have to do these things for him. In fact, a good definition of a painting, ancient or modern, is this: a painting is a flat surface to which pigment has been applied and that serves no useful purpose. Now since man leaves his creative sign behind in such abundance we seek reasons and are told that man possesses an esthetic nature, that he has an unusually developed sense of beauty. This is something like the invention of the term "ether" several hundred years ago, a word defined to accommodate physical phenomena otherwise unexplainable.

We should rather seek information from those who investigate basic human drives. Not many of these researchers are directly interested in art, and experiments are difficult to devise. One of the problems is that of finding ways to evade or shield out subjective evaluation in order that results will conform to classical standards of scientific investigation. A few experiments, however, suggest a direction of investigation which should interest us. R. A. Butler of the University of Chicago placed a monkey in a lighted box with two doors opening outward. Cards of two different colors were placed on the inside of these doors, with one of the colors always placed on the door which could be opened. In the experimental trials the cards were exchanged in random order. When the monkey chanced to push on the colored panel which opened outward, it could look out into the laboratory. When it pushed on the other colored panel, nothing happened. The monkey approached 100 percent accuracy within 20 days in picking the coded color, that which meant it could open the door and look out into the room. This was its reward, its motivation—to be enabled to look out into the laboratory, a richer visual field. We need to know more about the nature and power of this drive to obtain visual stimulation in man. It may account for the number of physically unnecessary windows in houses, and it may be a factor in the production of art.

Fig. 4 Venus of Willendorf, a Stone Age sculptured limestone figure. Motivation here is believed to center on a need to insure fertility, and hence group survival. This cast of the original figure is reproduced through the courtesy of The American Museum of Natural History.

Studies in activity restriction may also be pertinent. The psychologists Bexton, Heron, and Scott designed an interesting experiment in this area. Twenty-two young men were paid to lie on a bed alone in a lighted, sound-resistant cubicle for 24 hours a day, with short breaks for body needs. Subjects were fitted with goggles, gloves, and cardboard cuffs over their forearms. With all forms of stimulation thus reduced, the student subjects would not continue the regime for more than two or three days although they were paid $20 a day. They experienced distortions in time and space, the latter appearing to be two-dimensional. Subjects also reported a wide range of hallucinatory sensations, and some felt that their heads and bodies were detached.

Similar effects are reported by doctors whose patients were deprived of activity and visual stimulation during recovery from operations for detached retina. For a protracted period these patients must remain absolutely quiet, with eyes bandaged. It is a severe ordeal during which a patient may experience alarming hallucinations and other disquieting sensations. These reports suggest that the complex of electrochemical systems within the body which enables us to receive information and react to it needs to function in order to function correctly. Many activities fulfill this need (if it is a need), art activities among them. Art activities also fill a suggested need for visual stimulation. The faculty of memory may play a strong role in art production, also. These few suggestions are put down here as a reminder that studies on man as an individual must eventually produce some of the key pieces of the jigsaw in a satisfactory general theory of art production.

Now while it is clear that man has some kind of an individual existence, much of the character of that existence is formed by the other individuals with whom he lives. And people in groups do not move randomly like molecules in a cubic inch of gas (except in huge statistical surveys) but in patterns and sequences depending on a flux of interdependent forces determined by geographical environment and a rich variety of habits constantly challenged by the habits of other groups. Art is for the most part an element in this milieu, and the most certain and obvious statement that can be made about it is that art must necessarily provide an element of value to the group financing its production. Here we can learn from anthropologists who study whole groups. They produce studies properly long in description of art and occasionally concerned with the meanings of art within the group. Extensive reading in anthropology is recommended to the student. The pictorial material is fascinating and full of variety, and the student's views on current production may be elevated by a true sense of objective sophistication.

Let us list the functions of art as viewed in this light. The principal activities for the artists in so-called primitive societies are these:

1. Fashioning objects for magical or religious purposes
2. Fashioning objects to enhance the prestige of the rich or powerful
3. Making memorials to the celebrated dead
4. Creating useful objects
5. Making coded symbols.

Some anthropologists would not include all of these as art. Some distinguished scholars in this field would finish the list at the third line. Some critics would abolish the categories and set up an esthetic independent of any list. Nevertheless any general theory on art will have to account for all of the different kinds of marks that men make, explaining why certain of them are art and certain others not.

The oldest class of art objects in existence is a group of sculptured figures called Venuses. One of these, the Venus of Willendorf, is reproduced here as Figure 4. None of these figures classifies as a useful object; they are not weapons or tools. Instead they are thought to be connected with fertility rites. Certain exaggerations in the figure suggest this. Art here has a magical role. By the creation of a figure that possesses the properties of fecundity, a symbol of a desirable characteristic, the characteristic is believed to be transferred to an individual or a group. This stress on the one factor which might guarantee survival of the group suggests a rather low degree of control over environment. Of course very little is known about the early people who made these fetish objects, but it seems clear that art supplied something of real value in the life of the group.

Paleolithic cave painting is man's first electrifying visual production. In the now famed caves of Altamira, Font-de-Gaume, Les Combarelles, and Lascaux, our ancestors revealed the kind of drive and talent which had earlier killed off rival pretenders for the control of the world and which symbolized that preposterous explosion of the brain that raised men above the other animals in the mud. The bison in Figure 5 is from Lascaux, a cave in southwestern France, discovered in 1940 and containing paintings perhaps 25,000 years old. The bison is typical, in terms of subject matter, of painting and clay engraving performed before the emergence of settled and worn places of existence, of art before 5000 B.C. and ranging back into time perhaps 50,000 years or more. Existence through these centuries depended on hunting, and the reproduction chosen, while not revealing all the subtleties and elegance inherent in these works, does show an important detail: there are seven weapons in the bison. Here again we see the

wishful design forged by hard experience, a form alive wished dead like a woman form wished pregnant. This reveals the magical intent of these animal figures, widely agreed upon by the experts who have studied the caves. The art is wholly unnecessary in a technical sense (since eating depends on good knowledge of animal habits, clever hunting techniques, and effective weapons rather than on skillful drawings) yet clearly essential to the group's belief in themselves. The art creates a visual symbol of success and serves as a buffer against failure as no weapon could. Thus art becomes a weapon of belief in survival, and since there are no sharply defined minimum requirements for art which functions in this way, it reaches high values in terms of power and subtlety. When a group trains and supports some of its members in performing these

Fig. 5 Paleolithic bison from the cave of Lascaux in southern France, discovered in 1940. Group survival depended on the hunt, and most art of the period reflects this concern, serving as a magical device to insure success to the hunters. From The Lascaux Cave Paintings, *by Fernand Windels, New York and London, 1950.*

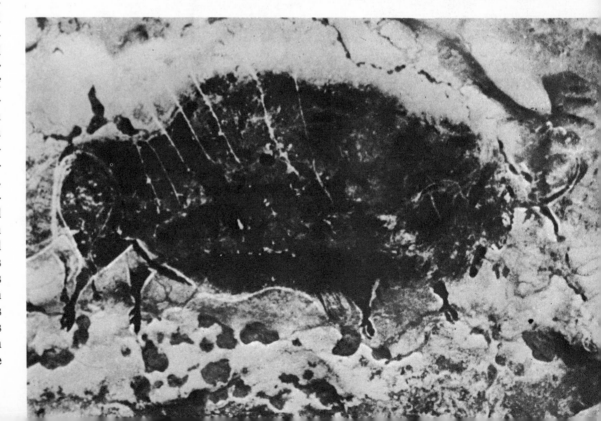

Fig. 6 A page from the great 8th-century manuscript Book of Kells, now in Dublin. A wondrous amalgam of geometric and symbolic content, this highly elaborate capital letter deliberately obscures meaning in order to communicate a quality of mystery. By permission of the Board of Trinity College, Dublin. From a facsimile by Urs Graf-Verlag, Olten und Lausanne, Switzerland.

acts of art, the performers, through constant practice and in order to please themselves and those charged with supervision, seek to exceed in subtlety, boldness, or difficulty forms previously acceptable.

Later, when the hunting culture is left behind and men settle down to raising crops, the art changes. The great fears of the unknown, the uncertain element in life, no longer center around the hunt. Plant forms appear in the art. Rain, fertility, and harvest are matters of concern in survival. Art here serves to stay the capricious hand of the elements, through ignorance attributed to supernatural beings whose helpful intervention is sought through the creation of images, dramatic ceremonies, and dances. Again, such imagery lacks common utility but nevertheless contributes something of real value to the community.

Then as man's thoughts turn inward and he thinks on the capricious nature of life itself with its attendant catastrophies, sickness and death—dark and strange, patterns of religious behavior emerge, again centered on the belief in supernatural forces. Art serves to create the images on which belief is riveted and secured. Over many parts of the world and through many centuries of time, art activities in the service of religions have produced visual material of great power and richness. We see an example of this in Figure 6, a reproduction of a page from the great *Book of Kells,* an 8th-century manuscript copy of the Gospels. The intent behind this involved play on a theme, at base a capital letter, is to draw a veil of obscurity over clear discernment. Perhaps the term "difficult beauty," borrowed from literary criticism, applies here. No simple peasant from the field is to walk in and declare himself a member of that inner circle having intimate knowledge of God's obscure works. Thus the air of mystery and awe, of humility before unseen power, so effectively communicated in cathedrals, is translated to the flat page. Early Christian art, while magnificent in terms of dignity of forms and richness of over-all effect, varies markedly in clarification of meanings. In Early Christian art, the lamb means a human creature whom God looks after, thus a symbol so plainly derived from daily experience as to serve as a model for this form of communication. It is clear that Figure 6 represents no utilitarian object but instead an instrument of belief, the church supporting the artist who in exchange contributes images of great value to the aims of the institution. Thus it is clear that "useless" art provides a society with a quality of high value, since it reflects beliefs and aspirations beyond mere physical existence.

our visual heritage

Our opinions on products of the designer's hand are shaped by the society in which we hold membership. It is therefore appropriate to examine some of the characteristics of our point of view before going on to work produced in other parts of the world. In terms of richness of imagery, the visual inheritance of Americans is relatively bare. Our ancestors were preoccupied with other matters, first, pushing back the frontier, and later, commercial enterprise. One interesting source, Indian art, went neglected. Perhaps a more telling reason is the absence of pictorial forms in the earlier American churches. Protestant tradition in America stresses the exercise of the verbal arts and gives little heed to visual stimulation. Virtuoso performances in the use of language have been the mark of Protestant churches in America. Interminably long at times, as some older citizens well remember, sermons helped shape the verbal fabric of our

culture. The political arena, too, has seen (or rather heard) some bell-ringing orators in a tradition still alive, especially in southern regions. We have had strong writers like Melville, Poe, and Faulkner, and a respectable tradition in the verbal arts of the theater. Since we participate in a tradition which places a strong emphasis on the skillful and precise use of language, the people who have come to us from predominantly non-Protestant cultures, those placing a stronger reliance on the power of visual motivation, have helped restore a balance. But in spite of the demonstrated power of visual symbols to stir people to belief and action, in spite of the daily bombardment of pictorial messages reaching us from the advertising world, virtually no college requires any study which might sharpen discrimination in nonverbal areas of communication. Many students thus exclusively indoctrinated in verbal arts learn to live by the word, distrusting other forms of communication as unreliable, and while a few intellectuals develop strong powers of discrimination in the fine-arts area, most are vulnerable to advertising imagery. Thus few college administrators bring to their offices the realization that pictorial symbols, like verbal symbols, are not merely pleasure-giving forms but weapons to be understood and controlled.

Many other peoples whose art we study are not so clearly bent by language concepts. Most "primitive" peoples possess no such well-developed verbal structure as ours, and they accept pictorial forms as a natural, needed form of communication, a part of life. We, by contrast, seek to translate pictorial forms into words, and if we can't, suspicion is cast on the obstruction. Scientific method has also made the strongest kind of impression on us. It is molded into our every fiber, and we tend to ask logical questions of every object, quiet or mov-

G

Fig. 7 a. Roman letter from the capital alphabet most familiar to Western culture. b. A Chinese brush character. Comparison reveals logical and poetic approaches to symbol design. Author's collection.

ing, in order to glean from it the information which explains its place in the order of things. Suspicion is cast on objects and activities which defy such precise analysis. As we have already seen in the few examples shown, art may not be too amenable to the action of logic, any more than is animal or human behavior in general. Whether this situation will obtain in the future remains to be seen.

esthetic considerations

One of the design activities of man centers around codified communication symbols. Those we are concerned with here are marks on surfaces with assigned meanings agreed on by two or more people. Such signs may be devised and agreed upon by any two people. Two lovers may agree on a sign which means "Father is home; stay away." Members of our society learn that a plus sign (+) means add. This form of communication is at once the easiest to start and, once started, the most difficult to change of all visual forms. Educated Chinese can read language forms many thousands of years old, and our capital alphabet is virtually unchanged (somewhat by accident) from that used 2000 years ago in Rome. In Figure 7 we observe a Chinese character and one from our alphabet. Our own alphabet reflects the logic and efficiency we might expect to find in forms acceptable in Europe and America. We have but 26 or so symbols to learn, and while the number could be reduced, the alphabet stands as a remarkable achievement for the person or persons who invented it. Chinese is a pictographic language with a different sign for each idea or object. Thus a model of inefficiency, Chinese is a poetic language both in meaning and symbol form. Even in an area so open to cold efficiency, we find evidence that other cultures tend to think poetically rather than logi-

cally. This characteristic makes much of the imagery of primitive groups seem strange, bizarre, and full of riddles to members of our society.

In our society only a few people are concerned with the visual form of coded systems, but those who are spend considerable effort on producing satisfactory forms. Here esthetic considerations embrace legibility, one of the problems in designing forms in coded systems being that of avoiding repetitions of form. No two symbols should look alike. Our Roman alphabet is fairly good in this respect. Its subtlety of form largely stems from the wide-tipped pens employed during the 2000 years of its development. Our children might well be trained with this traditional tool in order to achieve the maximum in legibility and elegance, as Chinese children are taught to use brushes in the tradition of that culture. Instead, our pencil-using children produce symbols lacking in character and indifferent in form. Thus, later in life they are often able to produce genuine wonders in the way of illegible and ungainly lettering and writing.

Coded symbol forms are not generally regarded as art except in cases where they are used to implement magical or religious imagery (see Fig. 6), or in objects which are designed to enhance the reputation of the wealthy or powerful. We will examine the communicative potential of this kind of design in Section 13.

Perhaps we could best use our heritage of the practice of logical analysis in the design of useful objects, those which appear on the surface to lack symbolic content. In the area of machine design we do well. Here the designer can come close to defining needs, and thus the form the object is to take. If a machine for cutting grass is needed, a succession of logically related questions can be asked and

10

answered about the way in which the machine should operate. Then, assuming that the machine fulfills everything required of it, a unique visual form is created which takes its place with other forms born of necessity. Its esthetic lies in the ingenious correlation of parts, its economy of means, and its usefulness to man. A useful object fitting these specifications needs nothing changed. For example, an oboe has a certain visual form, and the suitability of the instrument lies in the quality and range of sounds that it will produce in the hands of a good player. The visual character of the oboe is a subject for idle comment only, since it is the form the oboe *has* to be. Its visual character was not considered in the definition of the design problem.

In like manner, a house should provide certain qualities for living. The following list suggests minimum qualities for the function of a house. A house should

- provide protection from rain
- be vermin- and bug-proof
- provide proper heating and ventilation
- be easy to clean
- provide adequate storage space
- provide privacy for occupants
- be adequately insulated against sound
- provide convenient traffic patterns
- provide space for recreational needs
- provide adequate lighting
- be cheap to maintain
- provide a tranquil visual environment
- provide a feeling of spaciousness

Designing for these among other needs should determine the form of the structure. After these needs are provided for, the visual character of the structure can be discussed. The esthetic quality of the house is inextricably woven into the total living experience, even down to the quality of sound produced in the house. Thus in logical theory the form of the house would be what it has to be. But wait— we forgot to list one all-important thing that a house must do: communicate a sense of the owner's status. It must do this whether or not the owner has any, and it must do it by means of exterior visual form. Now there is little one can do to the basic structure of an oboe to have it communicate owner status. The instrument must be made of wood which vibrates well and is resistant to cracking. Holes in the bore must be drilled at specified intervals. Oboe reeds must be made of reed and the metal in the key mechanism must be neither brittle nor too easily bent. Status considerations do not enter into the design of the instrument to any great extent, and an entire section of an orchestra may use identical instruments. *Individuality* is almost inevitably expressed in performance, but logic dictates the form of the instrument. Here the old ideal of form fitting function comes close to realization.

In architecture, we generally require the exterior to exhibit signs of impressive design, although most of our living goes on inside. The picture window must be on the street side even though the flower garden is in the back. Redwood siding provides a sign of elegance superior to that of metal, although the former requires expensive and time-consuming maintenance. Even in basic structure, custom and status considerations rob us of space and mobility. Houses are still built with enough two-by-fours to hold up the Taj Mahal. In terms of basic living needs as outlined, there is little logic in our building procedures.

Status considerations interfere with logic in the design of nearly all useful objects. In Figure 8a we see the representation of the works of an 18th-century clock. The static forms are quite an interesting variation on a theme and might very likely be even more interesting in

Fig. 8 a. An engraving of the works of a clock. The sheer involvement of repetitious form makes an interesting piece, but the works lack the visual signs of status. b. Face of the same clock with proper ornamentation to reflect the social position of the owner. From Gallon Planches, *a French book of inventions published in Paris, 1776.*

movement. The works do not reflect any qualities of owner status, however, and so are hidden. Figure 8b is the aspect of the clock that the observer sees. In this the fleur de lis is repeated at an approximate ratio of one to one with the gears, and repeated in a duller manner, it might be added. But this prolixity of symbolic material assures the owner that the object fits his status-based visual habits. For machine forms are the forms of necessity, and forms of necessity suit the poor. Again, 8b is the art object, a fairly dubious one, to be sure, but much more likely to be found in a museum than are the works. Such a choice is even likelier today, when interesting and expressive mechanisms are hidden in "esthetic" boxes.

When radios were first manufactured they had a strange look to them. Queer pieces of apparatus, odd buttons, and dials stuck out here and there. As forms, they were quite arresting. For a few years radios gained distinc-

tion because of their rarity. Before long, however, as more people purchased sets, radios were made to fit the environment of front-room veneer. Even period radios were and are made. Now, no object we own is allowed, like the old lawn mower, to exhibit the curious forms of necessity. Instead it must be encased in materials designed to enhance its acceptability as a symbol of status. The idea that a perfectly functional entity fulfilled esthetic requirements, that a functional object was a beautiful object, received some acceptance 35 years ago but has lost ground since. These arguments drawn from familiar experience point up the fact that design problems are not solved in a vacuum. The logical idea behind the expression "form fits function" is intruded upon by the structure of our society. Our social needs are often at odds with the reasoned dictates of function and the designer must study both to solve design problems.

Designers themselves are not immune to status considerations. The entire fields of jewelry design was formerly in hire to the wealthy and powerful classes. Jewelers are still hired by the rich to make unique pieces which are unrepeated and give special status to the wearer. But the rich do not live so ostentatiously as they once did, so jewelers just work for those who aspire to higher status. Jewelers use silver rather than stainless steel, gold rather than brass, and precious stones rather than common stones of equal beauty. The designer of jewelry does not have the albatross of utility hanging around his neck and has no difficulty in having his work classified as an art form. A man who plans a lawn mower can use logical analysis to define his problems. Problems faced by jewelers rather defy precise definition. Each problem can be solved in many different ways. We should expect to find a rich variety of forms employed by jewelers and we do. We also find a rather curious enterprise going forward in the field of jewelry design—the practice of conferring status on an individual by selling him a mass-produced article, like cuff links, a contradiction in terms tinted with absurdity.

Potters, too, are beset by problems of status but in a little different way. Some potters show little concern for function and descend to the odd practice of making teapots that won't pour properly. This practice stems from the concern which potters and other three-dimensional designers have over their position in the arts hierarchy. Some years ago, grouped in a crafts category, these designers were not so highly regarded professionally as were painters and sculptors. Somehow tagged with a "handwork, no brain" label, they found it difficult to become associated with institutions of higher learning. The aspect of utility in their work was seen as a handicap. Since their "superiors" in the hierarchy produced only nonuseful objects with a visual esthetic, it seemed best to some potters to classify their work in the same way—as objects untainted by utilitarian considerations. Now in competitive exhibitions of pottery, pieces are judged in the same way painting is, on visual content only, instead of through the totality of experience which their form and tradition makes more plausible. Weaving, too, increasingly becomes a wall hanging, judged as one would judge a painting. The danger here is that pottery, to be like sculpture, must engage in the vulgar extension of its resources called the tour de force. To be like painting, it must be spotted and crackled without relief. Ceramic art then becomes a form in search of an esthetic, a reason to be, for it will never have the potential of painting or sculpture in terms of power to direct emotion. If the status problem were solved, such designers might find greater satisfaction in working out that careful marriage of form and function which so dignifies the ceramic tradition.

Earlier, mention was made of memorials to the dead as one of the functions for which societies employed artists. Our services and memorials are lacking in flamboyance, although coffins are often given the spurious connotation of wealth, a custom particularly devoid of merit. The artist is out of it and the student artist is not encouraged to get into it. For while there is a potential market for his services, the particular tradition we are in inhibits the employment of reason, talent, or any other facility he might have. Henry James once said that habit is the flywheel of society. To which he might have added that it is also the anchor. The student is encouraged instead to pass by a graveyard, to note in passing the acres of stones marking the dead, to note the occasional Egyptian obelisk towering over all, and to go about his work. The pattern is set.

Fig. 9 Ikon painted by a member of a tribe in northeast India. These paintings appease gods and protect the house. The form reflects a unique need. From The Religion of an Indian Tribe, *by Verrier Elwin, 1955, courtesy Oxford University Press.*

definition of problems in two-dimensional design

In order to proceed with designs so that the end result may be fruitful, it is necessary to define the problems. We have seen that in the design of utilitarian objects it is possible to proceed in a reasoned way except for unique intrusions of status necessity. On the other hand, in nonutilitarian design, problems are often established by cultural attitudes of belief. Logic as we think of it may be only remotely involved in the formation of these attitudes. This fact is of considerable importance in analyzing the art that we see. Consider the ikon in Figure 9, a work commissioned by a chief member of a tribe in eastern India. According to this tribe, such an ikon pays homage to ancestors and protects the house. This particular ikon was made to appease a god who had made a tribal member sick. A hill on which live various animals is represented and the animals are readily seen although perhaps not so readily identified. The rest is a melee of images half-endowed with the quality of reality woven in with those of symbolic content. In the lower central section there is a tiny representation of a policeman with a bicycle, put in because he had been a nuisance in the area and his inclusion might occasion a more permanent absence. The all-important question here is this: *What determines the form of an object designed to placate a god?* The answer is: Whatever form the group comes to believe will do the job. There is no limit to the number of forms that can cast out spirits. Figure 9 represents a unique kind of image which will not be repeated in other parts of the world. The persistence of the form, in a general way, no doubt depends on the group's assets in regard to the means of survival. Members of our society, thinking on the problem with a de-

gree of objectivity based on more information, think that they know that sickness, in terms of microbes and bacteria, is not to be driven out by images. Yet ignorance is a permanent condition everywhere and we owe a great deal to it. We are not smart enough to explain exactly why a child may cling to a dirty old blanket, nor can we as adults rid ourselves of the need for symbols of security. In this area the design problem is vague, veiled in uncertainty. This is in marked contrast to the use of reason in the design of useful objects. It is a distinction of the greatest importance. Through rational definition of the problem, useful forms may come close (when needs of class prestige are eliminated) to ideal, static, universal form, as in the safety pin. Intrinsic to the form of useful objects is survival, not the symbol of it. Useful forms undergo changes as living forms do, with inefficient variations dying out—a process involving reason. Thus many tribes evolved the fish hook form, and those groups who cannot work steel accept steel fish hooks because they work better, as the American Indian accepted the rifle.

esthetic standards

It is futile to assume that our esthetic views can be imposed on other groups. People in our society may regard the forms in Figure 9 as unsatisfactory but they are satisfactory to the people who commissioned the work. We cannot change the fact that we are part of a society which seeks to put things in order. When we look at art from other cultures, it does not fit. The forms are strange to us. They are likely to be judged in terms of our own visual heritage which is primarily based on Renaissance perspective and accompanying illusionistic spatial devices based in logic. Since peoples in many primitive cultures tend to think poetically, *we must learn to be receptive to imagery which reveals essences instead of outward appearances.* Young students ask of an art work questions which demonstrate their expectancy that it should consist of a string of outward appearances capable of verbal interpretation. It is hard to put the answers in verbal order because the experience is not to be explained in this way. After the student has had a few years of visual experience, he learns to see for himself, to interpret forms in nonverbal ways. A painter need not have great verbal aptitude, but art departments, surrounded as they are by the verbally skilled and reason-oriented, encourage students to read and ask questions, which teachers must then be prepared to answer. The proper question to ask of art works from around the world is: What did it mean to the people who made it? There is an intimate relationship between esthetic values and ethical values throughout the various cultures, and since ethical systems around the world are various, we should be concerned with what is considered right or wrong within the culture. Let us put it this way: would we accept any visual form which perpetuated the ends and ideals of Adolf Hitler? Not likely. The swastika, formerly a harmless symbol of good luck, now is charged with sinister meaning. No doubt the object in Figure 10 would find many admirers around the world. We characterize these forms as flamboyant, ostentatious supports to claims of social position. Yet, as the anthropologist E. R. Leach points out, the widely admired totem poles of British Columbia and much of the elaborate form from the Pacific area serve the same purpose. The tattooed man of Figure 1 represents something of this extravagance of form. Now in the 20th century we have had a rather violent rejection of art forms which in their elaboration (and thus expense) symbol-

ized social position. Rejection was as much against a way of life as simply against the elaborate visual form, which we gladly accept as exciting and stimulating if it comes from another culture where our ignorance hides the motivation behind the work. Explorers and commercial agents were able to pawn off any kind of sparkling junk on native peoples intrigued with the visual glitter. And while we must become sympathetic with the poetic visual language of other cultures, we must not fall into mere exoticism, the acceptance of glittering trash regardless of motivation, a practice as absurd as a derby hat on a native chieftain. There are, then, no universal standards of acceptable visual form, and a little study is necessary to discern those art forms motivated by the deeply felt beliefs of other peoples.

Even within our own social order we should expect to find a considerable difference of opinion on the acceptability of certain forms. A member of a synagogue would be quite likely to assert that the menorah, a candleholder charged with symbolic content, is a good and proper form, while nonmembers might be expected to express a range of opinions including approval, indifference, and disapproval. Even individual emotional states color perception. The psychologist Warren J. Wittreich, writing in the *Scientific American*, describes a series of experiments centered around the famous Ames distorted room. One experiment showed that under certain controlled visual environments married people "see" their partners as larger than strangers. The series of experiments seemed to reveal that the way in which we perceive the size and even the shape of others is powerfully influenced by our emotional relationships with them. In everyday experience we verify this by noting the change in our interpretation of an individual's appearance depending on whether we grow to

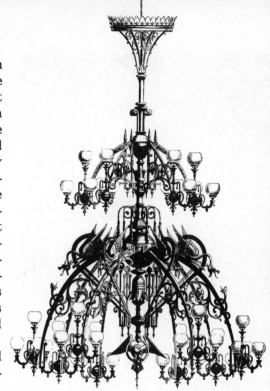

Fig. 10 Chandelier engraved around 1875. Elaboration of form reflects social position of the owner. Ostentatious design does not meet the approval of contemporary critics, although elaborate forms of other societies which serve similar purposes are accepted. From Household Taste, *by Walter Smith, 1876.*

15

Fig. 11 Garment from Tahiti. Contains form on several levels. Some of the forms are purely geometric, some are highly stylized, still others quite realistic. Few artists in our culture combine design elements in this way. From Sculptures Africaines et Océaniennes, *Librairie de France, Paris, 1929. The object is now in the Musée Ethnographique du Trocadéro, Paris.*

like or dislike that individual. Suitability in form thus has an individual basis as well as a subgroup basis and a culture-wide basis.

esthetics and painting　In our society, often termed Western civilization, we have come to expect certain qualities in art objects. In painting, our logical traits of mind influence what we expect to see rather strongly. We expect a painting to be complete, wrapped up, self-contained, with a consistent spatial conception and no loose ends. These qualities are expected of painters as different from each other as Mondrian and Delacroix. All the forms of a painting are expected to demonstrate a logical relationship and an over-all unity of treatment. This last is most important. A painting is not to change its spatial idea in midstream, it is not to switch surface treatment too radically, and it is not to change color keys suddenly

without clever modulation. To put it another way, a painting is something like the mathematician's "elegant proof." When a scientist speaks of elegance he means that the solution was neatly contrived, with clumsy trappings absent. Einstein, commenting on a theory in higher physics, once said that he couldn't disprove it but that he didn't like it because it was ugly; it contained so many bulging parts to accommodate known phenomena. When explanations of phenomena fit together like a jigsaw puzzle, scientists are delighted and relieved. Another analogy might be that a painting in our society is something like the works of a clock, with major structures and submechanisms contributing a calculated effect to the total.

Consider by way of contrast the reproduction of a piece of cloth from Tahiti (Fig. 11). It is true that there is a kind of over-all unity here based on geometric shapes, but notice the quixotic development of the subplots, the curious repetitions, and the sudden jumps between formal (geometric and symbolically meaningless) shapes, codified symbol patterns (zigzags meaning water), and realistic interpretations of grain plants. To our eyes it would almost seem as if the six basic visual themes, together with their possible mutations, had been fed into a computing machine, and of the billion or so possible combinations one of the more unlikely had been chosen for execution. Since this rich work contains several levels of communicative form, parallels might be found between it and literature, but not between it and most contemporary painting. But Picasso has shown the way here. One has but to note Picasso's knowledge of the daily scene, his acquaintance with the realm of classical mythology, his absorption of forms foreign to the culture he was born into, his acknowledgment of the changes in the theory of the nature of matter, his compassionate feelings for outraged humanity, and his virtuosity in form manipulation, to realize that the fusion of these faculties in visual form thrusts some challenge on his audience. There is a difficulty, a richness and variety in his imagery. Ugliness, grace, force, brutality, delicacy, majesty—all are there. Painting done in the United States is very strong in terms of paint quality and sometimes vigorous in striking out in new directions. It is also probably more restrictive in terms of involvement, in levels of meaning (compare to Fig. 6) than at any time in history. In some current canvases there is much paint but no idea. Earlier it was mentioned that primitive art was used in several different ways—in religion, in service to the wealthy, and in memorials to the dead. The current painter seldom has connection with memorials and he no longer serves to link our esthetic with Christian mythology. He claims little interest in the wealthy (either in terms of enhancement or disfigurement of reputation), seeks no change in the social order, but rather is interested in communicating SELF as never before.

Patronage for present-day painters of merit generally comes from individuals with college degrees who live in cities and whose incomes fall well above the national average. The painter seeks approval and status from other painters, college administrators (who employ many artists), commercial gallery owners, a few foundations, museum curators, and influential editors of magazines of art. Businesses, governmental agencies, churches, architectural firms, magazines, and advertising agencies employ painters very infrequently. National reputations are made in part by exhibitions of work, by the personal exchange of opinions among artists, and by press agentry centering in New York City. This last is in the American tradition of cheerful and exuberant outcries on the merits of the product being sold, the artist as much as the art. It is a gentler form of show-business exploitation and has not reached the hilarious stage attained by entrepreneurs of popular musical entertainers because there is not enough money in it. Certainly less than 10 percent of the population is in any way concerned with the work of serious painters. Counteracting the instability of the tastes of aspiring middle-class sponsors of the arts are museums that constantly reaffirm our links with the past, the personal integrity of the best of our art dealers, and teachers of art and art history in our educational institutions—a thin line of defense. Here teachers of art in our colleges and universities could serve better than they perhaps do, since some of them are too involved in the market for the best functioning of objective appraisal.

design in advertising

If art has a lesser role to play in the maintenance of wealthy and ruling class prestige, it does serve to enhance the prestige of business products, services, and institutions. This form of visual communication is produced in multiple copies by the printing industry and appears on every television set. A complex of trades, skills, traditions and technical processes is involved. First of all, this kind of design is closely associated with language, with roots, of course, in the dawn of civilization. The alphabet which is used by most people from India across Europe and America to the Pacific coast is almost 4000 years old. Paper, the carrier for advertising art, and writing have a long history. Discovered by the Chinese in the 2nd century B.C., the art of papermaking was passed on to the Arabs in the 8th

17

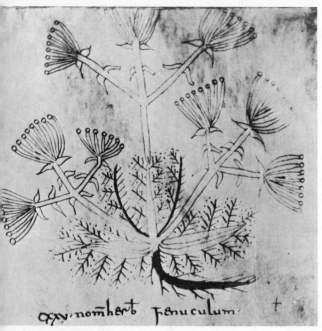

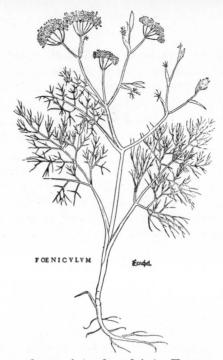

FOENICVLVM

Fig. 12 a. A version of Foeniculum by a 9th-century artist. While the forms are quite interesting, they are a long way from any approach to objective reality. Over the centuries, artists based their interpretations on other art rather than on nature. From The Herbal of Pseudo-Apuleius, *now in the Abbey of Monte Cassino. Courtesy of E. J. Brill, Leyden. b. The same plant in a version by the great Leonhard Fuchs from* The History of Herbs, *1542. This illustration is one of over 500 woodcuts in the volume. Courtesy Rare Book Room, University of Wisconsin Library.*

century A.D. and was introduced into Europe by the Spanish Moors. Paper as the carrier for writing supplanted animal skins, and its use was firmly established by 1400. Many developments pertinent to the printing industry occurred in the 15th century. Gravure processes (one of the three important means of multiple image production) developed in the early part of this century, although they have an older decorative usage. Relief printing processes (another of the three) became established in two forms. Pictorial block printing, with an earlier history in the Orient, came into wide use, and movable type was conceived and put into use in the production of printed books sometime around 1450. The third important printing process, lithography, was discovered a few years prior to 1800 and became very popular as a pictorial medium by 1850. Photography has been in development about 120 years and now is a central process in printing. Photoengraving, the process of converting photographic images to printing plates with the

18

aid of chemical reactions, is a development which began shortly after 1850. This development was climaxed by a technical achievement of paramount importance, the half-tone grating, in 1888. With this technique, subtle gradations in black-and-white material can be reproduced. It is well to remember that throughout history, before the development of photoengraving, all printed images were hand-drawn or hand-carved. By 1900 the hand-worked plate was well on its way out, with an unfortunate loss in personal craftsmanship. Several examples of the hand-drawn plate are to be seen in this book, among them Figure 39. The 15th century saw great steps taken in graphic presentation, while the 19th century saw the technical development of all three of the principal processes of reproduction which led finally to elimination of the plate-drawn image.

Advertising design still draws heavily upon those skilled in the creation of pictorial matter. This kind of representation is called illustration and historically has derived its form almost exclusively from that developed by 15th-century artists who reaffirmed older material and created some new forms.

Here we must make some distinctions between illustration and those visual forms associated with the fine arts. There is, of course, no fine line to be drawn. We have seen in much of the work already shown that some other idea than that of accuracy is central in representing objects. The Renaissance saw a rejection of medieval conventions born of the notion that the human body is but a shell for the spirit, and men became interested in how they were put together. Bodies were measured and there came to be an interest in illusionistic representation for its own sake. Generally speaking, illustrators have taken their lead to try to communicate accurate information.

Careful observation and skilled delineation can be seen in 3rd-century herbals, books devoted to botanical illustration. The work in Figure 12a dates from the 9th century, while that in 12b is an illustration from Fuchs' *History of Herbs* published in 1542. The same plant is depicted in both drawings. Figure 12a represents a point of decline in herbal art. As late as 1485 drawings were so poor that few plants can be identified. The artist during this long stretch stopped looking at the plants and copied from previous books. By the 9th century the form had become quite conventionized, and to a designer quite interesting. Among botanists, however, the work finds few admirers, since their esthetic reactions are dimmed by illustrations which are too low in information. In this short span between 1485 and 1510 botanical illustrations shot up in quality to the level of other Renaissance pictorial work. Esthetic qualities creep into much of it, due to the vitality of the organic stimulus. How much the structure of art forms owes to natural structure is difficult to assess. Perhaps everything. These two plant illustrations point up two facts: illustrators by our definition are supposed to produce work based on careful observation and keep strongly felt bias out of it (an ideal difficult to achieve); to artists, accuracy is not necessarily the important quality, but to specialists in scientific subjects it is, and various levels of abstract form result when the apprentice artist in any culture copies the models of his predecessors rather than taking a fresh look at the living object. This is one of the important style-making processes throughout history.

As we have seen, all of the multiple copy needs of the entire society—science, industry, trades, business, literature and so on—were met by illustrators working directly on printing plates during the period between 1450 and 1900, with many of the skilled performers being replaced by photography during the latter half of the 19th century. Many illustrators continue today, surviving the camera because they possess abilities superior to the camera. Photography cannot replace illustrators for several reasons. A camera does not think, it cannot discriminate adequately between a predefined level of pertinence and gross material, and a camera cannot keep the entire field in focus, cannot portray material in depth at a consistent level of intensity and detail. Medical illustrators are necessary because they can make such fine discriminations.

Another kind of illustrator is essential to the smooth functioning of an industrial society. Nearly every object made in our society requires a plan, the indispensable form of visual communication between the idea and its realization. We need a draftsman to build a house, a radio, a toy, or an airplane. We must have maps, charts, musical scores, and diagrams of football plays. No camera can so translate thought into a visual form—only man can.

Illustration is a popular form of communication and thus often reflects the shallower tastes of any day. The lady in Figure 13 is a typical 19th-century example and represents a high level of skill. It is also a little silly—a quality held in common by much of the "fine art" of the period. Until twenty or thirty years ago, illustration was the backbone of high-quality advertising. Many individuals were highly skilled in drawing and painting at that time, and most art directors had been trained in schools which offered a curriculum strong in drawing and painting. European developments in graphic arts and other design fields during the 1920's foretold a change. The Bauhaus, the painter Piet Mondrian, the Dada fellowship (who made an important contribution in their typography play and no other), workers in

Fig. 13 A skilled 19th-century engraving, published in Graham's Magazine, *uses the illusionistic devices developed during the Renaissance but is structurally weak and lacking in content. Illustration often reflects popular taste.*

19

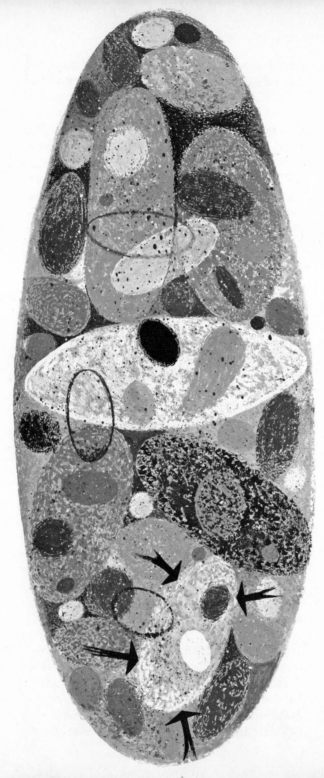

Fig. 14 Shapes representing major and minor groups in our population. Commonly held habits or beliefs draw people into groups. In advertising, the group is carefully defined before communication is designed. The free-lance painter finds acceptance among certain groups and his communication is subtly molded to fit. Author's sketch.

montage photography and painting-collage—all these innovators contributed to the enrichment of the communication arts which advertising was to draw upon. The ground began to be cut away from beneath the illustrator. During and after World War II the new language began to take hold in the United States and now has a firm footing in advertising. Illustration is a dying art. A few fine illustrators remain, veterans like Robert Fawcett, but few younger men are coming up in the field. Painters trained in the schools have greater opportunity to stick to personal expression rather than to go into the mass media arts.

The new advertising designer is a man of many parts. Competent but not especially good in illustration, he knows lettering, typography, photography, and printing techniques. He is also a student of the meaning of words and visual symbols of all kinds, of the entire range of visual history. The new advertising designer is an architect rather than a bricklayer, a composer rather than a trumpeter—thus we find the rejection of the old, reliable, and rigid format. Illustration/typography has made new demands on students going into the field. In one sense they are lucky, because anything they choose to study will be useful. This new form of visual communication may include several images differing in technical origins and carrying several related meanings—a synthesis of visual elements. It puts new demands on skill and intelligence and is a challenging field for young people willing to put in the necessary work (Figs. 87 and 124, pp. 80 and 110).

thoughts on communication

Design for industry and business is primarily a procedure of solving special problems, differing in kind from those faced by painters. Let Figure 14 represent the total population of the United States with various subgroups possessing special characteristics. Some of these larger forms might represent income groups, rural or urban dwellers, educational levels, various age levels, political affiliation, and church membership. Smaller forms might represent steel workers, fishermen, business owners, airline travelers, Negroes, owners of houses without central heating (the geographic factor), nondrinkers, and people who eat tomatoes. Spiraling downward in ever-increasing rarity but with common ties are such subgroups as violinists, Armenians, proponents of the single tax, college presidents, readers of poetry, elephant hunters, hoboes, and students of Sanskrit. It is clear that there is a considerable overlapping of groups, or rather, one individual is a member of several. First procedures in advertising design include determination of the group at which the communication is to be directed. In Figure 14 such a group is defined by arrows. Then all possible information is brought to bear in defining the design problem. Income level, educational level, the aspirations and common habits of the group are all considered. The finished design should contain images which are received and held and not those which cannot be comprehended by the observer. Each communication problem is different, and thus challenge is a daily feature of this area of design. Weaknesses lie in the habit of gearing images to the stupidest member of any group, the acceptance of pragmatic standards in judging excellence (anything that works well must be good, including outright deception), and dull repetition of what are judged to be the chief concerns of our great middle-income group: class status, sex, motherhood and babies.

Student painters, through ignorance, often come to believe that mass art media are too restrictive, too lacking in freedom. There are frustrations for the designer in the mass media, but lack of complete freedom is a condition of life found everywhere. Young painters cling to the illusion that they are a free, classless group with no strong ties to hamper their form of communication. The thought that the painter has no obligation to communicate to any particular group is romantic nonsense. As we have seen previously, those who support the painter attract his effort and subtly influence his color and form. True, in the field of painting, no handful of people sits around a table discussing the use of paintings as a status symbol for certain groups and mapping campaigns to gain entry into the market. Rather the student's visual language is subtly molded to acceptable standards by the eroding action of teacher criticism, by the examples of success which he sees in magazines, and by the sharp barbs he receives from "hep" fellow students. Our lack of ability to resist social pressure is rather alarmingly demonstrated by experiments such as those devised by the psychologist S. E. Asch (writing in *Scientific American* for November 1955). The painter's communication is thus certainly directed to a particular group within our society, represented by the black spot in Figure 14, although his aim lacks the deliberate and precise quality of advertising campaigns, where errors and income loss are directly connected.

Still another mistaken impression on the part of the student artist is the notion that art for hire is bad art. Here the history of art tells the opposite story.

an idea in visual form   How does the creative individual go about his work? The Paleolithic painter apparently had no model in the cave which might have served to sharpen his vision. Nor can we possibly suppose that cave artists made sketches in the field to be brought

21

Fig. 15 Design elements appearing in blankets of the Tlingit Indians of the Pacific Northwest. These highly simplified forms carrying rather definite meanings are learned and repeated again and again. Original material collected by Lt. George T. Emmons; this image is from Primitive Art, *by Franz Boas, courtesy Dover Publications, Inc. His essay first appeared in an 1897 Bulletin of The American Museum of Natural History.*

back to the cave to bolster impressions of animal forms. Instead, through repeated visual contact with the subject the cave artist was able to recreate his subject from images formed and carried within himself. These artists also learned the method of their teachers. Over a period of time such details as hooves and horns came to be delineated in a certain way. These conventional forms were combined with those more closely related to fresh experience. Thus such events as animal dismemberment, too accidental in nature to become conventionalized, are woven in with predetermined forms.

Tlingit Indians of the North Pacific area contribute highly conventionalized forms which almost possess the characteristics of codified symbols. These forms are a long way from that of the animal (see Fig. 15), and the artist learns the form by heart, so to speak, from his predecessors. They are often carefully drawn and filled in, a process not highly admired when carried out by members of our society.

Much has been written on the way Japanese artists proceed. Brush-stroke technique is carefully absorbed from teachers and older paintings. The Japanese painter gets close to the natural object and studies it for a considerable length of time before placing a stroke. He thus hopes, through slow absorption of the material, to arrive at a conception of the essence of the object to be represented which will serve to eliminate nonessentials and facilitate direct and authoritative statement.

Cézanne liked to get his ideas through direct observation of the living subject, reforming value, color, and contour to conform to his strong ideas on the internal structure of painting. Many contemporary painters start work with a well-formulated idea of the method of spatial illusion to be used but no fixed image in mind. They would rather work it out as they go along. Of course the way in which most contemporary painters apply pigment is very much like that used by a long line of painters going back to Renaissance times. Our artists spend considerable time learning some of these techniques before they do good work.

To most designers in both the two- and three-dimensional fields, the indispensable tool in the design process is the sketch. Given various names—study, cartoon, rough—the sketch serves as a link between the vaguely seen image in the mind and the finished piece of work. Most things, such as an architectural unit, a painting, or a machine, are too complicated to be seen in a single mind's image, or if seen rather distinctly once, may dissolve not to reappear again. Often, important parts of a final work can be visualized, but connecting links and details will be missing. Designers therefore stabilize part of the image by drawing it on a flat surface so that it may not escape. Then by a process of trial and rejection, connecting parts and substructures are fitted in until they seem satisfactory. In architecture, machine design, and many other three-dimensional areas of design, the sketch evolves into a precise drawing made up of coded parts to insure accurate and identical interpretation by others. Two-dimensional designers of printed matter use several different kinds of sketches. An idea may begin life in the form of a thumbnail sketch, a miniature image of the important structural light-and-dark elements. Sometimes a glamorized version of a sketch is made to show clients. Somewhere along the line an accurate sketch or mockup has to be made to provide absolutely reliable information to the printer.

During the decade between 1935 and 1945 the federal government commissioned a good many mural paintings for public buildings.

22

The artist was required to furnish a full-scale, detailed, light-and-dark study of the final work. Many artists of the past used the sketch or study to work out important elements of structure. That pictured in Figure 16 is by Poussin, the 17th-century French painter. The main point here is that colors have inherent qualities of light and dark. Lemon yellow, for example, is very close to white. Thus a sketch in value, in light and dark, furnishes invaluable information on the prospects of the finished work. It is difficult to learn to use the value sketch in working out design problems. In the early stages of development, the student believes that line can describe anything, but once he learns to use the light and dark sketch he will find it an indispensable aid in communicating meaningful ideas.

In this brief review we have touched on some of the background material of concern to designers. We hope this discussion will stimulate thinking on these problems as studio work goes forward and will suggest pertinent areas of study which may prove enlightening.

summing up

Many of the art works of other cultures are images of myth and belief, with the form internally defined and existing independently of the internally defined esthetic standards of other cultures. So-called "international styles" are products of one cultural area. Art in all parts of the world serves to enhance the prestige and conserve the power of individuals and groups that are at the top of the social, religious, and political structure and those that aspire to be. This practice is somewhat at odds with our democratic views but is generally accepted except where art forms become too flamboyant, although if such flamboyance is the product of another culture, it too is ac-

ceptable. The area of useful design represents the best opportunity to exploit logical attitudes, but here status considerations interfere. Visual forms in the service of scientific disciplines are freed of status or faith considerations but are not considered a high form of art. The same is true of coded information systems, from language forms to wiring diagrams, no matter how interesting. Let us agree to re-examine as many works as possible with one aim in view—to learn.

Fig. 16 Sketch made late in the career of the French painter Nicolas Poussin (1594-1665). Poussin used studies to test the structure of the painting-to-be. Here the various elements interpenetrate freely, allowing the action to flow. Other preparatory drawings by Poussin are models of form simplification. Courtesy of the Hermitage Museum in Leningrad. Taken from a reproduction in The Drawings of Nicolas Poussin, *5 volumes, edited by Walter Friedlaender, New York, 1939-1949.*

2 *perception and space illusion*

Most of the information we gain about the world and the things in it is gained by way of our visual processes. Many of the pleasurable experiences in life depend on seeing forms. People raise flowers because the sight of them gives delight. Those who take to the wilds do so partly for the satisfaction in body activity but also for the fresh visual stimulation. The spring season activates us for several good reasons, among them a change in the visual environment. Many fields of science depend on systems of classification based on visual experience. Indeed, most learning depends upon visual processes, and it is safe to say that man's progress up to now is predicated on sight as a minimum condition. Visual processes are of particular interest to designers since some of the devices used to form figures or create illusions are the same as or run parallel to principles involved in perceiving the daily scene.

The first condition necessary to the sensation we call seeing is light, the carrier of the information. A second required condition is that the various objects of the world absorb and reflect light energy in a variety of ways, thus setting up an information potential. The third minimum condition to sight is a mechanism to receive the information potential inherent in number 2 and to interpret that information. The energy we interpret as light is part of a broad band of energy waves. Those we are able to decode have wavelengths of between 400 and 800 millimicrons ($M\mu$). Wavelengths around 400 $M\mu$ are interpreted as violet and those around 700 $M\mu$ are seen as red. The wavelengths for other hues lie in between. There are energy waves on either side of the

visible band; infrared wavelengths are longer and ultraviolet are shorter, but we are unable to translate them into visual sensations.

On the second condition, when white light from the sun strikes the various materials in our environment, it undergoes changes. Depending on molecular makeup, certain materials absorb very little energy from light and thus reflect it largely unchanged. Such materials are seen as white. Other materials absorb much of the energy in light and are seen as black. Thus light and dark, both positive factors in perception and in design activities, result from light or the lack of it. Darkness results when light is absent. Fortunately for us, still other materials exhibit selective abilities when struck by light. An object that we see as orange has the capacity of absorbing almost all wavelengths except for those around 600 $M\mu$, and so on. (A more detailed discussion of color will appear in Section 14.)

The fact is perhaps too well known to dwell on, but cameras are based on the structure of the eye. Eyes have an opening, the pupil, through which light is admitted. This opening is automatically adjusted to admit the proper intensity of light, which then passes through a lens whose muscles automatically flatten it or bulge it, depending on the distance of the object of our attention, in order to focus the light beam on the inside back of the eye. Here the retina contains masses of two kinds of light-sensitive visual receptors. One type of receptor, the cone, is receptive to bright light and starts the photochemical process that is translated into color sensations. The other kind of receptor is the rod. These tiny structures, many times more numerous than the

Fig. 17 Bushman painting of a dance. Such rock paintings are numerous near the southeast tip of Africa and are believed to have been executed during the past several centuries, some time before 1850. The spirited, incisive work reveals a knowledge of two important space illusion clues: relative apparent size and relative position in the field. These clues in combination communicate a convincing spatial reality. Courtesy South African Museum, Cape Town, South Africa.

Fig. 18 "Shock Troops Advancing under Gas," an etching by Otto Dix, drawn from experience during World War I. Visual power inherent in strong light- and dark-contrast is clearly evident. Also illustrated is the way a strong light source tends to simplify individual forms by cutting them in half.

the light and the dark

Perhaps the most important word we could use in describing what we see is contrast. We are able to define an object visually because it has a different look about it than has the area surrounding it. As noted previously, this difference is caused by variations in the way materials react to light. Sunlight itself is seen as white at midday. Toward evening certain wavelengths are absorbed by the atmosphere and sunlight becomes more red. One object may absorb a considerable quantity of the light that strikes it while the material next to it absorbs a lesser quantity. As light is reflected from these two surfaces and reaches the retina, the light from the material which absorbs less excites the receptors more intensely. Thus light from dark materials is a kind of shadow, shielding the receptors from a high degree of excitation. Since most materials are also selective in the kinds of wavelengths absorbed and reflected to the eye, the possible combinations of hue and value (the term used by artists to designate light and dark content) that we can perceive are very, very many. In a world in which only hues were perceived and those hues were all of equal light and dark content, our environment would lack definition. It is the dark and light content which gives power and impact to our surroundings. In pigments, of course, certain colors are darker than others. Red is darker than yellow. This means that when using the full range of colors, a student will automatically get some definition in the light and dark content of the work. It is necessary for the designer to understand the value equivalent of hues so that he can usefully apply the fact that when he is using a certain color he is concurrently using value.

In terms of power and impact in art, black

cones, do not seem to play a part in color perception. Instead they help in light and dark discrimination at lower levels of illumination.

In its role as part of the third necessary condition for perception, the front part of the eye is a somewhat mechanical system and is therefore fairly readily understood. Beginning with the retina, processes become more complex and proceed into the area of the unknown. It is clearly not necessary for a designer to know as much about perception as need scientists whose special preoccupation it is. On the other hand, the student's work will go forward more quickly if he avoids confusion in the area of perception.

and white is the maximum contrast, as it is in the natural or man-made environment not connected with art. Thus, for dramatic power, many artists use black and white contrasts such as are seen in Figure 18, an etching by the German artist Otto Dix. When we stress the power of black and white contrast, we have to remember that the shape element plays a part in the ultimate effect. It is virtually impossible to discuss black and white (or any other kind of contrast) without also including a discussion of shape content, because one cannot be presented without the other. Of course, then, some of the dramatic quality in the Dix etching depends on the diagonal forms carrying the light and dark contrast.

Black, of course, also reinforces and strengthens color areas. In full-color printing, the three primary colors are used for hue content with a fourth, black, run through the press to add power and definition for sharper impact. Black outlines add power and definition in stained-glass windows and in the work of Georges Rouault, for example. Since contrast is a fundamental condition in the perception of any form, it is used in all forms of design, and the figures in this book will demonstrate the many ways in which contrast is exploited. Special emphasis on certain forms may be obtained by giving them a dark (or light) value when the field against which they are seen is predominantly opposite in value. We can obtain a simple example of this by putting a small black square on a piece of typing paper. The contrast is great and the field uninteresting, so that one's attention must be drawn to the square. Something of this can be seen in Figure 17 at the beginning of this section. Here the field is more interesting, but our attention is still drawn to the dancing figures. These have special emphasis partly because of strong contrast. Variety of shapes also

attracts our attention, and a recognition factor is also present. The figures have a special interest for us because we know they represent human beings doing something interesting.

As time goes on the student will become more aware of the key role played by contrast in art and in our visual life generally. As we interpret the world through its contrasting elements, so too do other living creatures. Visible contrasts work for and against living forms and serve as a powerful force in shaping the evolving form through time. An animal often uses contrasts in value to perceive its prey. The principle called countershading protects many animals. Fish are light on the bottom and dark on top to match the value of the material against which they are seen. Leen de Ruiter of the University of Oxford mounted countershaded caterpillars in a facsimile environment in the laboratory. Half of the caterpillars were mounted upside down with their light side out. Ruiter found that birds ate more of the conspicuous caterpillars. In England a species of moth changed from light to dark to match the value of trees whose bark had become darkened by soot spawned by the industrial revolution. Some fish not only can change value to match environment but can match geometric patterns. One fish (*Synodontis batensoda*) is darker on the bottom than on the top and swims upside down to be inconspicuous. Countershading is not the only principle used by animals and insects in becoming adapted to an environment. Color, pattern, configuration or shape, and a false recognition factor also play a part in nature's deceptive art of camouflage. Natural processes and designers use value, color, and shape, then, to control visibility, to blend or contrast forms. Control of contrast means the control of visual interest. Through this control spectator attention is directed, within limits, by the designer.

Fig. 19 Portion of an Arabian manuscript, executed about 1220, illustrating fables. Positive forms (the birds) receive major attention, but negative forms (spaces between) are seen with sufficient clarity to demonstrate their mutual dependence. In sophisticated work the designer is always aware of the shape, color, and value of the negative form. Because of the absence of a ground plane, spatial order depends on overlap. These clues, slight as they are, indicate that the larger birds seem farther away. Thus the work has a rather flat spatial feeling. Courtesy Bibliothèque Nationale, Paris.

If we look back at Figure 17 we will notice again that the dark figures hold our attention quite exclusively. We are aware of the nature of these shapes, the way in which they change, taper, and end. It is probable that if we looked at them for a time we could turn away and draw a figure something like one of them. Now of course the total visual experience depends not only on the dark figures themselves but also on what goes on in the spaces between. In this example these spaces are part of a rather uneventful ground and seemingly lack importance. Even if one were to examine these between-shapes quite carefully they would be very difficult to draw from memory. They have an abstract characteristic which makes them harder to grasp than those shapes which represent human figures. In Figure 19, a 13th-century Arabian manuscript illumination, the between-shapes are a more vital part of the whole and impress their particular flavor upon us. Because the field is again relatively undeveloped, because the contrasting darks have dramatic and involved contours, and because of the recognition factor (birds), the darker shapes take the major share of the attention. It is quite easy, however, to ignore the black birds and look at some of the light shapes. In the central part it is possible to read the picture in a different way, focusing on the light shapes, the enclosing dark shapes becoming the field. To get rid of the recognition factor, turn the illustration upside down, and you will find that the light shapes can be read much more easily.

In some geometric art, where dark and light patterns separate each other and where their distribution is approximately equal, it is possible to see the white pattern with black as the field or to read it as a black configuration on a white field.

It is clear that it is not possible to take a brush and make a shape on a piece of paper without creating the dual relationship of drawn shape and outside shape. Since designers must talk about these relationships, the black shapes in Figure 19 can be designated as positive forms and the light shapes as negative. Probably maturation, study, and practice are necessary for full control of the negative areas. A fully mature artist is aware of these relationships at all times and knows that in changing one he changes the other. As children we love the positive image. There is excitement in taking a piece of paper and a crayon and creating the image of a dog. Manipulation of the negative areas is not inherent in the material and method and is beyond the comprehension of most children. And of course the child as he grows is usually restricted in his learning about this problem because he is not presented with the necessity of manipulating field areas. Those who have seen movies of Pablo Picasso at work notice that he often spends more time painting the spaces around a human image than on the image itself. Too often the beginning student in painting spends all his energies on the positive areas, not realizing that this endeavor solves only part of the problem. All the relationships of a work must be on the same level of importance; indeed, in the paintings of Cézanne one gets the notion that each square inch of the painting is as important as the next. Publication designers who correlate photographs and type habitually examine the flow and shape of the white spaces around the positive elements to determine the total effect.

Awareness of the problems involved in the design of positive and negative shapes is shown in Figure 20, a detail from a fresco by the great 15th-century painter Piero della Francesca. There is an illusion here of one form existing in front of another in space, but positive forms and spaces between are woven together in an inseparable flow of harmonious shapes and elegant contrasts. The artist is very much in control of the negative spaces and uses them to advantage. This is a step in advance of the artist of Figure 19, who could be described as being quite aware of the nature of the negative spaces he created but did not make them contribute as much, although there is genuine grace and vitality in the work.

There is no particular harm in putting figures on a simple field. Designers sketch this way all of their lives. It is important, however, for the student to become aware of push-and-pull relationships involved in positive and negative form manipulation. Good projects are those which start from a surface neutral in value and which encourage the student to develop both positive and negative areas by placing both on the paper. That is, the student must get involved in the relationship whether in value or color. Using cut and pasted paper in values from black to white might be a good place to start. The eventual aim here is to develop a mastery of this problem to the extent that the terminology may be dropped. Mature artists do not need to think of positive and negative areas as such but merely as different parts of a whole problem.

graduated values in illusion When a source of light impinges on an object, the conformation of that object determines the degree of complexity of information waves which reach the retina and excite the photosensitive structures therein. Since these minute elements are numbered in the range of 100,000,000 and since each one reacts individually to light on an on-or-off basis, it is clear that the eye is normally and automatically capable of fine discrimination. The severe blackout restrictions in World War II were wisely initiated, since

very small sources of light can be seen from a hundred miles away if atmospheric conditions permit. A man cannot draw a line as fine as he can see.

If an object receives graduated quantities of light subject to its contour, this information will be passed on and subsequently recorded by the cortex as a subtle image. In this way a tree trunk receives a light source strongly at right angles to the source, to a lesser degree on the sides, and little on the contour hidden from the light. This is recorded as a continuous graded band of light and dark and creates the

Fig. 20 Detail of The Adoration, *a 15th-century fresco by Piero della Francesca. In a model of clarity, this great artist shows how the light source creates the illusion of solid form. In the natural process, lights are "placed" on the form. The designer most often reverses the process by placing the graded darks. Here positive and negative forms are elegantly interwoven into a homogeneous image in which all elements play an important part. From* Piero della Francesca, Gli Affreschi di San Francesco in Arezzo, *by Mario Salmi, Bergamo, 1944.*

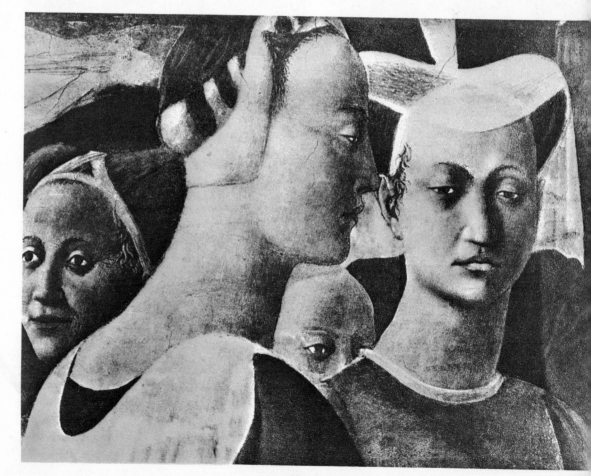

image which we have learned to associate with rounded form. Of course we know that the eye can be fooled—or perhaps it is not the eye but the human creature who wants to be fooled. At any rate, we can imitate the graduated light source by putting graduated values on a flat surface and thus create the illusion of volume. Usually dark values on a flat surface image are placed to correspond to points which in a natural setting light could not reach. Although this is sometimes reversed by using a dark field and directing the light parts, the world-wide habit in volume illusion is to assume a light value field and to place the graduated darks. Although nature molds forms by putting light on them and man molds forms by putting darks on them, man's illusionistic practices follow the fact that he is a daytime creature.

For a good illustration of clear modeling technique, again turn to Figure 20. In order to achieve the illusion of solid form, the artist assumes a source of light similar to a daylight situation. There is a source from which most of the light comes, and also a lower level of illumination from other directions. Seldom do we experience a sharp, direct, single source of light. When we do (the half moon, for example) is serves to remind us that such a light source can make form rather less comprehensible. Since no light reaches the dark half of the moon, the half without light is invisible. We see a flat hemisphere only, and if we didn't know that the moon was round we would assume it to be a flat half-disk. Something of this kind of simplification is seen in Figure 18.

So, it is light from more than one source that describes forms most completely and subtly. If we take a few simple forms—cubes, cones, spheres—and a single light source, perhaps that of a slide projector, we can see how this single light source distorts form. It is interesting to note the use by Braque of this

distortion. As different light sources are brought into play on the geometric solids, it is made clear how light makes different interpretations possible, how eventually the artist uses the light source arbitrarily to avoid static conceptions and attain a richer play in the light and dark pattern. Chiaroscuro, the control of light and dark forms, is one of the strong characteristics of Western art. For its controlled use for dramatic effect see Rembrandt.

Any particular light source can be said to be an accident of the moment, since it changes or can be changed moment by moment. Therefore, rather than be a slave to this visual phenomenon, we should prefer to use it where and when desired.

An interesting and at times important issue arising out of the use of light and dark to create the illusion of solid form is the fact that some people are skilled at interpreting difficult inanimate forms but cannot interpret the human head successfully. Since the human head is a good deal simpler in its conformation than many of the objects one experiences and draws daily, it is clear that something odd is at work here, some so-called psychological block. A possible solution is to realize that modeling the head can be analyzed on a logical basis, in the same way a rock can be analyzed.

monocular clues in space perception

When two eyes observe a close object, two slightly different images are projected on the respective retinas. It is possible to see slightly more than halfway around a pencil with two eyes, impossible with one eye. When the images are fused, a heightened perception of spatial depth is experienced. This experience lessens as we observe objects at greater depth and has little effect at distances of 30 feet or more.

For the binocular principle to be effective at

great distances, we would have to have eyes as wide apart as range finders on a battleship. Fortunately other factors at work in space perception also apply to the creation and perception of images on flat surfaces, our chief concern as students of design. These other factors are monocular clues to the perception of space, working as well for one eye as two. And a person with one eye can understand the illusion of space in a painting perfectly well.

The monocular clues are five: 1. relative apparent size, 2. overlap, 3. relative position in the field, 4. light and shadow, 5. aerial perspective (see left margin).

relative apparent size Relative apparent size refers to the fact that objects appear smaller at greater distances from the viewer. It is apparent that the painter of Figure 17 has made use of this effect, as those figures which appear to be closest to the viewer are drawn larger. Clearly the so-called primitive peoples were as aware of some of these clues to space perception as we are. Another part of this same effect is experienced on looking down a straight railroad track. The rails appear to converge. Similar seeming convergences of parallel plane edges can be seen in low buildings, streets, towers, and tall buildings. The visual effect of relative apparent size is everywhere operative. No object is excluded. It is most obvious when objects are lined up like fence posts, in which case it can be seen that relative size and the railroad effect (sometimes called linear perspective) are one and the same.

During the Renaissance, certain kinds of objects were found to have a conformation which allowed their representation to follow rather strict rules based on the convergence effect. Perspective, a process of expressing solid forms on a flat surface, leans strongly on

the observed effect that parallels come together at a point. Figure 21 is a 15th-century perspective study, again by Piero della Francesca. The Renaissance system works best on forms bounded by plane surfaces whose edges can be expressed by a line. While complex curved volumes need lights and darks to be expressed with clarity, many architectural forms can be brilliantly delineated by one of the several versions of linear perspective. Painters in the Renaissance, often called upon to decorate walls in an architectural setting, learned to correlate the illusion of space on a flat wall with the "real" space of the building. Since the development of the rules of perspective in the 15th century, perspective has been one of the cornerstones of art teaching. Certain designers in architecture and engineering find perspective indispensable to their work.

The development of the rules of perspective reflect the rational tendencies in Western art after 1400. No other cultural strain has relied as heavily on this particular device of representation. Certainly there is positive value in learning about perspective if the student will remember two things. First, the formal rules of perspective are but one of several important ways of revealing entities in space; and second, perspective depends upon some suppositions which violate experience. On this score, imagine that we are to use two-point perspective in drawing a skyscraper 60 stories high. Our position of observation is 30 stories up on another high building. As we look up, the parallel edges of the skyscraper appear to converge, and as we look down we notice the same effect. In drawing this building as we see it, we are forced to render it in a long, thin diamond shape, yet we see no such thing. A camera equipped with a wide-angle lens would probably record the building in two curves, and that may well be the retinal image pro-

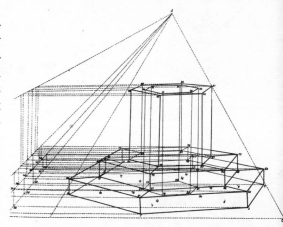

Fig. 21 Linear perspective study by Piero della Francesca. Linear perspective is a special case of the spatial clue of apparent relative size. The development of this illusionistic device is an attempt to rationalize man's environment by making it satisfy a set of assumptions. A knowledge of this kind of drawing is helpful, even essential, to certain kinds of designers, but it should not necessarily be regarded as identical with truth. From C. Winterberg's 1899 edition of the original Parma manuscript on perspective.

perience tells us that overlap is a constant and necessary phenomenon, even an inevitable one. Yet it is not absolutely essential in designing spatial relationships on a flat surface. In Figure 17 the dancing forms do not overlap one another or block out anything of significance. So we see that if a single entity is presented or if a number of objects are separated in the visual presentation, overlap need not be employed. On the other hand, overlap is used most effectively in Figure 22, a section of the Bayeux Tapestry showing an English shield wall. Here the human figures are arranged into an emphatic spatial hierarchy by use of overlap, but apparent size difference is absent. Those figures in the back are as large as those in front, as was typical of much design before the 15th century, when apparent size difference became important. Overlap becomes an important element in design when large areas in value or, color are used. In winter when a fine pattern of small branches is seen against the sky, the fact that some of the branches cross one another is unimportant. The branches are not large enough to block out forms of visual significance, as they are when in summer leaf. Overlap has been used in a preponderance of paintings since the Renaissance, and the student can benefit by close examination of the ways in which it is used. Picasso is one who uses it in as frank a manner as that in Figure 22.

relative position in the field   The effectiveness of the monocular factor of relative position is a function of viewer position. If the spectator has his eye at ground level he will not experience it. If he stands up he will observe that those objects closer to him are positioned differently than those farther away. A projection of his image on a flat screen would reveal that those objects closest to him would

Fig. 22   Detail from the famous Bayeux Tapestry illustrating the conquest of England. The main clue to space illusion here is overlap. Figures do not diminish in relative size—in fact, the contrary is true—nor do they occupy positions higher or lower in the field, but a spatial hierarchy is established by showing one figure in front of another. This device was much used in medieval pictorial work. Notice the inventive alteration in light and dark which sets one figure off from another. Courtesy Phaidon Press, Ltd.

duced by our lenses. Still, as we focus on various edges of the skyscraper we see straight lines. Thus it is seen that perspective is a convenient device but hardly the last word in vision theory. Contemporary painters for the most part rely on other monocular factors in their work, though certainly not by reason of ignorance of perspective.

on the overlap effect   In daily experience spatial relationships are established by one object being in front of another. This works even when apparent size difference is not particularly effective, as in the instance of a group of unfamiliar objects varying markedly in size and placed in close juxtaposition. The object closest to the viewer blocks out the view of the other objects, which in turn overlap others, and a spatial sequence is established. Our exbe in the lowest position on the screen. Objects farther away would be in successively higher positions. Within limits, the higher the observing station the more pronounced the effect. Of course it becomes quite inoperative when the observer's position is up in the air looking down. Presumably the maximum effect would be noticed at an angle of 45° to the ground plane. It works nicely as a space clue at a much smaller angle than that. As we are standing on the ground we can experience the effect at various angles since we can look straight down or at various angles out, to an exceedingly slight angle as we look at the horizon where again the effect is slight. Thus we shift our vantage point constantly, and when one factor becomes ineffectual we automatically give more weight to the others.

Now when we design images for the flat surface it is not so easy to shift points of view. It can be done, as we shall see later, but for the most part flat surface imagery depends on a single point of view and that very much shaped by man's physical stature. Until fairly recently artists have been rather conservative in the use of view point. In Figure 17 there is a group of four figures each one of which is in about the same position in the field. To the right are four more figures slightly higher up, while on the left eight women are positioned higher still. The extra man has a position a little closer to the viewer, while the unidentified creature is low down in the field and too close for comfort. Relative apparent size correlates with relative field position here to provide quite definite spatial clues. In Figure 19 the relative position factor isn't working. The birds are flying. Overlap, occurring slightly, tells us that the largest birds are farthest away. Curiously contractory, the spatial clues in Figure 19 serve to flatten the work, to reduce the spatial illusion.

Notice that in Figure 22 the heads of the figures rise on the field but the feet do not. The only conclusion is that some of the warriors pictured are taller than others, which is reasonable enough except for the inclusion of one figure who is much smaller than his colleague though seemingly closer to the viewer. Remarkable. Actually the several clues present in this fine work are contradictory and add a note of wit to the proceedings. It ought to be noted here that these contradictory elements in no way detract from a great work. Sometimes works of art possess the virtue of consistency and no other.

Figure 23 is a Japanese woodcut dated early in the 19th century. Here our point of view is rather high, so that those horses and grooms farthest away appear rather high in the field. Overlap is certainly a clue here, but in terms of relative size far and near figures have about the same measurement. Hence a curious flatness to the piece.

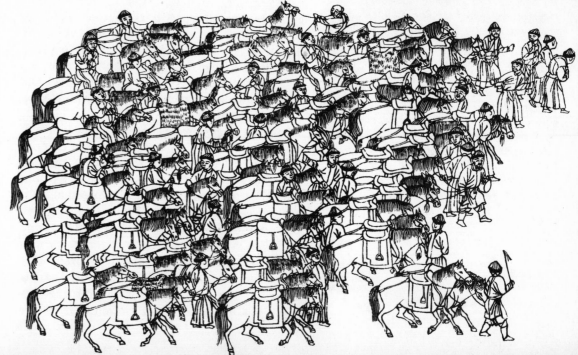

Fig. 24 When solid forms cut off a strong light source, cast shadows appear on neighboring forms. Since these shadows are stronger in light-and-dark content than the graded values which model the solid, form tends to be cut up and destroyed. Cast shadows do, however, create interesting, even fantastic, images which some artists use to advantage. Author's sketch.

Fig. 25 When other spatial clues are absent, relative apparent size communicates a spatial relationship only if the viewer possesses foreknowledge of the relative size of portrayed objects. The dog can be assumed to be closer to the viewer, but the spatial position of the object on the right remains ambiguous. Author's sketch.

light and shadow The fourth monocular factor has to do with the illusion of volumes as expressed by light and dark and with cast shadows. We have already discussed something of the role played by light and dark but we can refresh memory by reviewing Figure 20. Clearly the creation of volume illusions through graded light and dark directly implies space. Volumes occupy space. Cast shadows also give us information on solids. For this effect a rather strong, direct light source is needed. If this light impinges on an opaque object the light is stopped and the relative absence of light creates a dark image on the plane on which the object sits. The information obtained from cast shadows can be useful. Cast shadows emphasize the position of an object in the field and can inform us whether an object is on the field or above it. They can also reveal one of an object's profiles. On the other hand, the information provided by cast shadows can consist of half-truths up to fantastic exaggerations. A disk, a globe, a cone, and a cylinder can under special conditions cast identical profiles. And toward sunset on a clear day a man can throw a shadow a hundred feet long —a shadow that can at once creep over the ground like a ribbon, curve over a barrel and bend vertically to span a wall. This is certainly quite unlike any normal image of man. Artists who use a camera sometimes make good use of cast shadows, and one can always see them in the menacing moods of the motion picture. Designers working with flat surfaces utilize cast shadows less frequently. A version of it can be seen in Picasso's famous Guernica and Salvador Dali often uses it, but these are exceptions.

For one thing, the cast shadow is rather hard to handle. It cuts across solids with sharply defined darks, arbitrarily destroying the continuity of the form. Painters find that its use

may create the illusion of a hole in the canvas, or at least require an undesirable reduction in value. It is also a rather accidental, temporary kind of effect, less permanent than a form that can be felt like a rock and trusted. At any rate, most contemporary painters prefer other spatial devices. But cast shadows sometimes create interesting patterns of light and dark out of an ordinary set of forms. Figure 24 shows something of this possibility.

aerial perspective The last of the monocular clues, aerial perspective, refers to a rather prosaic phenomenon—dirt in the atmosphere. Light on distant objects is scattered, absorbed, and reflected before it reaches us. As a result the distant object is seen less distinctly. Values are shifted toward middle gray; color is grayed and weakened; contours become vague. Many landscape painters of the last several hundred years made use of the effect, but the group who seemed particularly sensitive to the play of sunlight and atmosphere were the French Impressionists and Georges Seurat. We shall see an example of Seurat's work in Section 6.

As we close our discussion of the monocular clues we use in our daily lives and in designing spatial illusions, it is well to remember that experience contributes a great deal to perception. Familiarity may breed contempt but it also aids knowledge of scale. We know the size of a man, so when we see one at an apparent smaller size we know about how far away he is. We do not need all the clues to establish a spatial relationship. The sketch in Figure 25 does not employ any but the first clue. Because we are somewhat familiar with the size of dogs and automobiles, we do not need clues number 2, 3, 4, and 5 to reach the conclusion that the dog is closer than the automobile. However, we do not know what to make of the image on the right because its identity, and therefore its scale, is unknown. We would clearly need more clues to know its spatial position relative to the dog and automobile and hence to assay its scale. In design we need not, as we have observed, use all the different clues, but under some circumstances more than one is needed. And we can tell space travelers that they will have to get along without number 5.

All artists who put forms on flat surfaces use the same five devices. Part of the distinctive flavor of the work from different cultural areas depends on the changing emphasis on the various clues. We can add to our store of knowledge on this important phase of illusionistic practice by subjecting works to analysis of their spatial structure.

The whole subject is brought to a rather nice conclusion by William Hogarth, the British artist who created Figure 26. Here he pictures a segment of a rather surrealist world by getting all of his monocular clues mixed up. At the bottom of the piece, Hogarth gives us this solemn advice: "Whoever makes a DESIGN without the Knowledge of PERSPECTIVE will be liable to such Absurdities as are shown in this Frontispiece." It is well to know how to handle space illusion; and given the basis for analysis one will enjoy the scrutiny of works from around the world because he can see for himself how it is done.

notes on the formation of images

The way in which the human creature forms a complete image out of very slight and unpromising visual material is amazing. If one will draw a semicircle with the open end to the left and add three dots as if to complete the circle, the formation will be seen as a circle. Where many would see ragged patches of ground and foliage, Cézanne saw pure curves and straight edges. So remarkable was his abil-

Fig. 26   Engraving by England's William Hogarth (1697-1764), in which he makes deliberate mistakes in the clues of space relationship. Sheep appear larger as their position in the field becomes higher. Readers will enjoy finding other discrepancies. Notice that, along with the profiles, both top and bottom of barrels are visible, which license is frequently taken by both primitive and modern designers, who are not necessarily bound by the images formed by an inflexible point of view. The Works of William H. Hogarth, Baldwin and Cradock, London, 1835-1837.

Fig. 27 Strong decorative markings by an artist of the Huichol Indian tribe (a group living northwest of Mexico City) fails to obscure the spare linear configurations which reveal the image to be that of a painted face. Seemingly meaningless daubs become animals when it is suggested that they are present, demonstrating that part of image formation depends on knowing what to look for. From "Symbolism of the Huichol Indians," by Carl Lumholtz, in Memoirs of the American Museum of Natural History, *May 1900.*

ity to see nature in complete, homogeneous images that he once said that if he shifted his gaze a few feet to the left or right in looking at a particular scene, he saw an entirely new total organization. An expert birdwatcher can read the image of a tiny finch, inaudible and immobile, out of a grass pattern which dwarfs the bird. When one first examines organic material with a high-powered microscope, one often observes a totally disorganized jumble of forms. Later on, after having learned clues of significant detail, one may discern whole and meaningful images. Astronomers have constructed total, connected (and highly controversial) images out of the vague markings on the planet Mars. Imagine looking at the markings on a tennis ball at 50 yards! This would be a parallel feat.

So we are rather good at making cohesive images out of slight suggestions of graphic content. This ability stems partly from an animal necessity to make sense out of a world filled with visual stimulus. An animal has to be able to pick both his enemy and his victim out of a random environment. The perception of whole patterns also reflects a desire on the part of the highest animal form to organize the world in certain ways, and hence has cultural and individual overtones. In order to simplify the discussion of this problem, factors of space illusion are omitted and we shall talk about images independent of overlap, and so on.

Because our eyes are unable to focus on more than one place at a time, our nervous system must make up for the deficiency. Rather than focusing on a thousand separate points and then adding up the impressions to see if there is anything significant in the field, we can interpret groups of things as a total, provided there is a special visual characteristic possessed by the group which is not shared by the rest of the environment. Again the clue is con-

trast. We can make an image out of green configurations if the field is another hue, out of gray markings if the field is darker or lighter, out of shapes grouped closer than those in the rest of the field (the factor of relative density), out of straight lines in a field of other kinds, out of squares in a field of circles, out of any one form in a field preponderant in another type, out of a black shape in a greater area of white and vice versa, out of one kind of pattern against a field of another variety, and by the location of a significant detail which gives away the image. An example of the kind of image completion we are able to perform may be seen in Figure 27, a painting by a member of the Huichol Indian tribe in Mexico. We have no trouble in discerning the fine line patterns which reveal the image of a face. Figure 27 represents a face painting. The fine lines in it are different from the other markings and constitute significant detail which gives us the clue, and the image snaps into being. If on some vague blob bearing some distant kinship with the human figure we should place a top hat, all would be clarified.

Animals can learn to pick out certain patterns from others, but human beings have special qualities to add to image formation. For one thing we can be told what to look for. Thus, regarding Figure 27, if we are told that on the right cheek and on around the chin are six deer (five male and one female) plus one dog, and that six bluejays are located on the forehead, we proceed to find some truth in the statement. Being told what to look for is a form of learning, and one individual can become better at obeying than another. Learning in another form, past experience, also plays a part in image formation. We tend to see familiar things in images which barely suggest them. Most people have seen faces in clouds. Many people have apparently seen faces on pieces of rock, judging from the names attached to various pieces of geology up and down the land. Individual differences obviously play a part here. In the Rorschach projective test, different people give various interpretations of the images presented to them, depending on their individual makeup. That an individual's emotional or motivational state has an effect on his perception has been demonstrated experimentally. It is no great wonder, then, that there is no one standard of interpretation in regard to paintings.

If we tend to see familiar objects in random forms, there is clearly a cultural factor involved. In a country where there are no sheep, one could hardly expect them to be seen in accidental configurations, projective tests, or dreams. Of course everyone sees those groupings of stars called constellations, but interpretations differ. In Figure 28a we see the star group called the Pleiades. Clearly, in their isolation, size, and close grouping they form a homogeneous entity. And we can make of it what we will. The skies, to the naked eye, present no such example of clarity, yet various peoples have constructed meaningful images out of the more or less random position of the stars, have named them with an identity drawn from daily experience, and have clothed them with a mythology of marvelous complexity and spawned the pseudo-science of astrology. What a richness out of so little! Figure 28b shows the interpretation of stellar events by the Huichol Indians. The arrow points to the Pleiades. Stars, nebulae, and planets play a part in the religious life of the Huichol, and these pinpoints of light are considered to be the dress of Young Mother Eagle. Thus in the configuration of stellar groupings and in the meanings given them we find a considerable variation between this and the well-established version which comes to us from a different

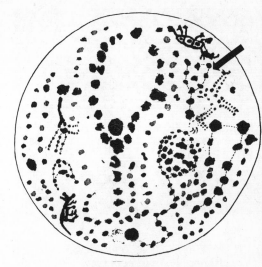

tradition of mythology. The animal forms suggest a part of the Huichol imagery.

For designers the meanings inherent in this discussion of image formation are several. First of all, one is impressed by the number of ways in which an image may be created and communicated. When these are multiplied by the variety of tools, surfaces, and pigments available, possibilities for unique expression are impressive. Then, too, it cannot be expected that everyone will see a particular image the same way. Even a dot may mean different things to different people. We can therefore learn a great deal by letting others see our efforts in design. We all get in the habit of projecting, of seeing things in our work that just are not there for other people—a phenomenon common to the creation of images. A person in the act of creation may be so intent on seeing a group of shapes in a certain way that the fact that he may have created a relationship with a different connotation entirely escapes him.

We can also expect to find that one kind of imagery is more arresting than another. Let us suppose that a page is designed combining

Fig. 28   a. *Formation of stars called Pleiades. The relative size and isolation in relation to the field makes for perception as a unit. The human nervous system fills in gaps and suggests meaningful forms. Courtesy Mount Wilson and Palomar Observatories. b. Completed figures on stellar formations by Huichol Indians. Letter b represents Pleiades. Unless borrowed from other cultures, completion of such abstract forms into meaningful images conforms to objects familiar in the environment. In a sense we see what we want to see. From the mentioned work of Carl Lumholtz.*

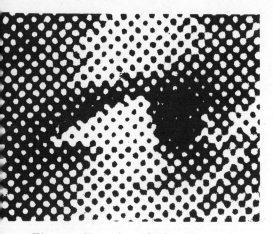

Fig. 29 Eye of outfielder Henry Aaron, from a newspaper reproduction. In the printing industry, reproduction of images containing the illusion of volume through graded values depends on our ability to perceive masses of detail as a total. All such reproductions are in reality small areas of pure black and pure white. If individual parts become too large, fusion of the image into its intended form is lost. If this image is seen too closely, its meaning as an eye departs.

Fig. 30 a. Detail of a 3rd-century mosaic. Large texture of the work may cause some trouble in fusing the image. b. Reduced image reveals a bust of Triton. Texture of painted works may also need distance for proper image formation. Both from Antioch Mosaic Pavements, *by Doro Levi, Princeton University Press, 1947.*

several different elements, and that one is a block of type stating that the building is on fire and that another is a laughing child. Do we have any doubts about which element will get prior attention? Under the same designation of scene-stealing images we can put babies or money or the young of animals. In designing with shapes which have subject content, one can never maintain all the shapes at an equal level of interest. A human shape in a landscape attracts attention, the recognition factor again. And it is perhaps only theoretically possible for a human being to maintain a level attitude toward all the forms in a work of art. Neither is it possible for a designer to lead the eye movements of a spectator in a planned orbit. The spectator will be attracted here and there and back and forth in an unpredictable manner. Perhaps a sure way to get a spectator to look at a particular place in a work would be to use a large red spot with a number of arrows pointing to it. A soft-drink maker once bought a full-page ad in a newspaper, and the only image which appeared on the entire page was a bottle cap. One can be certain that anyone reading that paper saw that cap.

In forms which do not have a subject content, one can expect observers to see resemblances to objects within their experience. This is to be expected and is a normal part of image formation. Some spectators will complain, however, if they do not experience familiarity in the imagery. An analogy can be drawn between such a person and one who goes into an Italian restaurant and is astonished to find that he cannot get egg foo yong. The painter Poussin had a fine statement on this: "Painting is nothing but an image of incorporeal things, despite the fact that it exhibits bodies, for it represents only the arrangements, proportions, and forms of things, and is more intent on the idea of beauty than on any other." This is a nice way to put the idea that subject is a reason to use form and color.

the limits of image fusion A daily newspaper offers good proof that we perceive images as a whole rather than as separate pieces. Figure 29 is an enlargement of a newspaper engraving. It represents the right eye of Henry Aaron, that expert on "motion parallax," a principle of depth perception and movement. There are no grays in any halftone engraving, but there are many small black and white dots, some joined together and others standing alone. Our nervous system is able to fuse these pieces into a single image implying three-dimensional form through graded values. The image is seen quite clearly at 8 or 10 feet. If, however, the image were to be enlarged several times again, the viewer would see only geometric patterns instead of an eye. The same phenomenon occurs on looking at many paintings, when apparently gross and meaningless daubs become elegant form as the viewer moves away from the painting. Figure 30a, a 3rd-century mosaic, may give the viewer some trouble. In it he may see only geometric patterns. A reduction of the same image gives us Figure 30b, and we have no trouble in fusing the image.

The point here is that designing sensibly involves thinking about the distance a viewer will be from the finished work. If a piece is designed to be held in the hand (as in a book illustration), the construction patterns may be quite fine. A painting that is to be hung in a large gallery could doubtless stand a coarser grain of texture. Most beginning artists apply pigment and view the progressing work at close range, and find on viewing it from farther away that what appeared to be a strong form is too weak. Much beginning work is too finely grained in texture to have any visual interest. There is not much chance of making the relationships too gross for the nervous system to put together. Fear not to work boldly.

a start in image formation Taking the simplest visual element we can think of—a dot—we can start image formation without difficulty. Figure 29 (and all the reproductions in this book) are formed of tiny building blocks of black and white, and these reproductions demonstrate that any and all effects are possible. Mimeograph paper, black tempera paint, and a pointed stick will suffice for our experiment, and the paper can serve as a ground. For first efforts there is no need to try for anything specific. Perhaps it is better just to notice the way in which dots begin to congregate (Fig. 31a) and thus begin to form an image. Then, continuing, one can try for a formation containing a little more action (Fig. 31b), and subsequently try to get the whites to become identified as whites, thus increasing the dynamic potential. This is done by isolating white areas, by surrounding them with other values (Fig. 31c). As we have seen, the contrast

Fig. 31 a. *Manipulation of dots causes concentration of dark and light and the beginning of figure formation.* b. *Dots begin to suggest rhythms and a more interesting involvement.* c. *White shapes caused by surrounding areas with dark. Dark and light forms begin to communicate a sense of space.* d. *Globe formed by dots.* e. *Control of shape and value are the tools for the realization of any complicated form. Author's sketches.*

39

Fig. 32 "Birthday Child," a drawing by the 20th-century German artist Paul Klee. Space, form, and even human emotion are communicated with an impressive economy of means.

of light and dark is fundamental to the attainment of space illusion, and in Figure 31c we see the image acquiring a little more sense of in and out.

With this simple device, over which the designer can exercise good control at all times, more complicated forms can be built. By changing values along a line, a light source can be implied and a volume suggested. With gradual changes in value, curved volumes can be formed. Development of a globe (Fig. 31d) is a good exercise to demonstrate exactly what occurs in forming this kind of an illusion. No reference model or copying is desired here, because it is important to understand it in theory. Cubes, cylinders and pyramids may be created, and then more difficult problems undertaken. Assume that the local value of a solid changes—that is, assume that a sphere is painted half white and half middle gray. What should it then look like? Or assume that a cube of wood is partly dark wood and partly light. Having done these things, we may wish to try more ambitious projects. Figure 31e may suggest the kind of project that might be attempted.

Paul Klee, the great 20th-century German artist, used all of the graphic devices. In "Birthday Child" (Fig. 32), a poetic piece of great charm, Klee uses comparatively slight suggestions to create the illusion of space. The effect is somewhat hazy, as if to parallel our memory of such an event.

It is good to start simply in order to review and establish one important fact about light and dark. The control of the light areas is not dependent on a positive physical act but rather on observation and judgment. Because of the fact that physical participation is easier, that observation and judgment require discipline of the mind, most of the beginner's creative activity will center on putting darks on the

primary object and leaving the negative shapes alone. Even advanced artists, when making preparatory sketches for paintings, may put all the darks on buildings and leave the sky white. This practice is quite typical of the work of artists from primitive cultures (Fig. 17) and, as previously noted, of children (Fig. 154). It will be noticed that Klee does not do this. Because he wants the vase to come forward in space, just enough dark is put outside of it to create the illusion of space in back of it.

Control is the key to studies of light and dark. For this reason pigment materials which make the application of dark too fast or too easy are not recommended. For slightly larger projects than that with the dots, toothed paper and a black crayon or lithograph pencil will do, with no erasing or smearing. For excellent control of values, see Figure 33 by Dudley Huppler. In this work the artist wanted the pigeon to appear light in order to conform to the delicate lightness of the bird. Yet he wanted the contour of the bird to be clear, so the modeling had to be done gently inside the shape of the pigeon. To have put dark values outside the shape in order to make the bird look white would have flattened out the delicate volume suggestions within. A somewhat advanced project along this line is a value study of a plaster cast—head, bust, or torso. The entire study should be accomplished using only the upper one third of the value range. This can be assured by using only part of a series of graded chalks. This is a good exercise in value control, making use of good material.

It should be stressed that value control is the heart of illusion. And understanding of space illusion is not an undertaking that applies exclusively to the fields of drawing and painting. It is incumbent upon all who design on flat surfaces and who wish to do more than make repeat geometry.

40

There are three basic conditions for the sensation we call sight. First there must be a carrier of the information. Energy waves called light waves serve this purpose. The second condition, the necessity for an information potential, is fulfilled by the fact that various materials of our environment absorb and reflect light energy in different ways. A receiving and translating mechanism is the third essential factor in sight sensation. Our eyes are equipped with mechanisms to admit the intensity of the energy required and to focus it. The retina contains cells, some of which are activated by quantity of energy while others are sensitive to energy of long or short wavelengths. These latter initiate the electrochemical reactions which transmit information to the brain, where they are translated into the sensation of color.

Light and the lack of it, dark, are chiefly responsible for definition of form. For the artist, too, value contrast is the basic factor in form illusion. Black and white has the maximum power. The beginning designer usually applies dark to a white surface. He is usually aware of the dark shapes he is making but generally lacks appreciation of the white shapes he is creating at the same time. Mature artists are keenly aware of these relationships at all times during the creative process, and it is essential that beginners exercise to sharpen their sensitivity to positive-negative relationships.

Monocular clues in perceiving the environment and in the illusion of space on a two-dimensional surface are five: 1. relative apparent size, 2. overlap, 3. relative position in the field, 4. light and shadow, and 5. aerial perspective. So-called linear perspective is a special application of relative apparent size. In

implying space, all artists use the same principles, so it is necessary that the student of design use and understand each of them.

The formation of homogeneous images is forced upon us by the necessity of making sense or order out of the gross details of the environment. We have the ability to perceive whole forms created with a minimum of plastic suggestion. Implications for artists are very important here, since communication can take place with surprising economy of means.

Fig. 33 "Pigeon," by contemporary American Dudley Huppler, 1947. Use of dots to create subtle volume and contour through the control of values. Through careful editing in the design process, distracting detail is eliminated, causing the viewer to see what the artist wanted him to see. Collection of Professor and Mrs. John Wilde.

41

3 sources of design: the natural environment

Man's insatiable quest for knowledge has taken him to and fro on the earth, up above it, and down in it. It has caused him to drag the bottom of the sea and examine the contents, to offer rewards for strange fish, to travel across the world to view an eclipse, to calculate the force in the muscles of an insect—some men have even watched operations performed on their own bodies. It is not to our interest here to speculate on the nature of this drive (and anyone who has watched a child examine a turtle knows that we all have it), but it is pertinent to state that an artist's compulsion to examine the structure of form and matter is often weak in comparison to that possessed by certain others of human kind. These are the men of science. We have seen the result of the cave artist's reaction to his environment, which produced a visual form based largely on various superficial or external aspects of appearances of animals. And in spite of a Leonardo da Vinci and a few others pricked by a special curiosity about the inner workings of things, the artist usually remains, although certainly more knowing than his ancestor, in a definitely conservative position on possible forms. This is true as well for those artists who include themselves in the *avant-garde*. In short, the scientist can often open our eyes.

appreciation of natural forms

We do not need the elegant variations in Figure 34 to disprove the notion that our culture is devoid of an appreciation of natural form. Studies in the history of art will suffice on this point. Our (Western) artistic tradition has, however, taken a different approach from that of the Japanese-Chinese in special appreciation of the natural environment. Figure 35 reveals something of the depth of feeling attained by the Oriental artist, sensitively keen to the poetic image inherent in the natural object. Our culture is different, to be sure, but most young artists may have their childhood curiosity in living objects revived. An occasional field trip, preferably as a member of a group, will turn up a rich source of visual material for comparison, exchange of information, and argument. Thus encouraged, individuals, following their own bent, find ample material for projects. For challenge in technical control this may involve copying, which provides a confidence that the beginner is the master of these found forms. Careful observation is the groundwork for great art. Found objects may also provide the springboard for a graceful introduction into the formation of visually significant form out of endlessly repeated detail. The artist thus learns for himself that while some organisms have an apparently endless need for reproduction, the condition may be summarized. Thus the artist learns to edit, to shape material to his own needs and that of his visual heritage. It may even be that one or two individuals, in becoming interested in plant or animal forms, will find a career in their visual interpretation.

the scientist as an ally The man of science is usually devoted to the study of structure in the universe. He is interested in the relationships of parts to whole, in discovering the meaningful order in seeming chaos. In this broad sense the artist and scientist are traveling parallel roads, and the artist must heed the

Fig. 34 "Plant Forms," by Alice Bunch. This lithograph, an elegant theme and variation study, demonstrates that artists may get ideas from natural forms. In the past, particular training in the perception and appreciation of singular environmental structures has been a strong feature in the development of artists in Japan and China. Collection of the University of Wisconsin, Madison.

Fig. 35 Trees from a scroll by Hasegawa Tohāku (1539-1630). Oriental artists tend to be sensitive to subtle nuances of natural form. Courtesy Tokyo National Museum, Tokyo.

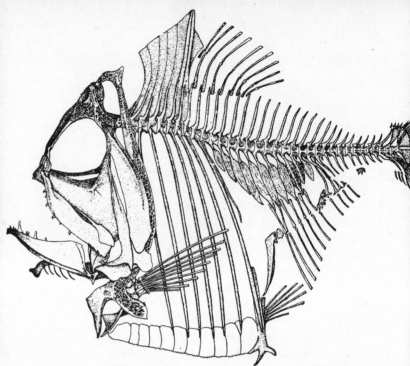

Fig. 36 Spiral nebula in Pisces, Messier 74. From scientists comes new and ever more reliable information on the structure of the universe, both macrocosm and microcosm. This information often upsets old concepts, including artistic ones. Thus, while there are fine works of art from Persia and elsewhere based on outdated notions about the universe, contemporary designers are bound to new truths. Accompanying these new truths are better and more interesting visual information. Photography by Mount Wilson and Palomar Observatories.

Fig. 37 Skeletal structure of a fish. Scientist and artist alike can appreciate the delicately balanced forms and the suggestion of precise articulation of parts in the living form. Drawing by H. L. Todd in The Fishes of North and Middle America, *Smithsonian Institution, 1900.*

work of scientific investigators. Figure 36 reveals that an apparent spot of light in the heavens actually consists of billions of stars in a patterned though ever-changing relationship, the image of which is out of date by factors ranging into the billions of years. Such truths about the structure of the universe make an artist think carefully about its pictorial organization. It may mean that for the contemporary artist such conceptions as that in Figure 28b, the Indian schema of constellations, are out of the question, save perhaps as humorous byplay. If at times the conservative artist allows himself somewhat reluctantly to be dragged down the road of truth, giving up with difficulty static conceptions of matter and space, he finds points where the views of artist and scientist almost coincide. Both can appreciate the subtle part-whole relationships, the implications of delicate articulation in the interdependent substructures of the living organism (Fig. 37). Beyond this meeting point,

the skeleton may have different meanings for the artist and the scientist. The former may see a chance to use the form in a visual study, while the latter may be interested in the way in which a particular substructure differs from that existing in a related form. His final study may therefore be executed in verbal, chemical, or mathematical symbols.

In matters of description and communication, however, the scientist often finds that pictorial matter works better than words. It is not surprising, therefore, to find that most scientists have a rather high appreciation of visual form. It is not their first order of business, but many find pleasure in the visual aspect of their work. If an artist were to bring a specimen to a specialist, disclosing the fact that he thought it to possess some unique visual qualities, the scholar might quite likely give him leads on other interesting material.

While it is true that we all must *learn* to see, many people in the sciences learn to see better

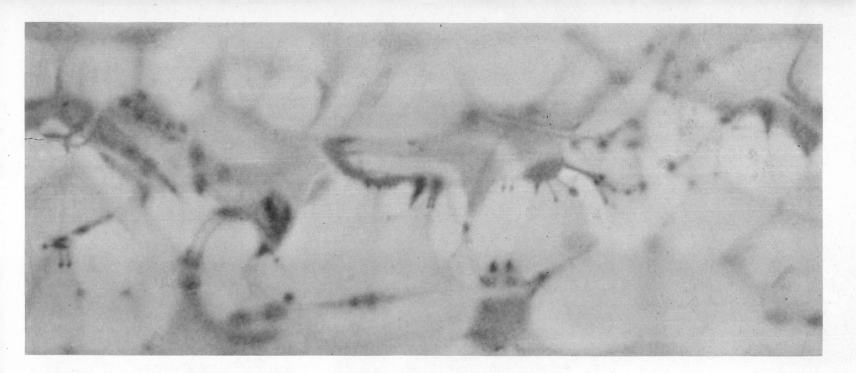

than do artists. For many of those not wholly engaged in a world of symbols, fine visual discrimination is a prerequisite. Gifted astronomers can resolve more detail than photographic apparatus. Figure 38 shows an example of this kind of talent. Those of us who are engaged in design fields can be helped to grasp the fundamentals of natural structure with the aid of those who are most closely associated with its study.

While placing an emphasis here on visual manifestations of natural structure, we have no intent to diminish the talents of those gifted in perceiving other kinds of relationships which have visual potential. A student draws a Cadillac parked in front of a shack. What does it mean? The student explains that the Cadillac and the shack are owned by a Negro. This kind of vision is rare and is of the kind that is passed over by most students of design and science. While the social structure is indeed grist for the designer's mill, beginners will

find such material difficult to execute effectively.

While artists and scientists of the present do have common interests in structure, in some eras art and science were much closer together. Erwin H. Ackerknecht, M.D., an eminent authority in the history of medicine, writing in the *Bulletin of the Medical Library Association*, states: "In early periods when medicine, like many other practical activities such as agriculture or husbandry, is profoundly pervaded by magic, and when art serves magic and is a part of it, the relations between medicine and art are particularly close." The anatomical studies by Andreas Vesalius, the great 16th-century Flemish pioneer in this field, with their echoes of morbidity on the subject of death, communicate considerable emotion. And certainly Figure 39 is more than a study in human anatomy. Here is the image of man the confident, in an imposing composition with elegant play in the substructures. The book

Fig. 38 Map of Mars, demonstrating a high level in the ability to see—an art which must be learned and which here goes beyond the resolving powers of photographic equipment. It is, incidentally, an elegant development in subtle shapes and accents. This is incidental, for the author's intention was to make an accurate map. Map by G. de Vaucouleurs of Harvard College Observatory, available through his courtesy.

45

Fig. 39 Anatomical study demonstrating the alliance between science and art. Here are clearly drawn analogies between human, architectural, botanical, and geological principles of support. In each of these features we find parallel development of detail, with subtle variations in the value relationships. Although shot through with philosophical content, the pillar alone is an elegant study in subtle value contrasts. This and other fine engravings are contained in Tabulae Sceleti et Musculorum corporus Humani, *by Bernhard Siegfried Albinus (1697-1770), published by Lugdunae Batavorum in 1747. From a copy in the Medical Library, University of Wisconsin.*

from which this work is taken, containing as it does many exquisite engravings, is an impressive one-man show. Such books are of especial interest to students of design.

Medical libraries contain visual studies of all the major systems within the human body and much pictorial work on details of tissues, operations, diseases, and so on. Some anatomical studies of animals will also be found. Works going back to pre-Renaissance times have certain terrifying aspects often relieved by humor, the practices of the times having been so outrageous. An abundance of interesting work will also be found in zoology libraries, where the several subdisciplines of ornithology (birds), ichthyology (fish), entomology (insects), malacology (mollusks), and other fields

are found to depend in part on a visual tradition. Botany, with a similar proliferation in specialization, has, as previously noted, a long and impressive visual heritage in herbals. Some of these pictorial works on plant life have considerable stature as works of art. Geology, too, provides fascinating visual studies on the inanimate structure of our environment. Cytologists (investigators who study matter on the cell level) provide much visual information on the flow of organic form. The fields of mathematics, chemistry, and physics also contribute visual material. Figure 178 (p. 170), the X-ray diffraction pattern of a single crystal of the mineral beryl, is an elegant and illuminating example of structure at a basic level.

design ideas in natural form

One of the striking concepts occurring in both art and the natural environment is that of symmetry. We are aware of the symmetrical nature of our own physical structure, imperfect though it is. Symmetry takes in the idea of completeness, of unity, of perfection. In Figure 40a and b we see two variations of this idea; in both cases large structures and secondary features repeat. It is simple to gather a good collection of symmetrical material. Many plants and animals have symmetry as a major feature of structure.

Another feature to be found in many design fields and in the living environment is the repetition of elements. Figures 17, 19, and 22 (pp. 24, 28, and 32) in the last section showed repetition of important elements. On some levels of natural structure, units are repeated exactly. It is sometimes desirable in design to do the same. The examples here are those showing repetition with variation, which is often more interesting. Figure 41a is a paint-

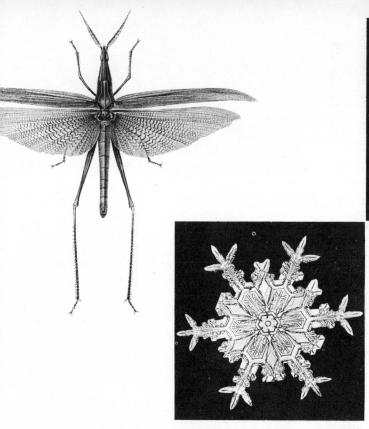

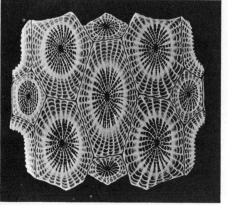

Fig. 40 a. *Grasshopper, illustrating symmetry of natural forms, a characteristic inevitably dictated by problems of support and movement millions of years ago. To be especially noted are the elegance of the wing shapes and the variations in the wing texture. From* Description de L'Égypte Histoire Naturelle Planches, *published by C. L. F. Panckoucke, Paris, 1826.* b. *Snowflake, an illustration of geometric symmetry. Principal features and substructures repeat. From* Snow Crystals, *by W. A. Bentley and W. J. Humphreys. Courtesy McGraw-Hill Book Company, New York, 1931.*

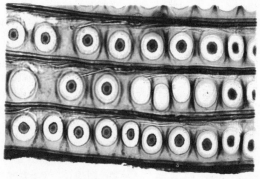

ing of a skeleton of a coral by the famous Ernst Haeckel, whose *Kunstformen der Natur* (Art Forms of Nature), published in Leipzig at the turn of the century, is a treasure house of natural form. Somewhat controversial as a scientist, Haeckel's masterpiece is said to contain examples wherein the truth is slightly stretched in the direction of art. Some of them certainly would be marvels of graphic invention had he improvised them, which of course he did not. In Figure 41a we see repetition with geometric overtones to the variations, which are in turn delicately embroidered. Figure 41b is a photograph of bordered pits in cell walls of pine. Again we see the repetition of form with variation.

If we are concerned with the contour, or perfection in shape, our environment provides examples in abundance. The shapes of leaves would provide an exhibition to the point. On elegance of contour, birds have their sponsors, as noted in Figure 33 (p. 41). Gulls or terns in flight are creatures of elegant form. While Audubon's works on birds are well known, libraries contain other fine studies on the birds of various areas. Birds and fish owe their structure to the kind of environment in which they move. Thus fish often possess a purity of form which we admire, since a cluttered form would be a handicap to movement through water. Basically the shape in Figure 42a is a simple one, with substructures echoing the

Fig. 41 a. *Skeleton of a coral, embodying a repetition of elements in a geometric pattern with subtle asymmetrical features and fine elaboration in closely correlated parts. From Ernst Haeckel's* Kunstformen der Natur (The Art Forms of Nature), *published by the Bibliographisches Institut, Leipzig, 1899-1903.* b. *Photograph of bordered pits in cell walls of pine, an example of repetition with variation—a frequent occurrence in natural form. Courtesy Forest Products Laboratory, Madison, Wis.*

Fig. 42 a. *Fish, exhibiting pure form shaped by physical forces in its environment. Substructures and texture echo the basic shape. Drawing by M. M. Smith,* The Fishes of North and Middle America, *1900, Smithsonian Institution.* b. *Pure form of a snake, with repeating elements, a phenomenon of its movement exaggerated by the artist. From* Description de L'Égypte, op. cit.

Fig. 43 a. *Drawing of living coral, a fine textural study of circular forms with interesting variations.* b. *Aggregate of crystals, a texture with a rectangular format.* c. *A geological form with textural ornament due to a manganese oxide stain. All examples are from* Description de L'Égypte, op. cit.

oval in various ways. Figure 42b provides a different sort of pure form, round and tapering with repeated geometric patterns, the whole arranged with repeated negative shapes by courtesy of the artist. Most cities support a zoo, possibly an aquarium, and many institutions of higher learning possess an herbarium and/or other facilities for the study of flora and fauna. Sketching trips to such facilities should be pleasurable.

On texture the supply of examples is better than good. Here we are speaking of differences in surface appearance—a phenomenon which adds richness to our visual environment and life to a work of art. Figure 43a is a representation of a living coral formation. As a rich surface it speaks for itself. In Figure 43b the minutiae are changed from circular to more nearly rectangular. We can almost feel the bite of the surface on our finger tips from this aggregate of crystals. Yet another texture is seen in Figure 43c. At first glance the pattern appears to have its origin in some kind of plant

life, but it is really caused by a manganese oxide stain on a rock. College departments of geology often house exhibitions of this kind of material. Sometimes a gem cutter can be found who will have an abundance of interesting rock formations. Libraries of course are full of good studies in textural qualities, but if it is a dry day it may be preferable to collect samples by way of a walk in the woods.

In discussions on esthetics a good deal of thought centers on the theme of variety within unity. This means that within the framework of a work of art, parts are bent but may not burst the framework and so destroy the central motivating idea. To show what variety within unity is not, artists sometimes play a little game which is not only exciting but to our point. Any number can play. One person makes a drawing and folds the paper over to cover it up, leaving two lines showing for the next person to improvise upon. He completes his drawing, covering it with a fold of the paper and again leaving two lines for the next

48

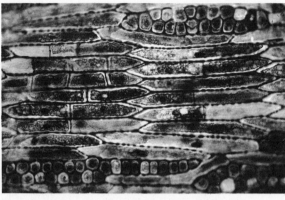

person, and so on until the game is finished. The resulting absurdities reveal what art is not: a conglomerate of separate ideas without valid connecting form. Here art and natural form run parallel, for in the natural form the parts are held together in a cooperative arrangement with a checkrein on independent action, an excess of which injures or destroys function. Cancerous growths in living form— aside from their disastrous effect in a physical sense—are repugnant in idea, for they are composed of cells running wild which destroy form existing for a reason.

This principle of variety within unity is seen in Figure 34 and in many of the other reproductions in the book. We see it in natural form in Figure 44a, cell tissues of black locust tree. Variations in shape, texture, and value occur within a rather strictly unified whole to give a visually satisfying effect. Variations of a different kind are apparent in 44b, a photograph, taken through an electron microscope, of a chloroplast of corn. Here rectangular and cir-

cular subforms are neatly resolved in the total effect.

Along the same line is the principle of elaboration of form. In products of design it often means repeating a form over and over until all the space is filled, to make a strong point of embellishment for its own sake. Natural form, too, sometimes seems to defy the dictum of economy of means and go in for sheer complexity. We see this kind of elaborate play of form in Figure 45a. In this drawing of a clam the fanciful repetition of curved forms has an underlying unity. The baroquelike involvement in 45b with its apparently endless convolutions embodies the idea of transparency with windows cut in the surface through which more details are seen. The animal form pictured here is that of a sponge. Differing sharply from this flowing form, colonies of diatoms, or algae (Fig. 45c), exhibit a geometric complexity. This structure contains sharply defined pure shapes in a rather rigid depth pattern. Again, with all the elaboration there is a kind of vis-

Fig. 44 a. *Cell tissue from black locust tree. Courtesy Professors William F. Millington and Emma L. Fisk, and Burgess Publishing Company, publishers of* Atlas of Plant Morphology, *1959.* b. *Chloroplast of corn. A variety of form, rectangular, circular, and linear, resolved into a unified whole. Electron microscope photograph by Dr. Albert E. Vatter, courtesy of Upjohn Company.*

49

ual unity to the piece, just as there is organic unity in the living organism.

In the area of the visually fantastic we again find that natural form has a good head start on the artist. Some living forms put a strain on credulity. Fantastic indeed is the image of an oceanic planktonic crustacean (Fig. 46a). Perhaps it is a good thing that this organism is very small. The strangely suggestive forms in 46b are the result of the growth of ice crystals, a phenomenon familiar to all of us. A possible explanation of its quality of fantasy is that the individual forms have something of a human connotation and if construed in that light a kind of mad dance is seen. The visual material of this section concludes with the sea urchin in Figure 46c. Here again is unique and strange natural form, still embodying a perfect unity.

To expand this section into a book would not be too formidable a task; the material is certainly available. If we want to learn about line the natural environment can teach us something about it. On geometric form, what about the patterns seen on giant turtles? What about the honeycomb with its modular perfection? On transparency, our study of its use by artists can be augmented by noting its existence in living bodies. When we speak of harmony, of family relationships of shape elements, of articulation or connections between elements, of flow of form, of asymmetrical form, of sharp variation—we can bring the example of the natural image to bear on the question.

summary

Artists have always taken themes from that part of the natural environment most bound up in their continued existence. A later development is the appreciation of natural form for its own sake, an idea given special fulfillment in the art of the Orient. In Western art the

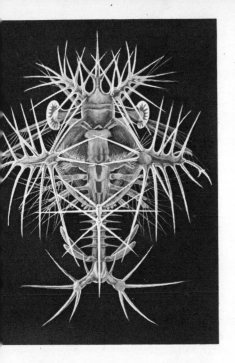
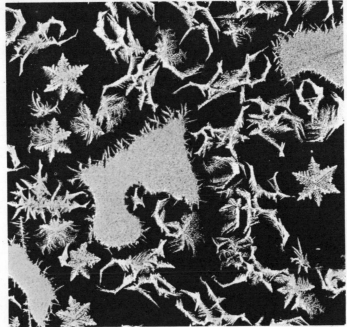

Fig. 46 a. *Planktonic crustacean, an ocean form and an example of a living entity so different from those seen in daily life that our impression is that of fantasy. From* Kunstformen der Natur, op. cit. b. *Formations of ice crystals. Images suggest living creatures, perhaps human, in an energetic state. Photograph by W. A. Bentley. c. Sea urchin, an electrifying symbol of the virtuosity expressed in natural forms. From* Description de L'Égypte, *op. cit.*

image of man has more often dominated the artist. The scientific fields of the Western world have long visual traditions evolving from their communication needs. Man's image is a part of this visual heritage but the scientist studies, draws, and photographs in ever-proliferating areas of investigation. Thus our culture produces men and women trained to see form with keen discrimination, and since designers too must learn to see, they can be helped by the study of the natural entity or its image.

Since we define art as man-made, natural form is not the form of art. But our environment does produce visual material which embodies some of the structural principles artists use in their work. This is valuable. Some of the forms we find can be introduced directly into the design process. This is valuable. And of course a curiosity about the structure of our environment is an enriching resource in life. And this is valuable.

4 *line*

If a point could move and leave a mark in moving, a line would result. This is a good way to think about line because it brings to the subject a dynamic quality. A line is almost always the result of something moving and leaving a mark. Because of this kinetic element in line, special qualities are associated with it. First, line is a go-or-no-go graphic element— it is either there or it isn't there. It has no vague properties and is therefore decisive and purposeful. Secondly, because line is a product of weight and energy, physical principles apply. It takes a certain amount of energy to start a line, and once started, a line tends to continue in the direction of its start. Given a sharp impetus, any tool touching a surface must describe a straight line or perhaps a slight curve. Because of this tendency for a body in motion to remain in motion, lines tend to be rendered in pure forms in a direction toward the straight or curved. It is difficult to find any applications of line from any source which are in violation of this physical principle. And lastly, because line is usually directed by some kind of intelligence, it seems to have a kind of destiny. Like an airplane leaving a vapor trail, line has some place to go. Our society uses line in many ways and nearly always it follows a predetermined course. It may describe a circle, the contour of a bird, the route to Los Angeles, the profile of an earthquake, or the face of an angel. Even the spider webs in Figure 47 reflect a meaningful purpose behind the use of line. These factors contribute to esthetic attitude toward the use of line. We expect to use line directly and forcefully. Subtlety is possible, but equivocation or hesitation are not qualities we usually look for in line.

line: the cultural aspect

We use line in lettering and writing and ciphering. During the last century many people became highly skilled in writing in the rather strict and elegant Spencerian style (Fig. 48a). Notice the emphasis, in form and message, on continuity of movement. This method stems from the fact that if the hand that is guiding the line is in motion, a bad line is unlikely to result. A flexible gold pen was used to obtain the thick-and-thin line which marked the 19th-century styles in calligraphy. The style was expanded to encompass various kinds of pictorial efforts (Fig. 48b). Pictorial work of this kind reached a level of high virtuosity. Foolish as these efforts seem today, they represented an aim of high merit—to teach the young to draw and write with the same tool, a tool which imparted character to either endeavor. In some parts of the Orient children are taught to use a pointed brush, and drawing and writing become part of one activity. In parts of the Middle East children are taught to master the broad-nib reed pen, the tool which created a great tradition in calligraphy and which developed our lower-case alphabet. In our schools we have no such close integration of the activities of drawing and writing, and the tools used, notably among them the graphite pencil, are generally lacking in distinctive character. But our children do use line at an early age, and we see its frequent use in play—drawing, marking off game patterns, and keeping score.

As adults we use line quite naturally in abstract or symbolic form. We make maps where line stands for a road, a building, a lot line, or

Fig. 47 Study of spider web reflects the purposeful quality inherent in line. It also demonstrates that line is usually a product of an object in movement and is therefore inextricably associated with kinetic rather than static concepts. Painted by Paul L. Taylor, Paton Studios, Indianapolis. Courtesy Eli Lilly and Company.

a bush. We figure our bills in linear scribbles keeping score with coded symbols made of line.

Specialists in our society rely heavily on line in communication. Engineering draftsmen learn to transfer complex machinery to the flat surface in order to teach others the relationships of parts in assembly and repair (Fig. 49). This kind of drawing is partly realistic and partly coded. Line may represent the actual seen contour of the machine in some instances, while another kind of line, pre-assigned in meaning, stands for a cross section. A third kind of line represents invisible structures, and this introduces the principle of transparency. Yet a fourth line, a center line, represents a totally theoretical value, since no such line can be seen on the machine. This system of imagery is by no means simple; the principle of transparency used in this connection is also used by painters. This kind of drawing is of more than passing interest to the design student. A collection of such material serves well in collage. Then too, it is necessary to master at least the rudiments of mechanical drawing in order to possess a well-rounded set of communication skills.

Architects use similar techniques in line to enable contractors and building tradesmen to follow plans accurately. Heating systems are planned in line, as are electrical wiring and plumbing systems.

Mapmakers rely heavily on line. We are most familiar with city and road maps, and recognize the difficult problems involved in being without them. Many maps, aside from their information value, furnish esthetically

Fig. 48 a. Page of an exercise book typical of 19th-century ideas on the teaching of handwriting. The whole exercise suggests continuity of movement. b. The flexible pen used in pictorial work gives a distinctive character to the picture. Handwriting and drawing require a similar flow of line. Both examples courtesy Wisconsin State Historical Society.

Fig. 49 Drawing of a machine. Line represents several levels of meaning, from realistic outlines to invisible parts and such imaginary entities as the center of parts. Courtesy Gisholt Machine Company.

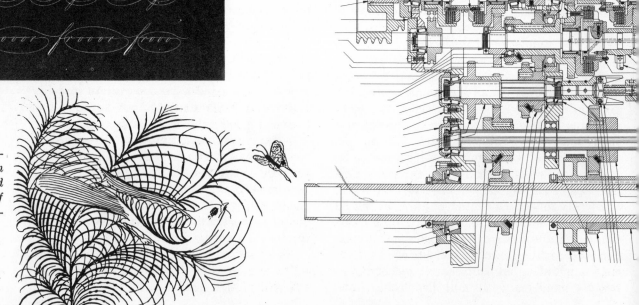

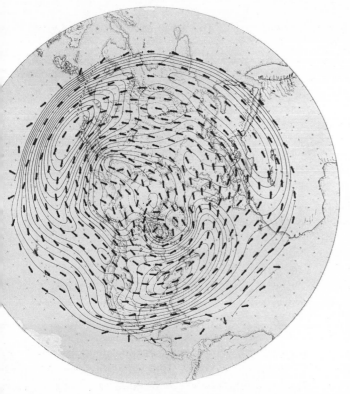

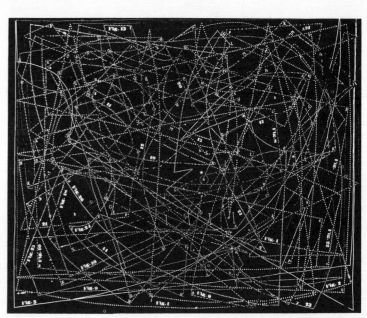

satisfactory visual material. They are often executed with subtlety and elegance, as in Figure 50, a study of wind characteristics in the Northern Hemisphere. Contour maps with their organic flow of line are not only fascinating but have taught us a valuable method of explaining three-dimensional forms. The technique used in Figure 51 can be applied to any solid form from a stone to the human figure. A foundation in design should include some study of this technique, for it is one in which line can be substituted for modeling in value.

A number of trades make use of line. In Figure 52 we see line as used in the patterns of a garment maker. This curious example, dating from 1873, contains at least ten different kinds of line for purposes of continuity in reading the pattern. Even at that it must have been a trying experience. Figure 52 illustrates in extreme form a principle widely used in design, that of simultaneous existence of images. Because line is essentially transparent, two or more images can occupy the same place at the same time. We will see examples of such interweaving of images, often designated by the term "interpenetration," later in this book.

Coded symbols used by many trades and professions make free use of line. The sign is an example of what is meant by the term. Meanings are pre-assigned as in a language. Pharmacologists use a set of these coded symbols, as do mathematicians, musicians, radio technicians, and hoboes, among others.

Mathematics uses line frequently to express solids and theories. In Figure 53a we see an example of line used to express a geometric

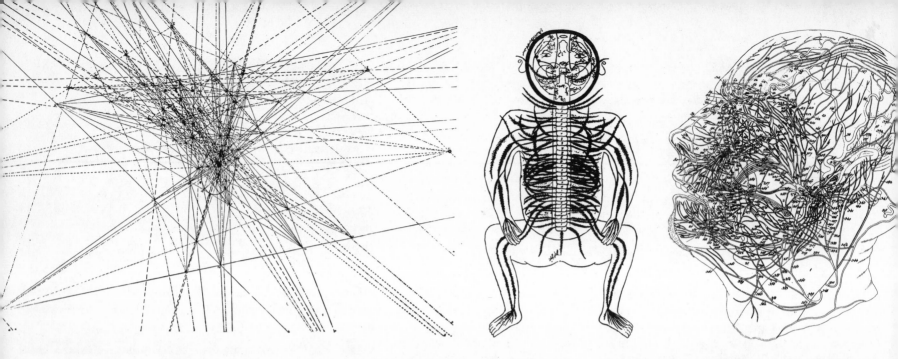

Fig. 53 a. Pascal's Mystic Hexagram, demonstrating the transparency of line. One form is imposed over another and the entire problem presented in one complex image instead of a series. From a thesis by Anne and Elizabeth Linton, University of Pennsylvania, 1921. b. Nervous system, from a Persian manuscript. The body is regarded as transparent and the line elements interpenetrate one another freely. From Sudhoff's Geschichte der Anatomie im Mittelalter, *Leipzig, 1909. Original Persian manuscript in the India Office Library, London. Courtesy India Office Librarian. c. Study of the nervous system of the face. Line is particularly suited to the expression of complex line-like material. From* Anatomische Tafeln, *by Iust Christian Loder, D., Weimar, 1803.*

problem, Pascal's Mystic Hexagram. Here again we see a number of different kinds of line used, and the essential transparency of line once again demonstrated. One set of lines is superimposed upon another, and the entire evolution and solution of the problem is shown in one complex image rather than being strung out in a series. Students will find many interesting linear studies in mathematics. Pure linear forms, the graphic expression of mathematical formulas, are often serenely elegant.

Anatomical studies provide a good source for linear techniques. There is probably more art than accuracy in the drawing of Figure 53b, part of a Persian manuscript, but as noted previously, the connection between art and medicine was rather close in earlier times. The contrast in line strength and character is very frank, particularly the formalized heavy line expressing the head. Many contemporary artists use just such contrasts. Again the principle of transparency is used—the figure seems to be made of glass, and interpenetration of

elements is seen. An added note of interest is provided by the incorporation of writing (Arabic) along with the line. This is a forceful and imaginative piece. Later and more accurate, the study in Figure 53c also represents a part of the nervous system. Because of its complexity, the use of line is a necessity. The interweaving of the many elements, over and under one another, is the kind of representation only line can accomplish. As is often the case in anatomical studies, the expressive qualities of the head exceed intent.

We see in this brief review that line as a communicative device is more firmly entrenched in our cultural pattern than we may have imagined. The reader will quite easily find more examples for his clip file.

line in natural and man-made forms

Some of the examples shown in the previous section on the design of natural form had strong linear elements. The rigidly spectacular form of the sea urchin (Fig. 46c, p. 51) contrasts with the delicate linear tracery in insect wings (Fig. 40a, p 47). As we wander about the landscape in moments of relaxation, interesting bits of linear form will come to our notice, particularly if we are properly alert. It may be the linear pattern of pine needles, the seed of a dandelion, the wing of a butterfly, or the swaying of long stems of wheat which arrests the attention. Figure 54, the structural elements of an oak leaf remaining after decay of the soft parts, is a suitable reward for diligent looking. On close inspection it can be seen that the patterns are by no means identical, and this variety together with strong and graceful major elements make a striking portrayal of natural structure. A different sort of line is seen in Figure 55. Rather than a clean, sparse, linear pattern, there is an intricate, dense, tortuous path of a broken line. Still another kind of line can be seen in Figure 179, page 172, fragments of macerated oak, in the section on transparency.

Probably no modern artist has been so knowledgeable in terms of natural form as Paul Klee, the 20th-century German artist. Klee collected and studied natural form and understood it not as isolated fragments but in terms of a whole environmental pattern. He appreciated the linear aspects of natural form —the seeking tendril, the relentless etch of line as revealed in cut sections of plants—and incorporated them into his own style of quiet fantasy. Fortunately the many books on Klee make this phase of his work available to all.

Many of the structures of man, too, have a linear content. Several good studies have been executed on the theme of television aerials, essentially linear structures. Wires are seen as line, and we see many examples of this in fences, telephone lines (see Fig. 78, p. 73), and electric power lines. Radio towers and oil derricks are other structures seen as line rather than shape.

From the paraphernalia connected with music there are music stands, pipe organs, harp

Fig. 54 Structural elements of an oak leaf, showing intricate pattern of support in living form. Courtesy Professor Herbert M. Clarke; photo by R. J. Williams.

Fig. 55 Transverse section of renal mass in fish bladder. This intricate pattern of natural tissue is delineated by a broken line. From "Parental Care among Fresh Water Fishes," by Theodore Gill, in the Smithsonian Report for 1905.

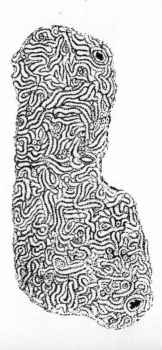

Fig. 56   Linear pattern made by crossing railroad tracks. Man-made linear sources are most often seen in straight lines and pure curves. Author's sketch.

Fig. 57   Line used to express a linear structure. Subject and technique of expression coincide. Both man-made source and drawing are essentially transparent. Brush drawing, "The Empty Studio," by American contemporary artist Ben Shahn for the Columbia Broadcasting System.

and piano strings. In fact, we will see line wherever we go—railroad yards (Fig. 56), shop, factory, dock or laboratory. We can learn a great deal about line and our society by being alert to its occurrence in the man-made environment.

limitations of line

The work entitled "The Empty Studio" by Ben Shahn (Fig. 57) shows what line does naturally—expresses a form that is essentially linear to begin with. Line also expresses the edges of forms quite easily (see Fig. 21, p. 31), providing the forms are composed of planes. Rounded forms where changes in direction are gradual are not as easily expressed in linear form. For example, examine Figure 58a. It expresses a circle. Now let us assume that we want this same line to communicate the sense of a disk. If we do not turn the figure in order to pick up the sense of an edge, we must rely on a flat value (58b) to express the disk, with only a fair degree of success. In trying to communicate the quality of a sphere with a line, we are likewise handicapped. If we try the method suggested by the contour map, we obtain the image in 58c. We don't know what we are seeing here. Is it a flat pattern of concentric circles? The contour method works best when the nature of the form is safely established. We could draw the contour of a head, for example, and use the contour technique successfully. In order to get our sphere we will have to give it some more attributes. By assuming that the sphere has lines traveling around its circumference, we get Figure 58d, a fair result. Perhaps the best way is to assume a circumference line or two and also assume the figure to be transparent. In this way we get Figure 58e, a fairly good result but not so good as that obtained by graduated values (58f), which can be built up of dots. Since designers using line may work on many rounded volumes, it will be instructive to see how they solve the problem.

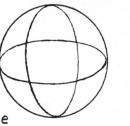

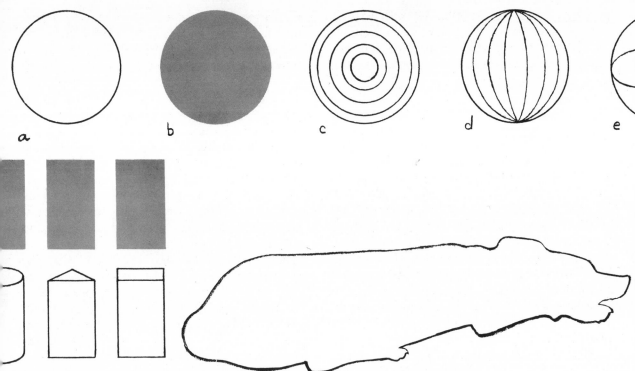

Fig. 58 a. *Circle.* b. *Circle can describe a disk with the aid of value.* c. *Contour lines fail to express volume of globe.* d. *Assumption of lines results in an improved sensation of volume.* e. *Assumption of transparency also improves three-dimensional sense.* f. *Gradation of value works better than any system of lines in communicating volume. Author's sketch.*

Fig. 59 a. *Identical profiles produced by three different volumes. Neither line nor value gives the needed information.* b. *Volumes must be tipped, or the point of view changed, to show the true nature of the volumes. Each object must be studied to determine its most expressive façade. Author's sketch.*

Fig. 60 Outline drawing of a sleeping dog, inadequate in information. A better aspect of the animal is needed, together with a more adequate explanation of articulation of parts. Author's sketch.

Line may also be unsatisfactory for explaining certain kinds of volumes. Figure 59a shows the identical profile shapes of three different volumes (59b). When executed in profile neither line nor value gives us the information needed. We can learn from this that some volumes need to be seen from an advantageous reference point. Thus, for the human being, the view from the top is most difficult and unrewarding. A French horn seen on edge is worth little. It is better in profile (see Fig. 68, p. 66).

Another example of line in a dubious venture is seen in Figure 60. It is commonly assumed that line is very good in contour, but it is clear that this drawing of a sleeping dog's contour is less than adequate. It communicates very little. A similar drawing of a seated hu-

man figure would be equally uninteresting. By changing the approach in two ways, the result can be improved greatly. First, a more expressive aspect of the dog can be chosen, one in which tail, legs, and head can be clearly seen. And then, with very little more work the articulation of legs and trunk can be established, along with such significant detail as the eyes and ears. Each object to be used in design must be studied to determine its most expressive aspect, the aspect which contains as much significant detail as possible. Notice that in Picasso's line study of a man (Fig. 61) the quantity of line is sparse, yet the information is adequate. Volume is expressed and a complete, rather sympathetic mood established with great economy of means. The artist has chosen a good aspect of a human being and has

59

Fig. 61 Picasso's drawing "Bust of Man" implies a rounded form with economy of means. The viewer already knows that a head is round, so that the illusion of volume is created chiefly by implication. Courtesy of the artist.

Fig. 62 A simple experiment in communication. Associate the following words with individual sketches: stable, lyric, foolish, nervous, dynamic. Line as well as other graphic elements communicates ideas independently of subject. Author's sketch.

included significant detail (eyes, nose, mouth, and ear) ; he needs little else. It was noted previously that line was not adequate to explain curved volumes. How does Picasso get around this problem? In two ways. First, he relies on our knowledge of form. We already know that a head is round, so that his image becomes complete for us with few additional clues. Secondly, when lines are seen on a curved surface they are curved and imply the nature of the surface. Thus the eyes and mouth in Picasso's drawing imply a curved surface. So with careful selection of material we can get around some of line's inherent weaknesses.

line and art

Picasso's drawing serves to introduce a discussion on the ways in which artists use line. We have seen something of the way in which modern society depends on line in communicating information; now we will see how the artist depends on line to communicate his ideas. First of all we want to establish the fact that formations of line have communication potential independent of subject. Let the reader examine the sketches in Figure 62 and see which item is most properly connected to one of the following words: stable, lyric, foolish, nervous, dynamic. Most of us will be able to connect the words to the appropriate sketch. These rather obvious sketches are in line, of course, but the principle applies to any method

or device used in obtaining images which transfer personal ideas. The graphic and plastic means determines the final result, and this means that nonfigurative work in which shapes are not identified in terms of cat or apple or angel still may communicate qualities which match our receptive abilities. An individual's ideas about darkness or a heavy piece of black in a painting may be shaped by what the rest of society thinks on the significance of black, and they may be shaped by personal experience, but black certainly cannot be seen as white. Analogously, a curved line conveys a different quality than does a straight one.

As might be expected, the use of line in an artistic or nonutilitarian way is old. The cave artist's tracery (Fig. 181, p. 173) in the section on transparency is a testimonial image. This work was created by moving fingers in wet clay. From the outset, line has been primarily action. Encouragement for the beginner is found in the bamboo engravings created by the inhabitants of New Caledonia, an island off the east coast of Australia (Fig. 63). The technique here is that of intaglio, cutting lines in large pieces of bamboo and either putting charcoal amalgam in the lines or allowing dirt to accumulate in them. Surely the method is associated with difficulty and sophistication, but obviously these artists proceeded to delineate what interested them in a very straightforward way. Line is used here to describe objects of linear structure, as contour, and to

build up value for the definition of shapes. Like black and white dots, crowded black and white lines are perceived as gray. An extension of this technique provides a method of obtaining the illusion of volume. (The superb modeling potential of line is proved by Albinus's anatomical study [Fig. 39, p. 46].) Notice the variety in the use of line in Figure 63. Although there is an over-all unity in the style, no two horses are executed in the same way. Individual differences in position, shape, dark and light tone, and muscle structure are suggested in a way which imparts an amazing vitality to each animal figure. It is this kind of fresh and bold approach to form simplification that has so intrigued the modern artist. Before passing on, notice one odd convention: both legs of the horsemen are implied to be on the side of the horse away from the viewer.

For use of line in fundamental ways we may turn to three works of Paul Klee. This gifted man always used line with clarity. Not that his view of life as reflected in his work was simple-minded, but rather, in each of his works, line has a single purpose, and this serves to teach us. In Figure 64a, "Children's Playground," Klee uses the kind of line one gets with a pointed stick and the figures are stick figures, with one line representing an arm gesture. The impression, that of sturdy but low-gauge cacophony, is remarkably apt. Of course there are knowing ways behind this seemingly fumbling approach. We can begin our projects in line with a similar approach. Using ink and a pointed stick or the wrong end of a brush, try drawing furniture and friends. Without hesitation and without worrying about overlap, let the line represent that part of any form which makes the strongest and most immediate impression. This begins to determine each individual's preferences in simplifying and editing form. As in many endeavors, the way to master the intricacies of

Fig. 63 Bamboo engraving in which line is used to build gray shapes. Crowded straight lines and crosshatching are used in interesting form simplification. From L'Art Néo-Calédonien, op. cit.

line is to put in a lot of practice. Paper is expendable, and if one line experiment comes out unsatisfactorily, we can throw it away and do another one—in fact, many.

In Figure 64b Klee uses an action line, one derived from the game of executing an entire drawing without lifting the tool from the paper. With this method we have an assurance that the line will have continuity and communicate a sense of action. These experiments can begin without reference to subject —in fact, without looking at the paper—in order to get used to the idea of continuous motion. Then, choosing live subjects only (and later moving subjects) put the action down without picking up the drawing instrument. This teaches us to make decisions quickly and act on important structural features. It sharpens perceptive abilities, besides furnishing instruction on the fluid properties of line. One requirement for this kind of study is a drawing tool which can go in any direction. Here at last is a use for the ballpoint pen.

In stressing line as action we do well to remember that muscles and hinged joints produce this action. Action in the muscles and joints of the thumb, index and middle fingers provides excellent short-range control. Here, writing provides a routine of ordered movements for these tissues. Right-handed persons have best control when on a down stroke and poorest control moving left. We have only fair control in up-and-down strokes, poor control in other directions. After the finger joints, the wrist hinge provides the next largest radius of action and our control here is less precise. It has been shown that different cultural sitting habits tend to train and to neglect different sets of muscles. Perhaps our routines do not provide enough work for the wrist in terms of ordered movement. The largest radius of action likely to be needed for line work is provided by the automatic correlation of hinges and ball joint in elbow and shoulder. Good control is provided, and large, smooth movements are possible, although we do not go to our left and up quite as well as to the right and down. In manipulating line we sometimes have a little trouble in moving from one sphere of action to another. Often the wrist is almost completely bypassed in moving out of the action range provided by the fingers. Now if in speaking of going to our left and right the discussion seems to have shifted to baseball players, it is quite in order. It is not enough to know where we want the stroke to go. We must practice the necessary moves. Much clumsy work by beginners is attributable to lack of control over the body. Constant training is needed to perfect our stimulus-response organization, to perfect the correlation between perception and action.

Figure 64c shows us a rather stiff, pure line. Here Klee demonstrates handling of curved forms. He uses line for contour and for edged forms (eyes, lips, nose); he uses line on natural wrinkles, giving them equal strength with other forms; and he also uses line for gradually curved forms. The zygomatic bone and base of the nose do not furnish sharp breaks in the direction of the form but Klee makes those changes decisive by adding a bold line. He thus takes advantage of all of the geographical information in the physiognomy and shows us how to handle the gradually rounded surface with line. We can try this approach to form, using the same kind of line on every possible kind of visual clue. Again, we do not wish to equivocate with line. On perplexing curved forms the formula is: look, make a decision, and act on it. We need to do this in order to achieve the kind of directness we see in Figure 64c.

Like the work from New Caledonia, the "Study of Insects #3," by the American printmaker Barbara Ellison Fumagalli (Fig. 65), is created through an intaglio (cut-in) process. Instead of crab teeth and bamboo, the printmaker uses steel tools and a copper working surface, and rather than creating a single image takes a number of prints from the plate. This is accomplished by forcing ink into the incised parts of the plate, cleaning ink from the surface, placing paper on the plate, and with the aid of pressure and absorbency, transferring the ink from plate to paper. Mention is made of the process as it has everything to do with the graphic content of the work. The subject content is four stages of a cicada. It is immediately apparent that the four images are constructed wholly of line, and close inspection reveals that the line varies in intensity, in its degree of blackness. Such an effect, which adds vitality and strength to these elegant studies, is quite impossible with pen and ink. But a deep cut in the plate holds more ink than a shallow cut and will therefore deposit a greater quantity of ink on the paper. Light and graceful yet strong and clear, the line in

Fig. 65 Intaglio print by Barbara Ellison Fumagalli. Called "Study of Insects #3," it is a representation of four stages of a cicada. Variation in line intensity, a feature of the work, is obtained by variation in depth of cut in the plate. Courtesy of the artist.

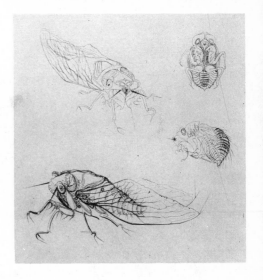

Fig. 66 "Café," by George Grosz, executed in Germany in 1922. A study of postwar society requiring the use of a direct, abrasive quality of line. Grosz's influence has been strong. Courtesy The Museum of Modern Art.

Figure 65 teaches something about observation, sensitivity, and control.

A bristling line, in marked contrast to the line used in the previous example, features "Cafe" by George Grosz, Figure 66. This pen and ink study was done in Germany in 1922, and the harshness of the line reflects the artist's view on a deteriorating social structure. Here, then, is need for a line which is direct, abrupt, and even jagged. Arms, heads, and hands are seen clearly and simply. Grosz's statements with the pen instructed many contemporary artists, and stereotyped versions of his line appear frequently in newspapers and magazines.

Social commentary of a contrasting sort is that by Saul Steinberg, contemporary artist whose work is well known in the United States. Mr. Steinberg has the ability to use line humorously. His study of musicians, Figure 67, reveals something of his selective eye and keen hand. There are very few people who have the ability to communicate humorous qualities through graphic means. Obviously the skill cannot be taught, although to be sure there is

some instructive value in trying to execute the ugliest possible work. It is obvious, too, that any young person who can produce humorous work should be encouraged. We are not speaking here of the cartoon leaning ponderously on funny words—the gag; the reference is rather to the brush or pen applied with wit. It is difficult to analyze humorous work—to take it apart and recompound it as a chemist might a pill. There is too much essence in it for that, too much personality. However, if only to judge by Steinberg's single example here, humor in art does not depend on ignorance of form. Let us take a close look at the left hands appearing in Figure 67. They are rather simply drawn—contour, overlap, contour—with no obviously indicated bend at the wrist. Is it that easy? It is in reality one of the hardest drawing problems one can imagine, and one has only to try it himself to test the truth of this. Years of careful observation and practice stand behind this apparently easy manner with line. Distortions are born of knowledge; the handling of arms, faces, and music stands is simple by design—that is, by deliberate plan.

It is hoped that the beginning designer will find himself in a studio which encourages some experimentation in terms of tools, pigment, and surface. Sticks, pens, and brushes come in many shapes and sizes. Thick pigment makes a kind of line different from that made by liquid ink. There are colored pencils, charcoal pencils and grease pencils, to mention a few of many. Smooth papers facilitate a fluid line while toothed papers give a rough-edged one. One can try waxed paper, pastel paper, rice paper, and blotters. He should try papers both wet and dry, with any instrument which will leave a mark. It is in this way that we build up a vocabulary of linear possibilities. In designing, the time always comes when a special application of line is required. If we stockpile knowledge of line, we will have the stuff when it is needed.

In this discussion we have seen only the tip of the iceberg in terms of total line potential. Those interested in enlarging the boundaries of their visual experience will quite easily find additional material on line which when assimilated becomes experience. Stress has been placed here on line in its direct and pure state, and the suggestion is made that the student examine the informal sketches of the master artists for ramifications. The role of line in texture and the illusion of motion will be taken up in later sections of the book.

review

We learn to use line at an early age in play and in learning to write and cipher. Because of this we have some abilities in the control of ordered movements of the fingers and arm which are necessary in the manipulation of line. Line is seen in the landscape of man's creation—in telephone wires, railway tracks, musical instruments and radio towers. It is also observed in the natural environment, as structural elements in the wings of insects, in leaves, and in the stalks, tendrils, and branches of plant forms. Line has wide application in communication, in coded symbols used by many trades and professions, and in the work of engineers, architects, mathematicians, and cartographers. In the nonutilitarian area—art —line is used as contour, to build up shapes and textures, to model form with value, and to describe a gesture or action. Different kinds of line are used to communicate various kinds of moods and ideas. Because of its versatility, line is a designer's indispensable device.

Fig. 67   Untitled drawing by Saul Steinberg. Humor through knowledge of structure. Courtesy Duell, Sloan and Pearce, Inc., New York.

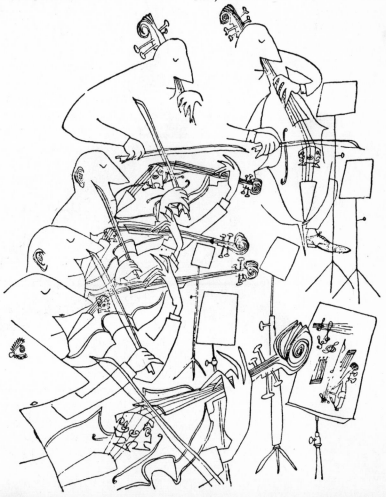

5 *sources of design: man-made*

In Section 1 there was some comment on the interesting forms of a clock mechanism (Fig. 8a, p. 12). With its interwoven theme and variations, the works overshadowed the accompanying façade. Then in the last section we were shown the result of Ben Shahn's perceptive eye in his version of chairs and music stands in a studio bereft of human warmth. The French horn (Fig. 68) presents a marvelously intricate variation of straight and curved tubes, beginning and ending in the same way. Rather than occurring in random order, the forms imply a logic which conveys a unified total. When we consider these examples we may wonder if they represent isolated, rare cases. Are coldly utilitarian forms really of interest to an artist? In answer we must consider volume and percentages. Our national enterprise turns out so many different products that some of them are bound to be interesting visually. Then too we must realize that human paraphernalia has come to make up our visual life. Houses, factories, automobiles, and motor scooters overlap the horizon, hiding trees, shrubs, and wild creatures. In some parts of the United States trees must be imported by truck. Perhaps we will see that with perceptive abilities sharply honed, the visual aspect of the man-made environment is not so dull after all.

It cannot be pretended that man's self-made environment is totally his own doing. Almost everything we confect begins to be changed through wear and aging. Things become dirty, bruised, scraped, scratched, and broken. Chemical and physical forces are constantly at work on our product, corrupting its purity and by slow attrition reducing it to rust and corro-
sion. Sunlight bleaches, rain swells, freezing bends, and thawing buckles. Metals contract and expand, glass flows, and painted surfaces crack, crawl, and peel. Both the artist and the writer need keen discernment in this involuntary but inevitable partnership of man and chemical which creates the true image of what has been called man's landscape. The writer Thomas Wolfe had an eye for it. He could talk for hours on the subject of rust, for example, explaining precisely what it looked like and what it meant.

We, too, in looking at a man-made structure, are concerned with two things: what it looks like and what it means. For every object that man puts his mark on reveals something about him or his society. Our experience plays a part here—we know within certain limits what a run-down shack means. It is when we are in an area of intellectual blindness that form alone is appreciated. If an individual is looking at a plant and is ignorant of the fact that it traps insects, he can observe the forms of the plant and approve or disapprove of them as he chooses, on the basis of form and color. When the individual becomes aware of the purpose of the structures, he may have other ideas about the plant. In short, we may know enough to avoid bears and the teeth of a Northern pike but thereafter our information on organic form trails off, and unless expert opinion intervenes our appreciation must be on form alone. In perceiving the man-made scene we as artists have the task of separating form and meaning. Theoretically it is probably impossible to do so perfectly, but we try, because as artists we are chiefly interested in shapes and colors and new ways of

Fig. 68 Photograph of a French horn. Man-made forms are most often born of considerations other than visual but are nevertheless interesting to look at. Photograph by James Fay.

67

Fig. 69 North African town of Ghardaia with dominating mosque. Interesting play of light and dark planes with a sudden, dramatic vertical shape emerging from a horizontal group. Courtesy E. Haeberlin, Singen-Htwl., Germany. Photo by Peter Haeberlin.

Fig. 70 Fantasy in an old structure. Shapes have unity due to geometric origin but the order of occurrence is strange. Author's sketch.

putting them together, and as members of a group we are chiefly interested in meaning. When we see a hundred identical mailboxes in a building which houses professional workers, we can see in terms of form alone geometry repeated, symmetry and precision. In terms of significance such a set of mailboxes could suggest the leveling action of our society, since regardless of rank all boxes are the same size. Or perhaps it could suggest the lack of individuality in our pattern of living, with a parallel between the geometry of the mailboxes and that of a honeycomb, the work of bees. Such are the overtones of meaning which man-made structures may provide as we search for the means to communicate ideas.

architectural forms

Habitation reveals the ideas and aims of man. Buildings are a visual representation of his highest aspiration, of success, bad luck, necessity, compulsiveness, superstition, vanity, gregariousness, optimism, decline, and fall. An empty factory on the city's edge tells us of failure, or of progress. A factory without people speaks a melancholy tale. The Gothic cathedral often exercises a visual dominance over the other structures of man with which it is seen, and this tells us something significant about the people who built it. But architecture is of interest from a purely formal standpoint, too. The town of Ghardaia (Fig. 69) shows an interesting study in relative apparent size, with the shapes getting progressively smaller in direct ratio to position in the field. It is also a fine example of subtle shifting of light and dark with punctuating play of subplot. It teaches a lesson in how to set the stage for a large and dramatic change of pace without destruction of over-all unity. Besides the graphic content, there is also expressed an idea of a dominating force in the lives of the people who live in Ghardaia.

Some of our new buildings, with their identical patterns of metal paneling and fenestration, are studies in pure proportion and precise geometry. They are a fine source of ideas on the ultimate in repetition. One may find wonderful variations in color and rounded forms in the stone-concrete foundations of old barns. Old garages may be patched with several different patterns of tin. A number of different patterns of roofing material may be used on the same roof. Whole façades of unintentional collage, consisting perhaps of wood, tar paper, tin, and oilcloth, may be seen. Buildings being torn down are often fine studies in contrast, with whole walls of stained plaster contrasting with several varieties of old wallpaper. These are good sources because they often exceed in daring the artist's imagination.

Buildings may take on an appearance bordering on fantasy. We see something of this in Figure 70, a study of the roof of an academic building. Strange shapes emerge from the roof like black mushrooms, while the whole is dominated by a rush of related bits and pieces of geometry. An artist would find it difficult to create such a set of forms out of inner resource alone.

Factories, of course, are a fine source of combinations of shapes. Some large petroleum cracking plants are particularly complex. Buildings under construction present a play of thin rigid elements decorating space like the spider's web. Construction sites are fine places to sketch, but one must work before a masking façade is put in place. Figure 71, a study of an elevated railway, shows something of the interesting involvement in open structures. Here thin members join in an intricate spatial pattern with an embroidery of zigzags adding textural content. Such structures reveal

Fig. 71 Study of an elevated railway. Involved spatial play of thin forms with typical geometric adornment. Author's sketch.

69

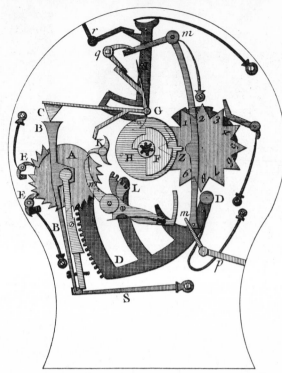

Fig. 72 An engraving of parts of a telescope. The circle shown in every aspect. From Atlas der Himmelskunde, *1897.*

Fig. 73 Engraving of an invention. The helter-skelter quality in the shapes makes this the buffoon among machines. From Gallon Planches, op. cit.

a good deal about the kind of society in which we live. A scouting trip around town will furnish much valuable design material from the architectural area of man's busy work.

machinery

There is so much visual material to be found in machine forms that one could almost list all the adjectives in the dictionary from abaxial to zymotic and find a machine to match each. Nearly everyone has seen cross sections of automobile engines in dealers' showrooms. What they teach the casual visitor is not certain, but they certainly are interesting in appearance. Full of cuts and recesses, thrusts and counterthrusts, such objects make excellent still-life objects for designers learning to control form. And for purposes of learning about a great variety of shapes, simple and intricate, the dump or junkyard can furnish loot to string

70

above and around the studio for handy reference.

Figure 72 presents the circular form almost exclusively. Disks, circular tubes, cones, cylinders, and spheres are shown as in a single atlas of pure round form—an astonishing piece of machinery, albeit a fairly static one. Although the modern truck is large (and dull) and the fire engine a splendid spectacle, nothing equals the railroad steam engine for sheer embodiment of power. Roundhouses full of the massive entrails of these mastodons provide fine sketching experience. There should be one in every museum, along with the old, fantastic threshing machine.

A certain poetic quality emerges from a machine found out of context. A railroad engine wrecked and on its side is a kind of tragedy. And then there are those melancholy fields of old automobiles floating above the long grass. The machine shown in Figure 73, on the other

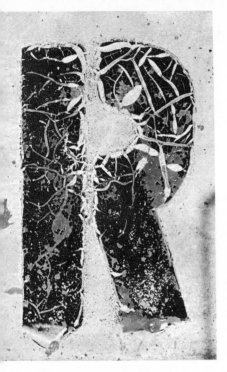

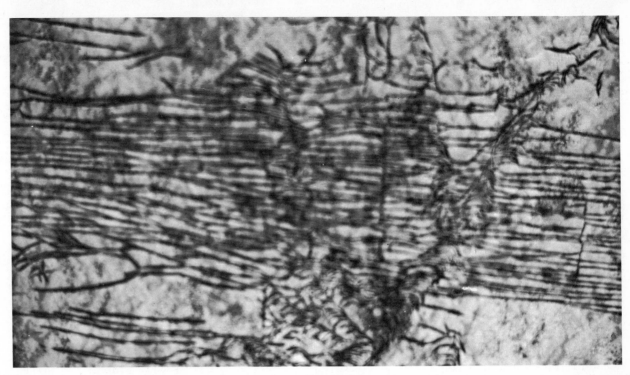

hand, possesses droll overtones. Rather than being pure and logical, the forms are ragged and tenuously connected. Then too, there is an inescapable tendency to read the casing line as a head. This being the case, there is little left to do but add an eye and a nose to achieve the old cliché on thinking. Digging around for old visual material is enjoyable, and rewarding as well, since one needs a file for collage purposes.

forms of attrition

Nature's war on man's works often provides fine elaboration of form which can suggest to the designer ways of varying the surface quality of a work. On the mailbox in Figure 74, two layers of paint are disintegrating in two different ways; the film of the gray layer is separating, and the black layer has become brittle and is breaking up into tiny crystallike flakes. This effect bespeaks poor painting technique but provides a very interesting play of texture and line. Similar play of form can be obtained by the use of incompatible pigment carriers, but there is no guarantee that the deteriorating process can be stopped while the results are satisfactory. Many of such effects are gross and lacking in cohesive pattern, but occasionally an example is found in which the development of elements seems directed and purposeful. Cracking linoleum (Fig. 75) may show the kind of change of pace, of variety within unity, that we expect to find in paintings. There is a graceful flow to the line. Since the piece of linoleum had been used in place of a window, weather was probably the disintegrating agent. In the event that an important "found" object is tightly secured, a camera is the proper recording instrument. Designers should learn rudimentary camera techniques early.

Fig. 74 Capital letter from a mailbox. Two incompatible paint surfaces are cracking, affected by sun, wind, rain, and cold. Photo by Gary Schulz.

Fig. 75 Linoleum used in a glassless window and cracked by the weather. Interesting flow in the line and good change of pace in the size of shapes help to hold the viewer's attention. Photo by the author.

71

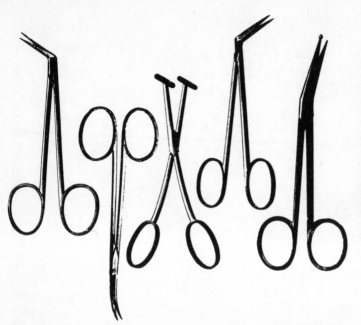

Fig. 76 Surgeon's scissors, a study in pure wirelike forms in repetition. Author's collage of old engravings.

Fig. 77 Garage front, dated 1936. Repeating circular elements play against rectangles. Courtesy the photographer, Walker Evans.

the shape of tools

No doubt most of us have seen storage boards on which are painted the profile images of the hobbyist's tools. They are a kind of symbol of our compulsive nature, our seeking for order. Homogeneous through unified treatment, these boards contain a fine variety of shapes. Tools are often expressive of their gripping, cutting, and sawing functions, and in form run the gamut from pure to bizarre. Surgeons' instruments, with their elegant refinement, are particularly interesting. We see a few of these lined up in Figure 76, engravings from an old book. Here we have a repetition of thin pure ovals and thin straight elements ending in birdlike cutting edges. Engineering draftsmen, too, use a particularly interesting group of tools. Families of French curves offer a flow of line; and ellipse guides, shape templates, and erasure shields show a variety of pure shapes in repetition. Telephone linemen have tools which serve particular needs, as do shoemakers, plumbers, masons,

72

carpenters, and sculptors. There are fine collections of tools in rich variety in every garage. Not only are tools interesting as forms, but in a communicative sense they symbolize the line of work through association. Signs for shops still use this device occasionally.

the look of shops and stores

It is recommended that the designer keep his eyes open while walking down the street. Sometimes there are strange and wonderful arrangements of forms to be seen. A shop full of lamps is one of these. Taken individually, lamps may be ugly, but standing and hanging like the numberless trees and branches of a forest they present an image of fantasy. Specks of shiny brass mix with floating balloons and bits of sparkling glass to produce a wonderful mirage. Butcher shops with rows of hanging sides of beef have intrigued more than one artist. Not only are the forms interesting but they inherently contain the image of death. Pawn-shop operators, with their catholicity of taste, are able to present wonderful mixtures of form. These shops are similar in a way to the scene on famous Maxwell Street in Chicago, where one could, if he cared to, buy a trombone, a necktie, and a live chicken in the same minute. Racks of clothing are a study in variety of color, shape, and texture. Watch repair shops are also fascinating. Walker Evans, the prominent American photographer, pictured a striking garage façade (Fig. 77). Here we see a forceful play of circular elements against rectangles, and a reminder that home-made lettering often yields versions of the alphabet that a designer, with his face in a type book, would never think of.

Storage facilities provide good material on repetition and variation. Places that store ceramic conduit pipes offer patterns of tubes of all kinds. Railroad yards with their acres of giant boxes deserve close study. Supermarkets are good. The rows of vegetable bins, super-green and mirror-imaged, provide a colorful display. Liquor stores and bars are a kaleidoscope of color and sparkling glass, with

row on row of repeated bottle shapes. And there are small mountains of coal and gravel, fields of oil storage tanks, acres of grain bins. The material is there if we but stop to look.

patterns in communication

Since we are all too familiar with telephone and telephone wires, we probably don't bother to look at the pattern the wires make. In Figure 78 we see this kind of pattern. Three dramatic vertical forms are opposed by a mass of horizontal lines—a good compositional idea. The few diagonal lines provide relief from the general severity. In terms of meaning, the picture speaks of numbers. We seldom realize how many human beings there are. A trip to the telephone company will also prove rewarding. There one can see the intricate system of relays which route the messages.

The wiring of radio and transmitting equipment has for many years provided a fascinating study in complex line. More recently, printed circuits have been developed,

Fig. 78 Telephone wires. Three dramatic verticals are opposed by a mass of horizontal lines. A symbol of human numbers. Courtesy U.S. Signal Corps.

Fig. 79 Advertising piece based on the printed circuit. Unity of treatment in symbol and typography is a striking feature. Courtesy International Business Machines Corporation.

DATA SYSTEMS TECHNOLOGY:

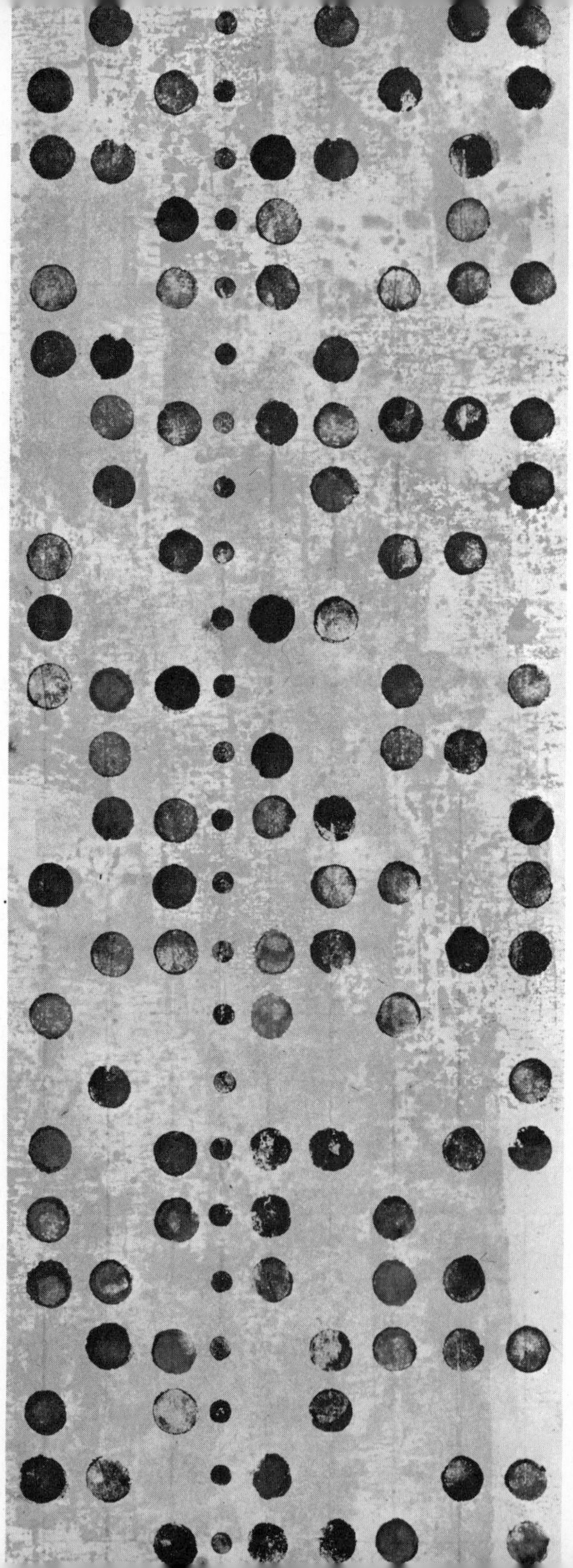

Fig. 80 *Staccato geometry of the information tape. Endless permutations in the pattern are possible. Author's sketch.*

and these create very strong and interesting patterns. The strong, rigid forms of Figure 79 are derived from those seen in printed circuits. Notice that the designer of this advertising piece has arranged the typography to match the other graphic material in size and strength. It is a unified whole. The simplicity is disarming, but it speaks of years of study, experimentation and experience on the part of the designer. Probably most people catch the import of this message, but it was designed to recruit professional people to whom recognition of the design source would be routine.

The staccato image of the information tape is shown in Figure 80. In the old days a man wrote in on a data sheet the color of eye; now the information can be stored in the form of a hole in a piece of paper. It is hardly comforting to note that the theoretical groundwork has been laid for a machine which on impetus of stored information can reproduce itself exactly. And make repairs. The assembly line has inspired more than one artist, and the newer "thinking" machines may also provide the idea for graphic commentary on a trend in our society.

Laboratories are constantly devising ways to translate invisible information potential into visible patterns—proof that seeing is next to believing. Raindrops which help to produce the rainbow are a natural reminder of the scientist's endeavor. Prisms and diffraction gratings produce similar images of greater complexity which reveal the chemical structure of matter. These varied patterns are interesting to the designer. Cathode-ray oscilloscopes make visible any information which can be put on an electrical circuit. Thus sound is translated into visible wave patterns. This order of translation was reversed by the composer Villa-Lobos who transferred the profile of a mountain to the musical staff and scored it for or-

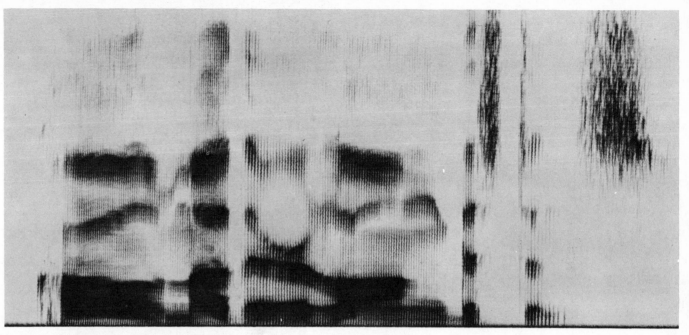

chestra. There is also a technique for making speech visible. Figure 81 shows a spectrogram of male speech, with a time duration of about 1½ seconds. Of course the configuration varies with the words spoken and the person speaking, so that the resulting patterns are endlessly variable. Here is another area where art and technology may collaborate.

Whether it be the rhythmic gyrations traced by automatic machinery, the fantastic elaboration of form in the apparatus of a chemical experiment, the visible static of the jukebox, the redundant mosaic of an airplane's instrument panel, or the leaping bridges of Robert Maillart, interesting form is all around us. Logical form, lyric form, capricious form—it is all grist for the designer's mill. But he must learn to see it, and this requires active effort. He must become keenly attuned to the meaning of what he sees, in human terms. Otherwise he will interpret the world like a seismographic pen.

summary

Man-made forms are generally the result of utilitarian enterprise not connected with art. These forms do, however, manifest the same visual characteristics as art—theme, variation, contrast, and unity. There are two considerations involved in understanding the manmade source—one is that of form and the other is that of meaning. We may admire the pure shape of a jet plane; its context in the social pattern is another matter. Some of the categories which furnish provocative visual material are architecture, attrition by chemical and physical agents, tools, machinery, shops and stores, storage facilities, and methods of communication. The list could well be lengthened, as the area to be covered is very large. Manmade forms are an important part of our environment but are so taken for granted that we must, if we wish to assimilate them, learn to see all over again.

Fig. 81 Sound spectrogram of male speech, with an interesting flow of light and dark. Patterns are endlessly variable. Courtesy Edward E. David, Jr., Bell Telephone Laboratories.

6 *the shape of things*

If a line describes a closed figure, as in the case of the contour of a dog (Fig. 60, p. 59), the figure is perceived as a whole and designated a shape. In line alone such figures are of limited interest unless the contour of the object described is especially involved. For greater visual impact, a shape is usually described with a value, which gives separation from the field. This accounts for the over-all dramatic power of "New York, 1947" (Fig. 82), a photograph of cracked paint by Aaron Siskind. We are forced to perceive this image as a total because figure and field are so inextricably involved one in the other that we cannot tell which is which. Our experience with shape is likely to have been on a more elementary level, perhaps a shadow emphatically isolated on an uneventful field. This effect of isolation is caused by strong light striking an object and casting its image on the nearby plane. A similar effect is seen on looking at an object against a strong light. Our eyes take in so much light that we cannot discern the internal pattern of the figure and we see a silhouette. It is possible to make shadows of animals and other figures with the play of a strong light on hand formations. Some talented fellows cut profiles of head and face, or create shadow plays. These are all part of the same idea. Our childhood experiences in art often centered on cutting out paper shapes and filling in shapes with a crayon. At first glance this emphasis on contour would seem limiting, and on certain levels of communication it is. A profile of a nautilus, the shelled creature of Oliver Wendell Holmes' famous poem, would prove fairly dull in comparison to a sectional or X-ray view of the same form (see Fig. 186, p. 177). Unable to discern the profile's connection with a nautilus, we would lose recognition. As a symbol of value the profile of a dollar bill is worthless. In terms of the nautilus, or any other object, we can judge profile on form alone; if the form is dull or unsatisfactory, we can throw the image out and get a better one. In terms of symbols, recognition is necessary in communication.

The young stag in the Neolithic rock painting (Fig. 83) is more interesting than the dog's contour of Figure 60. With its gracefully curved contour, its series of small shapes emerging from the large one, the stag is more interesting on graphic content alone. The recognition factor is also present—that quality sometimes referred to as "figurative." In connection with the dog's outline it was mentioned that a better aspect of the animal should have been chosen to make the line effective. Similarly, a curled-up, sleeping human offers little in terms of communicating through profile shape. In profile shape a dancing figure would be more expressive. Arms, head, and legs would not only improve form interest but would provide the recognition factor. In pure profile, overlap is not present, so that if an arm is "inside" the body it is not seen. If this seems like an insurmountable handicap, study Figure 17 (p. 24) again and be reassured. In order to be successful in flat profile work, designers take one of two approaches—either selecting an object with an exceptionally interesting form content or using the less interesting shapes in groups. Individual shapes in Figure 17 are quite fine, but it is the number and placement of the shapes that makes the work successful. In the selection of single objects we

Fig. 82 "New York, 1947," a photographic study of cracked wall paint. Line can describe a shape, but value provides the element of contrast between figure and field which gives visual impact. Here field and figure are interwoven. Courtesy of the artist, Aaron Siskind.

77

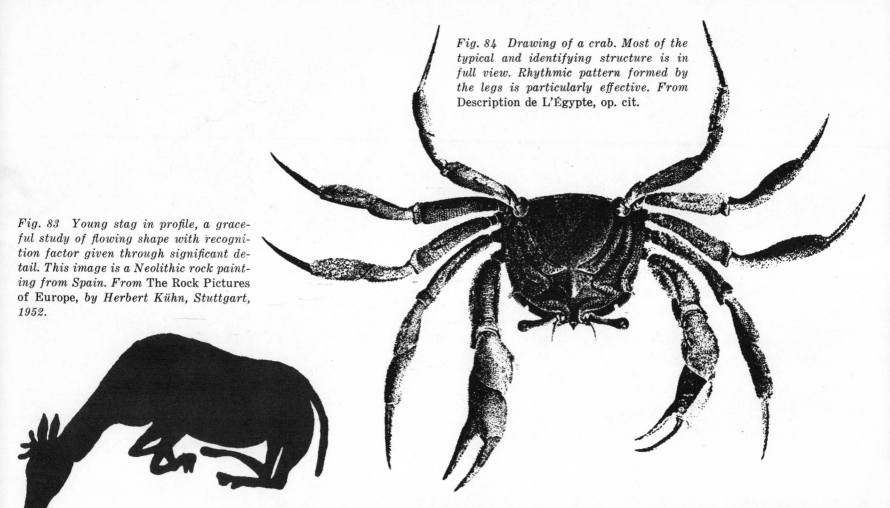

Fig. 84 Drawing of a crab. Most of the typical and identifying structure is in full view. Rhythmic pattern formed by the legs is particularly effective. From Description de L'Égypte, *op. cit.*

Fig. 83 Young stag in profile, a graceful study of flowing shape with recognition factor given through significant detail. This image is a Neolithic rock painting from Spain. From The Rock Pictures of Europe, *by Herbert Kühn, Stuttgart, 1952.*

look for a structure in which significant or typical parts emerge in full view, like an octopus. On occasion we can accomplish a good deal by editing and exaggeration.

sources of the flat image

As in most aspects of our trade, we must forever increase the acuity of our vision in order to perceive flat images. At first it may seem that we know of no such forms as those in which significant parts stick out. But then think of an airplane. Smooth and uneventful,

these machine shapes might well be expressed in terms of carefully chosen profile views. If we look around we will see other forms we can use. From the organic environment we have already seen birds in flight (Fig. 19, p. 28), the spiny form of the sea urchin (Fig. 46c, p. 51), the slim, elegant shapes of the grasshopper (Fig. 40a, p. 47), the sharply etched contour of a snowflake (Fig. 40b, p. 47), and the flowing form of a snake (Fig. 42b, p. 48). These have possibilities. From this environment we also have the crab (Fig. 84), with a fine rhythmic development in its legs.

78

Fig. 85 "Migrant Fish," a pen and ink drawing by Paul Klee, dated 1926. The shape and position of the forms suggest movement through the smooth variations of figures and field. Courtesy of Herr Rolf Burgi, Bern.

It took Magee 15 years of research to develop a miracle-yarn of two-thirds wool blended with one-third Avisco "15."*

Then we leaped into action! Well ahead of the blend trend we came out with two beauties... MERIDIAN and AVITEX. And we promoted them... hard and fast! With a fact-packed sales manual for the folks in your store ("Tips to Put You in the Chips"...ask and you'll receive yours). With advertisements on AVITEX...full page, full color, full of sales impetus... appearing this fall in foremost home magazines. If you're after top volume in carpets you need top values in blends. Why not hop to it... why not get busy with

magee *carpets and rugs*

*A revolutionary new, heavy denier, dull crimped rayon staple fiber engineered expressly for carpeting by American Viscose Corporation

The Magee Carpet Company Mills: Bloomsburg, Pennsylvania Sales Offices: New York, Chicago, Boston "The Mill of 2,000 Dinner Pails"

Fish have contours ranging from elegant purity to bizarre redundance. The fast-moving fish are streamlined, somewhat uneventful in contour. Another drawing by Paul Klee suggests, in terms of the kind of shape used and the placement of them, the movement of fish through water—an artist's idea (Fig. 85). It is more interesting than any mounted fish, the symbol of alleged prowess. Again the natural environment furnishes inspiration.

The cultural environment supplies the impetus behind Gene Federico's advertising piece (Fig. 86). This idea derives from a popular expression and makes use of the profile aspect of frogs. Notice that the placement and shape of the legs with their zigzag involvement suggests a lively quality by graphic content alone. Notice too that since the left margin of the piece is rather irregular, the typography follows suit on its right margin in order to preserve compositional unity.

Of course the man-made scene is a fertile ground for the expressive shape. We have already cited the interesting form content of tools—hammers, pliers, scissors, and so on. Keys have a most expressive profile, and such

Fig. 86 "Three Jumps Ahead," an advertising piece by Gene Federico. Inspired by a popular expression and expressed through profile shapes from the natural environment. Courtesy Magee Carpet Company and the artist.

79

Fig. 87   Advertising piece by J. Alcorn. Pure, flat shapes derived from a motorcycle, in a strong pattern. Courtesy Push Pin Studios, New York.

assorted objects as eggbeaters, trombones, scalpels, and drawing compasses have possibilities. As an example of the idea potential in the works of man we have the set of shapes in Figure 87. Designer J. Alcorn, taking inspiration from the shapes of a motorcycle, has simplified, edited, and arranged the parts into a striking image. And in Figure 88 we have a bold and varied pattern derived from the look of books on a shelf. The source would not be voted most likely to succeed, but the designer's sharp eye has seen something in it. So explicit is this piece of advertising that it scarcely needs verbal reinforcement, but the accompanying typography reads "take an olivetti back to school."

The last two examples show a singleness of purpose on the part of the designer. In both, the way of seeing form is consistent and the variations sustain the unity of style. Such unity is very important in any design field.

In Figure 79 (p. 73) we saw an example of the flat image derived from the communication field. Such patterns as are seen in the information punch card are interesting. There is also a large body of cultural material which pertains to communication. Here we refer to images derived from symbols—mythology, popular sayings, and language. Shapes of course are used in these cultural sources, as we see in Figure 89, a logotype by Gene Federico. The designer, using the positive shapes and negative areas of the letters, has by clever placement created an image of great strength and vitality. Notice that the small letters ornament the large, precluding an excess of heavy black. Letters come in many shapes and sizes, as any type book can demonstrate. Mature designers of course are fully cognizant of these forms and are able to use them in an imaginative manner. The flat image is derived from many different corners of the environment.

Fig. 88 Profile shapes of books on a shelf. The inclusion of the machine communicates a suggestion that the typewriter is as indispensable to the learning process as are books. Words could not express this idea so effectively as is done here. Courtesy Olivetti Corporation of America.

Fig. 89 Logotype by Gene Federico, making use of the shapes of letters. Placement of the letters increases the vitality of the finished work. Courtesy American Institute of Graphic Arts and the artist.

ideas for the laboratory

Simple shapes can demonstrate a number of ideas. With black, gray, and white squares of cut paper we can experiment with simple permutations to see what kind of pattern causes even balance throughout a page. Imbalance and isolation can be explored for effect. We see what happens when a single black square is placed on a page of gray and white squares. Then by overlapping the squares, experimentation in spatial illusion begins. Following natural procedure in overlap, black would be represented as being farthest back in the spatial structure, gray next closest to the observer, and white the closest. Then we can see the result of reversing the order. Show space by overlap but make the most forward object black, thus creating a dynamic flux of spatial illusion. If we use one monocular clue to establish the spatial hierarchy we do not have to use the others. Knowledge of this fact brings us the key to freedom in design. It is very much like saying that if a leaf shape is formed with a flat gray we do not also have to put a line around it.

Then, using square shapes of different sizes a spatial order can be created through apparent difference in size. In life we know in one sense that a grown cat is, for all practical purposes, the same size at all times and places. But in representing the animal in a spatial sequence we use a small image in order to communicate distance. Again reverse the size and value order of squares in order to determine the effect.

A horizon line can be represented by a black line in the middle of the paper. This device of the imagination serves to test the monocular clue of relative position in the field. To make relative position more secure, a light source can be assumed and cast shadows

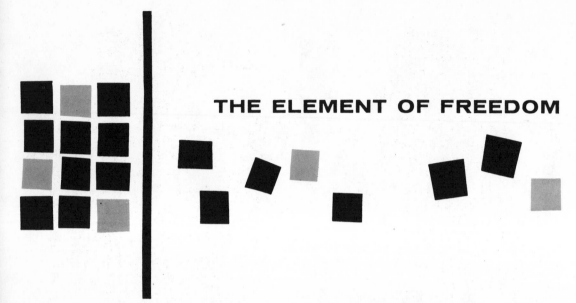

THE ELEMENT OF FREEDOM

Fig. 90 Recruiting message to scientists. The differing patterns suggest conformity versus freedom. Courtesy System Development Corporation and the designer, James Cross.

Fig. 91 Greek figured hylix, a ceramic piece. Interior development of the shape accomplished by line which echoes profile shape in clarity and refinement. Tail and legs are bent to repeat the circle. Courtesy the Trustees of the British Museum.

nition to the dual conditions of work in a visual language; the left-hand pattern suggests the rigid arrangement of a coded message.

Studio work utilizing cut paper and tempera paint can continue forward in various different directions. With the great variety of size and shape of simple geometric forms, areas of concentrated interest can be countered with areas of rest, and power countered with activity. Or interest can turn to arrangements of simple organic forms—leaf, fish, or bird—in studies suggesting the patterns of growth. Occasionally parts of the natural object can be pasted in for variety of treatment. As facility expands, more ambitious projects in communicating ideas can be entertained,

painted in. A complete contradiction in logical order may be communicated by assuming a different light source for each square. The shadows will assume the form of a partly hidden parallelogram. This helps to demonstrate our control of arrangements in space. The designer controls the concept of space. Monocular clues do not enclose the designer in a labyrinth which he must follow in order to solve his problem. In very rough indications of time sequence and geographical terrain, it can be said that only those artists at work in the European area (and the environs of its influence) between 1500 and 1850 have been devoted to designing with all the monocular clues in consistent relationship.

Figure 90 suggests the kind of sophisticated idea which can emerge from manipulation of squares. This printed device is a recruiting message to scientists. Management and art direction people assume that scientists like the freedom to initiate their own research projects rather than working along assigned lines. The arrangement of the squares gives sharp defi-

82

using graphic materials to convey such qualities as speed, torsion, stability, and impact. Or again, such moods or attitudes of mind as anger, tranquillity, and nervousness can be suggested. This last is important if we remember that design involves more than arranging pleasing formations. It involves learning to use graphic means to express ideas.

shape development

Our interest in shapes is by no means confined to even-valued silhouettes. We stressed shape in its simplest manifestation in order to see clearly what a shape is, and to see how different shapes imply different qualities. Now we become interested in developing shapes to increase interest and to supply communicating detail. Our simplest device here is line. In Figure 91 line is used to complete the profile image, to enforce a spatial interpretation and to echo the quality of the contour. Notice that in this Greek hylix the tail and legs are bent around to conform to the circular format. Endings of forms on the outside perimeter tend to describe a circle, as do the letters. This is an impressive display of skill in arranging details into a harmonious total. The figured ceramics of classical Greece provide a fruitful study area, having the merit of providing pleasure along with instruction. These works of art exhale the breath of life.

Notice too that Figure 82 features a rather linear play in the light shapes, while line is at once ornamentation and identifying element in Figure 88. In several of the advertising pieces, type is used to develop interest in the interior of a shape. In Figure 85 we have a slight textural play. For extreme elaboration of contour and linear crochet in interior development, however, it would be difficult to surpass that in Figure 92a. In this shadow puppet

from Bali there is no value play except that of black and white. In some places the line moves as line and in other places it bunches to form texture. The piece shows marked contrast to the restraint featured in the Greek ceramic. We see something similar in a woodcut (Fig. 92b) by Elaine Qubain, a contemporary American artist. In this work the artist used a third kind of line to elaborate the shape, one more direct and angular. Notice that the contour is at the opposite pole from that seen in Figures 91 or 93. Instead of pure curves we see the contour broken, piercing the field area with sharp knife thrusts of black. Thus, treatments of contour depend on the quality which needs communicating. This one bristles with energy.

Fig. 92 a. Balinese shadow puppet, featuring elaborate linear development of a shape's interior. Courtesy The World Publishing Co., publishers of Alphabets and Ornaments, *by Ernst Lehner. b. Woodcut of a hen by Elaine Qubain. Brush line used to develop the interior of the shape and to form the contour. Result: an image of intense animation.*

Value of course plays a major role in the interior development of shapes. Changes in light and dark define shapes and model form in illusion. It also marks the changes in local value of texture where needed. Spots on a dog are an example of local changes in the light and dark content of a shape. Value is used in a subtle way in Georges Seurat's drawing "Femme Assise" (Fig. 93). The contour varies from sharp to obscure, while the interior development is gentle. The work is strong yet delicate. As in Figures 92a and b, the treatment reflects the technique, here charcoal on rough paper. Figure 94, on the other hand, combines extreme subtlety of value treatment with sudden contrast. The horse's shape is divided into large subshapes, all of which are defined by curves. The shapes set up a rhythmic flow enhancing the suggestions of movement provided by the six legs. Movement is suggested in two ways—by the windmill forms emerging from the principal shape and by our knowledge that man and animal are running. Manipulation of value within the shapes and between shapes and field is so subtle that at times a line is used for definition. In many ways this is a remarkable piece of work. This sudden change in the value of large shapes, while preserving subtle development elsewhere, is not found in the Western tradition very often. It is a marked feature, however, of much Oriental art. Students will note a rather curious convention in this work. The horse is presented in profile, while two hooves are also twisted to show the rounded bottom view.

Here again we but scratch the surface. Value is used in so many different ways in shape development. It is hoped that the student will be alerted to look for these various treatments in the other illustrations of the book.

review

The structure of the various parts of the universe is often manifested in terms of an identifying form called shape. Besides identity, a projected shape may communicate qualities by form alone. Thus the shape of a sea urchin is a spectacular splash in graphic content, while that of a cherry leaf is quietly elegant. Shapes in variety occur in the natural environment, in man-made structures, and in the cultural area of man's endeavor. All of these sources have inspired the designer. The shape in its most elementary form is a flat silhouette. Manipulating such shapes can demonstrate the facts of perception and the validity of monocular clues as used by artists of all ages. Shapes in nature and in manufactured articles often reveal accompanying substructural detail which makes the form more interesting. The artist follows in endowing shapes with variations suiting his own purpose. These interior developments of shapes may follow the suggestions of the inspirational structure or may be purely personal, arbitrary inventions. Development of shape may be accomplished by use of line and/or value change. Outside of the area of symbolic devices like numbers, where economy of means is desirable, we seem to require an involvement of form to involve our attention. Thus the form of a pure disk requires at least repetition and possibly permutation to arrest our attention. Since this matter is central to most design problems, the beginning designer must study shapes and their inner involvement in the models presented to him by nature and talented artists.

Fig. 94 "Man Leading a Horse," a 17th-century Mughal Indian painting. Nearly all shapes are defined by some kind of curve. Sudden changes in light and dark occur but value changes within shapes are subtly handled. Courtesy Museum of Fine Arts, Boston.

85

7 *sources of design: world history*

It is assumed that the beginning designer will augment the ideas he gets from the studio, from his colleagues, and from his environment with those coming to him in the systematic study of world art. Since it is in part the history of cultures, with economics, religion, and geography playing roles in image formation, the history of art is a liberalizing area of study. Then too, the study of world art provides specific demonstrations on the use of plastic devices. Design effort is improved in this way. Such studies also show the relationship between the individual, his culture, and past cultures in terms of ideas, techniques, and talent. It is also well to remember that teachers and art directors are expected to have more than a chance acquaintance with world art. Knowledge of it counters the superficial and faddish.

It is quite understandable that our culture stresses the value of that period between the Renaissance and the present, with accent on the European-American traditions in imagery. An art history course on this period would tend to rely heavily on drawing, painting, sculpture, and architecture to explain directions and influences. For this reason this section will suggest (as previous sections have suggested) that there are other places to look.

what to look for

First, in the history of art we look for the image of man. The relationship of man to his environment and to other human creatures as shown in works of art helps us to solidify our ideas on where man stands in the universal flux and how to picture him in our own works.

In the earliest cave art man hardly makes an appearance, and he has disappeared from view in much contemporary painting. What are the cultural attitudes which cause man to appear and disappear? In some Chinese works the landscape dwarfs man's image and makes him insignificant. In an Arabian manuscript man may be just one shape among a dozen others. In Figure 39 (p. 46) he emerges as a confident giant, whereas at Chartres he is pictured as a spiritual being playing a cooperative role in holding up the edifice. From these various sources we learn that altogether different pictures of man have emerged at different times in history.

Then we should look at the total composition. What kind of objects are in the work? How are they related? What is the graphic treatment, stridently bold or subtly quiet? We should look for the systems of form simplification, for consistent ways of handling illusion which give stylistic unity to a work.

Techniques will be of interest since they often enforce the system of simplification. Look for technique to act as a stylistic governor in mosaic, weaving, stained glass and so on.

Look for principles and devices. See how line is used in conjunction with shape and texture. Watch to see how overlap is used and avoided. See where symmetry is used to good effect and where interpenetration of forms takes place. Examine the sources of transparency in art, and look into the communicative possibilities of distortion. See how contrasts in shape are handled and expect to see the use of sudden contrast of value. Most of the devices used in the modern movement are of ancient

Fig. 95 Beaded dance headdress, Bangangte Tribe, French Cameroons, West Africa. Geometry used boldly and inventively. Courtesy Chicago Natural History Museum.

Fig. 96 *Warriors fighting, from an archaic Greek lekythos. Repeated form of the circle relieved by diagonal lines of legs and spears. From* Journal of Hellenic Studies, *1889.*

geometric form   At the close of the last section it was mentioned that the form of a disk hardly merits our special attention, and that in order to gain such attention it would have to be seen in repetition. If we were to take 25 black disks and arrange them in five rows with five disks in each row we would get something a little more interesting. We could achieve more interest if we alternated black and gray disks in sequence *a b a b a, a b a b a,* and so on. If we change the sequence to *a b a a b, b b b a a,* we add still more interest. Then if we could get *c* somewhere in the proceedings we would be evolving a truly effective design.

Now in the proper connection there is nothing wrong with simple geometry in repetition —nobody quarrels with the form of a checkerboard. But it can be boring. It is well to remember, too, that certain techniques in design are limiting. For example, in simple tabby weaving the sequence of warp and weft is *a b* repeated ad infinitum. If the materials used are pleasing, we do not expect the cloth to exhibit more visual fireworks. But in other cases there is no such limiting technical rein

origin, and they are easier to use if they have been seen in a number of different connections.

on form—in painting on ceramics, for example, yet the zigzag patterns put on pots would reach around the world.

Many of the artists in African tribes know how to use geometry (Fig. 95). In a photograph of a beaded headdress used in the dance, we first have *a* then *b* on the hat itself. On the animal's side we have *a* inverted, *c,* and *a* turned 90 percent. Going up the neck we observe *b* (in variation), *a* inverted, *b, a* inverted, with *c* and *b* inverted on the bill, plus *d,* the eye. And notice the irregularities in some of the passages. There is clearly no oppressive drag on creative effort due to technique. But no matter what the technique, the African tribesman will find some way around the limitation to make the work varied and interesting. Besides beads, sea shells and seeds are often seen in African work. Something of this kind of talent was seen in Figure 11 (p. 16). The geometric form in variation can be seen in most parts of the world, but it takes more talent to make it work than one would suppose.

theme and variation   It may be that we get our ideas on a theme repeated from geometric repetition. Or it may be that our environment demonstrates ideas on repetition. We see sheep in flocks, quail in bevies, fish in schools, lions in prides, geese in gaggles, cattle in herds, and people in mobs. And whatever the term for it, automobiles by the thousand. One can see repetition at art's highest levels, at the Ravenna church of San Vitale in its Byzantine mosaics, and at Chartres in the sculptured figures. Scenes of battle as in the Bayeux Tapestry (Figs. 22 and 188, p. 32 and pp. 186 and 187) are good sources on theme and variation, as is Figure 96. This is a scene painted on an archaic Greek lekythos. Eighteen warriors are shown, along with eighteen shields. Always seen in full front, while the warriors are in profile, the shields, varied through overlap and position, are a study in clever permutation. Helmet shapes repeat those of the shields, so that we see circular forms everywhere. Only the diagonal leg and spear lines provide relief. A study of the history of art will reveal more of such variation on a theme.

the organic form Cave paintings of animals immediately suggest man's concern with his immediate environment. The forms the artist uses will reflect the forms of those objects and creatures most important to him. Thus in Figure 97 the smoothly rounded forms are derived from the form of the creatures. If whales came in squares, the image here would be different. Over a period of years habits of configuration tend to become established. Salient features of animals are stressed and agreed upon, and methods of interpretation passed on to others. This is the way in which styles are created. Here the flow and taper of the shapes suggests organic growth. Called "Thunder Bird with Whale," this study by a Northwest Indian exhibits two devices of art generally thought to have been invented by "sophisticated" artists. The interpenetration of one form through another carries with

it the idea of transparency. Marriage of contour, a device of coincidence, is seen where back of whale and the beginning of pattern on the bottom of the bird use the same line. The whole Pacific basin provides wonderful material on the organic form in art, much of which can be seen in applications in the modern movement.

symmetry and asymmetry The cave artist used the most expressive aspect of the animals he painted—the profile or side view. The profile of a bison happens to be asymmetrical, and this partly accounts for the wonderfully free-flowing quality of contour found in Altamira and Lascaux. Front views of animals, where symmetry prevails, are less expressive (and more difficult) and consequently are less often used by primitive artists. The front view of the eye, however, is more expressive than the eye in profile. So in Figure 97 we see the eye in front view and the animals in profile.

Fig. 97 "Thunder Bird with Whale," painting by a Northwest Indian of the Nootka group. Form concepts derive from the natural source. Manner of interpretation developed through time and mutual agreement. Courtesy American Museum of Natural History.

Fig. 98   Record cover, in an expression of pure symmetry. Courtesy Columbia Broadcasting System

Such conventions are typical throughout world art. It is seen in Figure 96, and although one can see the front view of a face in Figure 3e (p. 5), profiles of heads contain front view eyes. Front views of a face are expressive but lack the full flavor of the nasal contour. World art contains many examples of the combination of front view face and profile nose.

Symmetry came to art through sculpture in the round, and through the interpretation of such forms as the leaf, where symmetry is embedded in the only practicable aspect. Wherever it is found, symmetry communicates a quality of formality, of logic or solemnity. We see this quality in a record cover produced by the Columbia Broadcasting System (Fig. 98). Here the designer has arranged 24 elements on a page in perfect symmetry, except for the lopsided flute player and a very very small GLASER off to the side. The design suggests the formality of classical music but conveys the delicacy associated with the solo in-

strument, the flute. During the Middle Ages book pages most often exhibited an asymmetrical format in terms of the arrangement of letters. For the past several hundred years, however, symmetry has been the habit. Most lately, typographical design has gone the other way, back to the medieval pattern (see Fig. 86, p. 79). There is something in symmetry, even though one might not find it in a week of travel through contemporary galleries. Symmetry is a special condition in nature and art. Only the sphere presents the same image in turning.

notes on composition   In arranging any group of things into a unified whole we try to bend the material to fit the communication need. We want the graphic structure to express dignity, excitement, elegance, order. Learning to shape stubborn forms which demand their own identity is difficult. The rule here is that the whole is greater than the parts, and the latter have to be beaten and pushed into a submissive state of cooperation. Here is where the sketch comes in. This provides the means of trial and error in forging the complete idea, in eliminating and changing forms which insist on running off in a direction opposite to the demands of the idea. The artist must recognize that at first this is a real contest. Later, the struggle may quiet down and the relationship between the artist and his material may become less turbulent, even in rare cases serene.

Figure 99 gives us an impression of a battle scene. This Persian painting reflects the chaotic conditions of strife. To appreciate the graphic content of the work, turn it upside down. This procedure frees one from the compulsion to look at heads, horses, and other interesting details, and allows a total impression. From this vantage point the shapes, contrasts, and textural patterns are seen to form an image of riot, with little pieces of black strewn over the area in an apparently random fashion. This may disturb our Western sense of order but it is right order for battle.

Our tradition knows of nothing like this particular piece. The realistic attitude (in regard to decapitated heads), the asymmetrical idea of forms suddenly stopping at the edge of the work (which so intrigued Degas and Lautrec), the flatness of the shapes together with sophisticated handling of forms turning from profile to front view—all these are features of one phase of the Oriental attitude toward life and its interpretation through graphic means. Purity of contour is a feature of much Oriental art, and we see it here. The Persian artist of horses is as good as the Chinese or Greek. Contributing to the spatial flatness of this work, which makes it seem as if everything had been pasted to the picture plane, is the absence of apparent size differential and aerial perspective. Figures at the bottom of the work are same size and as clear as those at the top. Overlap and relative position in the field determine the spatial order. Similar kinds of visual material will be arranged and manipulated differently in accordance with the philosophical views and artistic habits of the various cultures. Studies in the history of art reveal these interesting differences.

ornamentation Throughout history, skill and craftsmanship have been at the call of those whose position in the social order requires visual manifestation. Thus we have crowns, maces, and ornamental swords. This tradition is marked by signs of value. Difficult and time-consuming execution; precious materials—gold, pearls and rare dyes; materials and techniques with visual flash—gold

Fig. 99 *Battle scene, by a Persian artist. Shiraz painting, Safavid period (1548). Forms suggest the confusion of battle. Courtesy of the Smithsonian Institution, Freer Gallery of Art, Washington, D.C.*

leaf, mosaic, and diamonds; size—these are the marks of art which support prestige. Areas of society in major association with this function of art are ruling groups, some churches, and propertied individuals. Persons in our society would probably vote the great pyramids in Egypt as the most outstanding waste of engineering skill on record, and we are a little sensitive about conspicuous consumption in our own day. Politicians appear in plain dark suits and drive the medium-priced automobile. The extras provided by high executive salaries tend to be hidden from public view. We should be able to judge prestige art on form alone

91

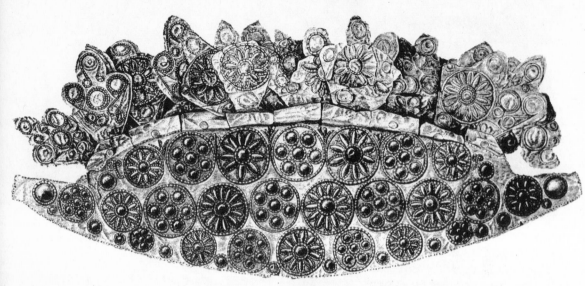

Fig. 100 Ornamental gold headdress from Mycenae. Art serving the demands of prestige shows the signs of value as expressed by size, precious materials, and difficult craftsmanship. From Jewish Symbols in the Greco-Roman Period, *by Erwin R. Goodenough, published by the Bollingen Foundation, New York, 1953-1958. Original is in the National Museum in Athens.*

but our judgment is somewhat warped by preconceived notions. Besides, some of the usual standards are absent. Economy of means, restraint—these qualities the ancient kings eschewed.

Still, there is a magnificence in this tradition, as we saw in the illumination in Figure 6 (p. 8). In an ornamented diadem from Mycenae (Fig. 100), we see several rosette themes alternated in the lower section. There are 40 circular ornaments in this part. The upper portion, extending the possibilities of the circular theme, makes the lower half seem quite restrained. To those who saw it worn upon the head of a king, it must have presented a splendid vision. There is also a strong tradition of ornamentation in medieval manuscript illumination, in the ikon of the Greek Church, and in the craftsmanship of India. In fact, art as an implementation of position is seen all over the world. We have to study this phenomenon and decide on form content whether we are seeing imagination in vigorous flight or tiresome redundancy.

the mark of technique It is clear from experience that different materials and techniques establish their imprint on art. As children we found that a crayon shaped a more definitive (and permanent) line than a finger moving through sand. We found that soap sticks to glass and that berry stains are sometimes permanent. Inks, temperas, and oils each mark the surface in a characteristic way. Thus materials and technical processes are inextricably woven into the thing we call style.

Students of world art see some of the great techniques used in communicating ideas—frescoes by Giotto, Piero della Francesca (Figs. 20 and 106d, pp. 29, 99) and Orozco; the great stained glass windows of Chartres and other cathedrals; the strong Byzantine mosaics; weaving, as represented by the Bayeaux Tapestry.

In studies on less developed communities, one finds ingeniously designed basketry, bead work, weaving, leathercraft, metal work, and sculpture. Anthropology places strong reliance on art to throw light on cultural patterns. As we have seen, sophistication in design is hardly to be claimed exclusively for industrial society.

Multiple-print techniques have become increasingly important to the contemporary artist. Lithography, serigraphy, the relief print, and the intaglio print all communicate distinguishing characteristics. The record here goes back well over 1500 years, and contributors include such figures as Dürer and Rembrandt.

That direct expression of human personality so important to the contemporary painter, the brush stroke, precedes him by a thousand years, as can be verified by a study of Chinese and Japanese painting. Figure 35 (p. 43) revealed something of this rapport, instantly expressed, between man, tool, and surface, in a hush of subtlety. Figure 101 shows it in sharp vigor. Oriental calligraphy, even more

92

direct and bold (Fig. 7b, p. 10), carves the path for Franz Kline driving the brush in right cross and left hook.

Technique is sometimes the fundamental force in abstraction, the reduction and simplification of complex and wandering detail to graphic relationships which can be grasped—to the form of art. The concept in Figure 102 is a cultural product, the expression of group belief. Too early to have been influenced by angels, this Peruvian winged figure is derived from an environmentally inspired image crossed with the wish of human capability grown to myth, but the embroidery technique helps keep it earthbound. Development of the face, the most complicated area of the work, is dictated by the medium of expression, producing forms of strength and visual impact. Modern painters, having no such limitation but feeling the need for it (see Picasso on Iberian sculpture), take inspiration from such works. Here again, form as determined by technique has laboratory application.

form through opinion The battle scenes previously shown undoubtedly display a certain bias. Only that of Otto Dix (Fig. 18) suggests no winner. In the others, truth has been altered to present the image which suits the patron, the image the patron wants others to see. Medieval history scholar Sir Frank Stenton, writing on the Bayeux Tapestry, states: "Even had he so wished, the designer of the tapestry could do no other than follow the tale most acceptable to his patron." This is not a comment on the work as a whole but rather one directed to certain parts. As Stenton puts it, some parts are "a story shaped by a purpose." This is as good a definition of propaganda as we are likely to find. Some years ago automobile manufacturers included small people in illustrations of their product in order to make the vehicle assume a larger aspect. In some cases the people in these ads seemed to be midgets. And when a portrait painter makes a woman look younger and prettier than she is, he is lying. But then one might say, what about Cézanne or Van Gogh? Were they lying? The answer to the question would probably be revealed by a careful analysis of (a story shaped by) purpose. If the artist is simply trying to interpret the world as it seems to him, we justify his excursions in form. If he has an ulterior purpose, we examine the purpose.

Why not judge everything on form alone and let it go at that? Because the way we per-

Fig. 101   "Tossed by the Wind of an Approaching Storm," a 17th-century Chinese painting. Intimate knowledge of the subject and of the tool expressed in direct action. From Bamboo, by Katherine M. Ball, Gillick Press, Berkeley, California, 1945.

Fig. 102 Paracus winged man with trophy head, part of a burial mantle. The technique, embroidery, plays its part in form simplification. Peruvian Indian, 300 B.C. to A.D. 300. Courtesy The Textile Museum, Washington, D.C.

ceive things is shaped by our emotional state and attitudes. If we find out that a lampshade is made of human skin, the knowledge will color our judgment of its attractiveness.

When we examine purposes we are drawn into a difficult area of personal ethics—good taste, opposing views, effect on society, even law, and the safety of the nation. Sharp lines are hard to draw, and the artist must come to his own decisions on how he should use his talent.

One thing is certain—art is a weapon. It can be used to persuade, to change men's minds. Like any weapon, it ought not be handled carelessly.

Then too, it is certain that much world art has a purpose other than that of creating beauty. These motivations of course are factors which enter into form content. Consider "General Agreement" (Fig. 103), a mildly satirical comment on pecking order symbols. The piece attempts to persuade the viewer to a particular point of view. Graphic means consist of exaggeration, the line building an amazing complex of textures—a hash of hash marks, ribbons, medals, epaulets, and so forth.

A study of world art in terms of the graphic techniques of persuasion and propaganda is valuable in two ways. On the basis of one's own criteria, one can learn to detect propaganda, to ferret out the hidden persuader so that belief and action become as far as possible products of the will. Then too, we learn to use the devices of distortion, understatement, emphasis, and exaggeration to communicate our own viewpoints clearly.

These have been some of the things to look for in the world source of art ideas. There are many more, of course. Again it should be emphasized that studio practice can be vitally enhanced with ideas encountered in the study of art history.

recapitulation

The history of art provides us with most of the knowledge we use in teaching and learning art. Studio practice provides the necessary trial and error activity which serves to sharpen skills. It is desirable, then, to correlate the two activities for best effect..

In that art of the past reveals ideas, its study is intellectually stimulating. World art also gives us facts on many facets of each society. Thus it broadens our area of knowledge and shows us what we are like now.

The beginning designer will be looking for graphic devices at work. Some of these are symmetry, overlap, interpenetration, and transparency. He will see the varied theme, geometry in repetition, and principles of composition.

He will also look for art as a symbol of position. Here size, difficulty of execution, expensive materials, and visual flash are important features.

Techniques and materials influence style and methods of simplifying form. The techniques of stained glass, mosaic, fresco, and tapestry, for example, all leave a characteristic imprint on the communicated idea. There are hundreds of techniques, some of which have studio application.

It is also wise to study the relationship of art and propaganda, the role of art in persuasion —how points of view determine graphic form and how the designer uses distortion, exaggeration, and understatement to make his point.

Fig. 103 "General Agreement." A poi of view determines graphic content. E aggeration is used to make the poi Pen and ink drawing by Jerome Snyd for the Columbia Broadcasting Syste

8 *the simplification of form*

Ambrose Bierce, in *The Devil's Dictionary*, gives this definition: "GEOLOGY, n. The science of the earth's crust—to which, doubtless, will be added that of its interior whenever a man shall come up garrulous out of a well. The geological formations of the globe already noted are catalogued thus: The Primary, or lower one, consists of rocks, bones of mired mules, gas pipes, miners' tools, antique statues minus the nose, Spanish doubloons and ancestors. The Secondary is largely made up of red worms and moles. The Tertiary comprises railway tracks, patent pavements, grass, snakes, mouldy boots, beer bottles, tomato cans, intoxicated citizens, garbage, anarchists, snap-dogs and fools." This striking description is a reminder of the random order we find around us—the order of coincidence and accident. Even internally related units seem disorderly when seen in depth. Your neighbor may have related his house to the terrain and vegetation to suit his own sense of order. Neighbors down the line arrange their things in a different pattern. The telephone company adds a row of wired poles which fits their scheme. The postal service truck appears. On the horizon is a reasonably placed water tower, and the scene is completed with the addition of an airliner, two dogs, and a swarm of bees. Such a common scene is visual hash. You are able to organize the scene depending on what you want to find out. If you are scanning the scene for signs of rain, irrelevant clues go unregistered. If you are checking on the neighbor's garden, other images fade. If you are expecting mail, hate dogs, or are curious about bees, you will exclude the nonpertinent information.

Order in nature is equally random in the total impression. We cannot untangle the cooperating and conflicting relationships and so make gardens wherein flowers bloom in sequence. We are most pleased when the natural environment expresses an order which can be comprehended in visual terms, as in the rhythmic seasonal changes attendant on temperature and length of day.

Our world is too complex to understand, keep track of, or express in total, so the problem is broken down into parts. Thus in Bierce's geology one will take up rocks, another bones, another antique statues. Still others take up red worms, anarchists, and the rest, with each stripping off gross material. Only in this way do we make sense of the environment.

An artist, then, is simply one of many who, in editing the environment, take from it that which they deem pertinent, leaving out much that confuses, relocating substructures, and summing up scattered detail into comprehensible units. The image presented to an audience is thus an abstraction, and the process outlined is the process of design. The word "abstract" has come to be closely associated with the modern movement, but it applies in some degree to all art.

As very young children we do not perceive complex relationships, especially those involving spatial organization. But we soon learn enough to select and concentrate on typical and identifying structural features. In a crayon drawing of a cat (Fig. 104) by a young student, we see concentration on the eyes, presented in the most expressive fashion in front view with the body in profile. Ears, legs, and tail are gently rounded forms. Claws are included but whiskers didn't quite get in. Notice

Fig. 104 Child's crayon drawing of a cat. Ability to select typical and identifying structural features starts early. Courtesy Cedarburg Public Schools, Cedarburg, Wis.

97

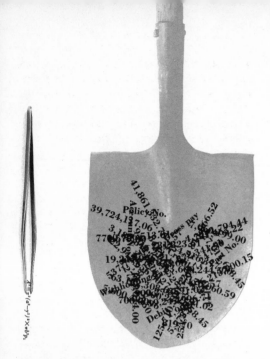

that the child is conscious of the shape and size of the paper and to get the tail in bends it back over the body.

The designer's task, then, is that of editing the gross and accidental material of the environment and synthesizing it into images of clarity and unity. This idea is given succinct expression in an institutional advertising piece for Burroughs Corporation (Fig. 105).

the gamut of possibilities

A human body is capable of many different interpretations, as we have already seen. To what degree the human body, or any other, is simplified depends primarily on the communication need, personality, and technique. No two artists will portray form in exactly the same way. Figure 106 presents a brief outline of the range of possibilities. At one end of the scale we have a prehistoric Japanese work. Human and animal form is represented by a crude line, but it tells the tale and is sufficient to the need. Contemporary artists sometimes find that such an extreme simplification suits their purpose (see Fig. 141a, p. 125). In the Eskimo painting, the figures are presented as simple shapes. The wolf is an especially fine interpretation. Form becomes more developed in the photograph of an African child—enough to excite our emotional involvement. More information, more involvement in light and dark are included in the fresco detail. Notice the wonderfully sculptured treatment of the garment. It is clear in form and inventively varied, yet shows the restraint typical of this

Fig. 105 Institutional advertising piece for Burroughs Corporation. A clear expression of the artist's task of editing gross material to obtain images which communicate order. Courtesy Burroughs Corporation and Carson Roberts Inc., Los Angeles.

master painter. In Courbet's "The Stonebreakers" we get still more detail, as can be seen in the handling of the garments and hands. Here we see the strain of tendon and muscle. In the study of circulation the artist approaches the limit in the amount of information which can be carried by one image. It must be emphasized, however, that this artist is still editing the material. He merely suggests the position of some of the substructures, and he is concentrating on one system only. We cannot even visualize a completed system of reality.

Now if we had a hundred examples in a graduated scale of simplification instead of six, it would be even more clear that the terms "abstract" and "realistic" would be rather hard to apply. If, in discussing art, language is to be used with any precision, we need ten terms or a hundred. Certainly two terms suggests a dichotomy which doesn't exist. It would be better to use a word for the scale, as we do in the case of the ruler.

the plane

If a straight line were to move in a direction perpendicular to its length and in so moving leave a mark, it would generate a plane. In graphic content this is a flat surface familiar in wall, table, and signboard. We can represent such a plane by painting a square in flat gray, and we can represent a cube by three planes and three values. This is fine for any group of objects, no matter how complicated, which are bounded by planes. Now let us perform a thought experiment. Imagine a group

Fig. 106   a. Prehistoric Japanese drawing. A stick figure technique tells a story. Courtesy Hachirō Ohashi, Tokyo, and the Tokyo National Museum. b. Eskimo painting. Man, woman, and wolf represented by identifying profiles. From Eskimokünstler, *by Dr. Hans Himmelheber, Eisenach, 1953. c. Photograph of an African child. Profile shape augmented by suggestions of volume. Courtesy Col. Laurens van der Post, author of* The Lost World of the Kalahari, *published by William Morrow, New York, 1958. d. Detail of Adoration fresco by Piero della Francesca. Forms shown clearly but with considerable development. From Mario Salmi's work on the artist, op. cit. e. "The Stonebreakers," by Courbet. The artist takes a closer look at texture and detail of form. Courtesy Staatliche Kunstsammlungen, Dresden. f. Study of the blood circulation system of the head. Limit in communicating information is approached. From* Anatomische Tafeln, *by Loder, op. cit.*

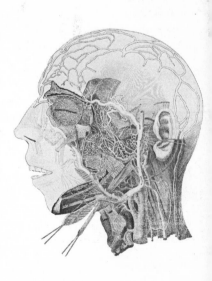

Fig. 107 Albrecht Dürer's drawing of St. Peter and two faceted heads, dated 1512. Rounded forms analyzed in terms of planes. From Dürer, by Erwin Panofsky, Princeton University Press, 1943. Original in Sächische Landesbibliothek, Dresden.

Fig. 108 Drawing of men in action by Luca Cambiaso (1527-1585). Planes used to describe the human form in many aspects. From Magazine of Art (now incorporated in Art News), September 1940. Original is in the Uffizi Gallery, Florence.

Fig. 109 Pen and bistre wash study for "Madonna on the Steps" by Nicolas Poussin. Executed in 1646, the sketch shows the plane used to explain curved forms. From The Drawings of Nicolas Poussin, op. cit. Courtesy Musée de Dijon, Dijon, France.

of solids on a table—cubes, pyramids, octahedrons, and so on. In the midst of these solids there appears a sphere. We know we can represent all of them in illusion quite easily. But how can we represent them and still present a unity of style? In representing the plane-bounded solids we have sharp changes in value, creating graphic content of power and excitement, while in the sphere the gradual changes suggest gentler, softer qualities devoid of emphasis. This thought experiment parallels the environment we encounter. Although our environment is infinitely more complex—veritably a junk heap of solids, profiles, lines, and textures—much of it can be clarified by extracting and using one element at a time. This we have seen. But we are left with this perplexing problem of unity.

As soon as artists are in complete command of the important monocular clues, they ponder the problem of a unified system of representa-

tion. The designer of the Bayeux Tapestry did not wait on the full development of aerial perspective, the least important monocular clue in the practice of illusion. Albrecht Dürer, pondering the problem of a unified system of representation, reduced the round form of a head to a complex of planes (Fig. 107). Cutting through the distracting hirsute adornment—hair, eyebrows, eyelashes, beard—ignoring vein and wart and concentrating on bone structure, Dürer reveals a method of analyzing any solid form.

In a later example of the analysis of human solids, Luca Cambiaso, a 16th-century artist, shows figures in action (Fig. 108). Planes, defined by line and value, explain the entire action. The two examples are isolated cases of experimentation on the part of these artists. Neither Dürer nor Cambiaso incorporated the ideas represented by such experimentation in their regular work.

Nicolas Poussin, on the other hand, regularly used planes in preparatory sketches for paintings. In a sketch executed in 1646 for "Madonna on the Steps" (Fig. 109), large areas of value are washed on to set up the important relationships. For an example of Poussin's manner of extreme simplification, notice the handling of heads. The quotation from this artist which appeared on page 38 attests to his concern for pure form. It is quite evident in the over-all structure of his paintings, although individual passages show no such straightforward handling. Poussin was not quite able to use pure form in his paintings, but his ideas on form simplification amounted to a great deal more than simply isolated experiment.

Cézanne found a way to describe all environmental forms consistently. In his mature work, curved and faceted solids appear side by side (Fig. 110). Small inconsequential objects are eliminated or raised to a stature which could play a role in the variations. Forms near and far are given consistent paint texture. Planes play a large part in Cézanne's method of simplification. Round forms are not smoothly graded in value; rather they are subtly faceted. Cézanne stated that all environmental forms could be reduced to the cone, cylinder, and sphere. This concept was central to his way of interpretation, which should be carefully studied by any serious student of art.

In a work executed nine years later (Fig. 111), the simplification of form is seen to have gone a step further. It is as if Picasso had taken Cézanne's words literally and set about testing them. This work can be studied closely to see how Picasso expresses a round form. There is some reliance on classical modeling technique but planes are boldly indicated. Painters are now clearly interested in form for its own sake, and the idea of subject iden-

Fig. 110 "Portrait of Vollard" by Paul Cézanne, executed in 1899. Round forms subtly faceted. Courtesy of the Petit Palais, Paris.

Fig. 111 "Bowls and Bottles," by Pablo Picasso, executed in 1908. Planes play an increasingly important role in communicating the illusion of round forms. Courtesy the Hermitage Museum, Leningrad.

101

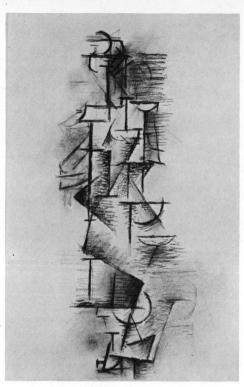

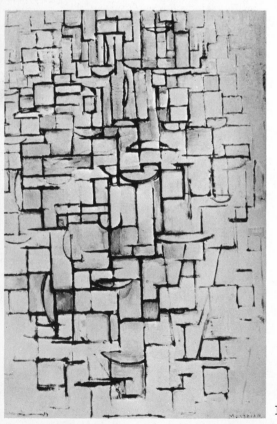

Fig. 112 "Nude" by Picasso, dated 1910. Form broken down into fundamental elements of straight line and curve, with contour line and linear modeling conveying the illusion of solidity. Courtesy The Metropolitan Museum of Art, Alfred Stieglitz Collection, and © S.P.A.D.E.M. 1960 by French Reproduction Rights Inc.

Fig. 113 "Composition" by Piet Mondrian, dated 1913. Curved and straight-edged forms in equilibrium. Again line and value define the planes. Courtesy Rijksmuseum Kröller-Müller, Otterlo, The Netherlands.

tity is secondary. Poussin's idea that subject is an excuse to present formal arrangements is now well established. Until late in life Cézanne treated subject with tender indulgence. He was dependent upon the environment. We begin to see man's theoretical conceptions dominating subject suggestions in Figure 112. It is at this point that the term "cubism" comes in.

Following Cézanne's lead, form here is pursued to ultimate conclusions. After experiments in recording solid forms in facets, Picasso continues his role as editor, deleting nonessential form suggestions from the environment. "Nude," executed in 1910, probably represents part of a day's work. An arbitrary stopping point in a river of painting, it shows us a figure composed of straight lines and curves with modeling, devised in stylistic unity, defining planes in suggestion. Traditional light-and-dark pattern is preserved but greatly simplified. Contour is used when needed, then dropped, the form to be established in another way. Instead of a spontaneous, intuitive expression we find in Figure 112 a reflection of that tendency in our society to test propositions with deliberate analysis. Hence the term "analytical cubism" seems appropriate in referring to this kind of work.

It was left for others to go on with the analysis. In Figure 13, "Composition," executed by Piet Mondrian in 1913, the last vestige of environmentally suggested form is gone, save that of curved and cubed volumes. Here, defined by line and value, these two live together in balance. Further restriction is placed on the rampant curve, always communicating more action than straight-edged elements, in "Composition in Gray," Figure 114, by Theo van Doesburg. Here there is no overlap, since all forms are placed next to one another in a rectangular format. Value is used to make the planes recede or advance. It is also used to give the planes a slight twisting effect which makes the substructures seem locked together in tension.

In the examination of pure form, distracting elements were discarded. Strong diagonals, strong color, involved curves—all these were eliminated in the drive toward ultimate reduction. Mondrian, for instance, finally abandoned the curved form, reinstated pure hues and, relying on black line and rectangular shapes, issued a long series of works marked by an elegant sense of balance. These well-known studies, while reflecting a special condition in environmental structure, were of great influence in page layout. Others went further in the simplification of form but came up against a blank wall. We are not inclined to accept the single round dot on a page any more than we accept a single note of music surrounded by rests.

planes and space Now we must retrace our steps and see what has happened to the spatial conception. In the works by Dürer, Cambiaso, and Poussin a ground plane is indicated, with perhaps the bottom third of the picture area so occupied. Use of monocular clues is normal, with relative size differential, relative field position, and overlap indicating the spatial sequence. Then in the Cézanne work and in Picasso's "Bowls and Bottles" the field or ground plane is elevated. In Cézanne it is near the top of the picture, and in "Bowls and Bottles" it fills the entire picture plane. This ground plane completely fills the picture area in Picasso's "Nude" and in the studies by Mondrian and von Doesburg. It is as if one were looking at a door lying on the ground. The door contains some upright flat doll shapes hinged on the bottom, with the door having hinges which fasten it to the ground on the edge near the viewer. The door is raised to a vertical position. As it is raised the hinged figures remain upright, so that when the door is in the vertical position the figures are against it, also vertical. More important, the figures are now seen as the same size. This is important for two reasons. First, one can scarcely form comparisons in configuration when two objects vary greatly in size. One dominates the other. No scientific experiment would be made on the communicative content of various shapes unless size were controlled. In a lineup of suspects in a police station the suspects are at the same distance from the viewer. Secondly, painting tiny objects requires a different technique from that used for large ones. A large brush cannot be used to describe a fly. In all these works on pure form analysis, a uniform technique is used throughout.

Overlap appears in "Bowls and Bottles" in a traditional manner. Thereafter there is a change. The reason for it can be seen by a simple experiment. Put one square shape down and overlap it with another. It will be seen that the square on the bottom becomes an L shape. Clearly, two squares cannot be compared in this way. On the other hand, if this same arrangement is drawn in penciled line, the L shape is not a positive factor and the shapes can be fairly compared. This technique is an assumption of transparency of matter: it allows one form to penetrate another without losing its characteristic and identifying contour. In Figures 112 and 113 we see overlap become penetration, with the accompanying transparency of space. In Figure 114 overlap is avoided, with space controlled by value, arbitrarily and not by the single light source. Now with these techniques of representation, spatial hierarchy is not dominated by the accidental and random conditions of perception

Fig. 114 "Composition in Gray" by Theo van Doesburg, dated 1918. Overlap eliminated as a spatial device; space illusion created by arbitrary control of light and dark. Courtesy Mrs. Nelly van Doesburg and the Peggy Guggenheim Collection, Venice.

103

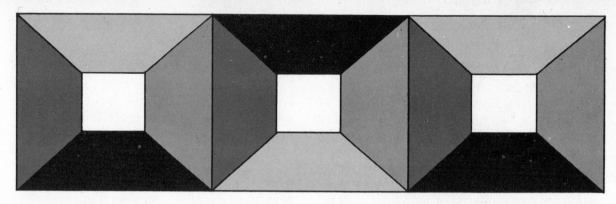

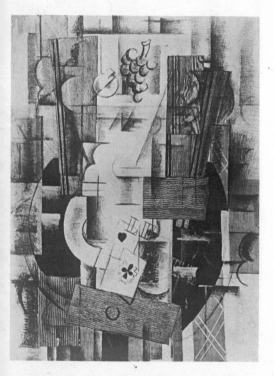

Fig. 116 *"Still Life with Playing Cards" by Georges Braque. The ornamented style of cubism combining old and new ways of expressing form. Courtesy Musée National d'Art Moderne, Paris.*

and environment. The artist is in complete control of form and space, and can maneuver shapes and manipulate space, in and out, as he pleases. It was mentioned earlier that the designer must learn to control shapes, from left to right, up and down, and in and out. These studies show how it is done.

Thus, the ground plane is reoriented by 90 degrees and loses its identifying features, becoming as a pane of glass. Relative field position, after "Bowls and Bottles," plays no part in the spatial structure.

suggestions for studio practice Since we have had some preliminary practice in maneuvering shapes according to the dictates of monocular clues, we are now ready to try more advanced experimentation. By assuming a fixed source of light we can, with the aid of planes and value, make forms go in and out of the picture plane at will. We see something of this in Figure 115. If we assume that light comes from above (a normal circumstance), then the volume at the left comes out, that in the center goes in, and that on the right comes out again. Such exercises help us learn to control space as with a gear shift.

Another exercise can be designed along the lines of Figure 114. Here the light source is variable and at the control of the designer. Compositions can be arranged in which the spatial flow is subtle and gradual, punctured

perhaps by sharp blacks. Violent fluctuations in the surface are possible, as are comparisons between uneventful and busy passages. Experiment and invention will turn up some surprises.

Then we will need some practice in transparency, perhaps using a group of geometric solids set on a table, with representation to be made on the assumption that the solids are transparent. The same group of objects can be used in an exercise in which planes are used to create the illusion. In this it should be stressed that curved and planesided volumes are to exhibit the same style and strength of expression. The approach of Dürer and Cambiaso can also be used, as capabilities permit.

planes in diverse application Having carried out an analysis of environmental form which stripped it of all nonessentials, Picasso gradually turned to a style of painting which put the nonessentials back in. Working closely with Georges Braque, he returned to the use of color, texture, ornament, and symbols. But these elements were not to have the same role as in the painting of the previous centuries. Picasso and Braque revived one old device which combined two points of view into the same image. If we see a bottle from the top we see roundness but no identifying profile, no elegant curve. If we look at a bottle in profile there is no indication of roundness. The cubists merely combined these views, showing the bottle in profile and the lip as an ellipse. In illusion, where one cannot pick up an object and turn it around, this provides more information. This we can do in the studio. They also revived an old practice of combining paint and pasted-in materials, as in medieval manuscript illumination which combined letters, paint, and gold leaf.

"Still Life with Playing Cards" (Fig. 116), by Braque, is dated 1914. The ground plane is still oriented at 90 degrees and is perpendicular to our line of sight, although now indicated. Space is handled by pre-Renaissance clues. Apparent size differential is absent (compare Figs. 22 and 99, pp. 32, 91). Overlap is used, along with transparency. All the environmental material that had previously been stripped away is combined in a new order. Forms are suggested rather than completely stated. Although pure curves and straight lines dominate, with diagonals at a minimum, there is a new richness of image, a new freedom of expression, without loss of internal unity.

The influence of cubism was felt throughout the civilized world, especially in Europe and, to a lesser degree, America. Cubism was misunderstood by a great many artists who, disregarding its very careful handling of space, took it as an excuse to throw a lot of geometric bric-a-brac on a flat surface. One who used its ideas well was Charles Demuth, a much underrated American painter. One of his works, titled "Stairs, Provincetown," is seen in Figure 117. Like Cambiaso, he does not fully explain the relationship of the ground plane to the rest of the structure, and Renaissance methods return in the form of the rather dramatic use of apparent size differential. Demuth realized that others sometimes grossly misapplied the devices of cubism, and once commented that he (Demuth) had dipped into them with care

and "never spilled a drop." "Stairs, Provincetown" represents a careful application of the principles of cubism on a ready-made subject, but the whole is perfectly unified.

Also using the ground plane and deep space is "Winter Sea" (Fig. 118), by the English painter Paul Nash. Here the elegantly organized forms which make up the ground plane grow smaller in size going away and make up a larger shape which recedes like a railway track, reaching a contrasting curtain of atmosphere, the return of aerial perspective. In the studio we can create a play of elements in deep space by cutting truncated triangles of paper and pasting them on a surface in appropriate places. A simulated horizon line may be used, or the shapes may focus on a spot or spots. Lines can be drawn in so that one plane may cut through another. Several vanishing points may be used at once if a difficult project is required.

Rufino Tamayo, the contemporary Mexican painter, gives us fine simplification of human forms in "The Flute Player" (Fig. 119). There

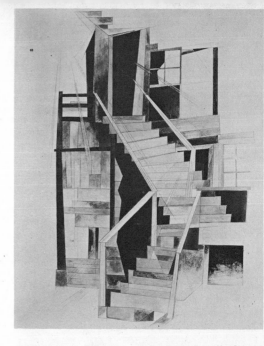

Fig. 117 "Stairs, Provincetown," by Charles Demuth, a 1920 work executed in gouache and water color. Limited use of cubism's precepts in stylistic unity. Collection, The Museum of Modern Art, New York. Gift of Mrs. John D. Rockefeller, Jr.

Fig. 118 "Winter Sea," an oil by Paul Nash, the British painter, dated 1925 and 1937. Planes used in the illusion of deep space. Courtesy City of York Art Gallery, York, England.

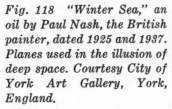

are fine changes of value here, together with a most subtle purity of line. Often when value is used to describe a form, line in the same function proves a dreary redundance. Notice here, however, that the artist has made the most of the natural curved forms of the body, repeating them and unifying them into a family of harmonizing shapes. This is something the cubist brotherhood did not accomplish, since it would have represented to them a condescension to the flowery curves of previous centuries. They threw the baby out with the bathwater. This work deserves close study, since the simplification of the human body is extremely difficult for beginners.

Many American painters have contributed greatly to our knowledge of form and how to reduce it to understandable dimensions. Among many who deserve close study are Walt Kuhn, Max Weber, John Marin, Karl Knaths, Robert Gwathmey, and Philip Guston.

As we move out from experiments in pure form, with the knowledge that they provide us with the plastic equipment to interpret our environment, we may ask, What is there to work on? What is there to say? The answer is,

whatever you believe. If one is a devout member of a church, say so in print. Whatever you have to comment on, art is murmur, conversation, speech, or proclamation, as you will. Central to the point is this fact: all the things we need are in the immediate environment or within us as opinion. Whether it be a study of leaf forms, the juke box, or a jail, all are available. Figure 120 shows a study in which the daily routine of family life is outlined. Form is simplified in various ways. The table is turned toward us so that we see the top, the stove is seen with its top almost in full view, while the coffee pot is in profile. In similar manner plates are in oval line, pitcher in profile line, and heads in profile black. Here is a lesson in the way technical means serve to express our environment.

It is recognized that the art of children is candid in self-revelation. When a child comes into adolescence he realizes that his outrageously honest commentary may not continue if his position in the family and social environs, school, playground, and church is not to be marred by scenes of violence. We put away that which is childish and speak, dress, and act in adult fashion. In speech, which is ephemeral, more care is taken, and in art, a permanent record, it is "No comment," a complete blank. Control of fine movements improves but the expression of personal view declines. It is important to realize that this particular problem exists. It is both possible and necessary to rediscover areas of personal interest in the environment which can be successfully explored.

the power in simplicity

If one compares Figures 112 and 113 with examples coming before and after, it will be seen that the pursuit of ultimates in form resulted in loss of variety and, perhaps, impact. These qualities, abetted by large shape, strong value contrast, and pure hue, returned to Picasso's work during the World War I decade, as can be seen in his well-known studies of three musicians in 1921. Picasso's explorations took him off in several directions but when he needed maximum power he returned to the use of planes and extreme simplification of individual forms. This is evident in his famous "Guernica" (Fig. 121), the execution of which followed the bombing of the town. In this huge oil Picasso used only black and white, the graphic expression of tragedy. All spatial clues are used with great flexibility, and combined aspects add force to the expression. The head and lamp-holding arm represent a concept of form new to us. Here the shapes express the path of a volume through space and time.

These various examples show how form came to be simplified in the modern movement. This period, starting (perhaps arbitrarily) with Cézanne, should be studied carefully, because each designer will want to develop his own way of expressing form, and to do so he must know what he is doing with space.

In our studies on the simplification of form we necessarily press forward in a limited direction. This of course does not mean that elaboration and complexity are negative qualities in graphic expression; we have already seen examples which confirm their virtues.

review

Simplification in the expressions of children comes through concentrating on salient features and lumping lesser features together. On occasion this method produces good results, but it is insufficient for the adult designer who must organize his material in a consistent spatial system.

A rational approach to form simplification begins with breaking the curved volume down into a system of planes. This is inconsistent in the Renaissance spatial system of atmosphere and results in studies reminiscent of puppets on a stage.

The modern movement revives and purifies pre-Renaissance spatial construction, dropping out apparent size differential in the strictest of the experiments on form analysis. With this they revived transparency and interpenetration, which had not been a part of Renaissance methods of interpretation. Another revival was the use of two viewpoints in the same image, with profile and top aspects combined.

Using some of the ideas developed in cubism, artists then attacked the problem of deep space. The subject of form and space must be studied carefully because it is central to unity of style in art.

Fig. 121 Picasso's "Guernica," an oil executed in 1937. It was inspired by the bombing of the town of Guernica during the Spanish Civil War. The simplification of form as an instrument of power. Courtesy of the Museum of Modern Art where the painting is on extended loan.

9 *symbol: the cultural source*

Sam Snead, the golfer, in commenting on a defeat, stated, "I thought I had the fish on the hook when I got a birdie on the first hole. But then came the 10th, 11th and 12th holes—and the fish had got away." Here the fish image is a symbol of victory—which eluded him in this case. No poet, Snead in this remark reminds us of the indirection in everyday communication. We hear: he iced the game; he salted it away; he brought home the bacon; he served it up; he wrapped it up; he socked it away; he pocketed the win. We constantly speak in parallels, using simile, metaphor, and hyperbole. These are drawn from sign language, religion, mythology, superstition, fable—from every area of experience.

Occasionally we hear or read expressions like "Don't put your halo on yet," or "She's an angel." Such expressions can be put in verbal or printed form. The idea admits of graphic expression as well, as Figure 122 reminds us. It reminds us also that communicating in parallels may become quite complex. Here wings import a divine mission, haloes represent divinity, two circles the dual nature of Christ, human and divine, and so on. Even the four evangelists are represented in their symbolic guise. Note incidentally two important graphic devices: the dominance of Christ's image through size, and reinforcement of impact through the use of words. This latter idea is important to our discussion.

It is not our desire here to become involved in Christian symbolism but to point out that graphic representation and literature have common ground in ancient and recent material evolving out of the cultural flux. Where there is common ground the artist is interested, as he is interested in any ideas which increase his graphic vocabulary.

graphic communication

sign language In sign language we have a communication potential drawn on by writer and artist alike—perhaps the oldest in existence. The wrinkled brow, tightened lips, squinted eye, the drawn look of terror (see Fig. 121, p. 107)—all these communicate directly. Hogarth, the creator of Figure 26, made frequent use of the communicative potential in facial expression. The thumbs down sign has the same meaning in life and in the drawing of it. We may express a bad odor, lunacy, command to quiet, approval, retreat, advance, excess noise, strength, and "Stop!" through body manipulation. The study of this adjunct to verbal communication will be profitable to students of design. Even in stick-figured expression it is possible to put on an outrageous drama.

speech This next oldest form of expression is seen daily in the comic strips, in TV commercials, and in advertising art. Speech is seen coming out of the mouths of drawn figures. This convention allows animals, as well as ghosts, trolls, alter egoes, and vegetation to speak. It is a very old and seriously used graphic device dating back to at least the 15th century, where it was used in a painting of the Judgment Day by the Rohan Master. We see it in action as part of a recent advertising piece for Link Aviation, Inc. (Fig. 123). It makes the most of the shape idea and includes a textural note pertinent to engineers, the au-

Fig. 122 Embroidered cloth in the Byzantine tradition, dated 1605. The work is saturated with symbolic content. From L'Art Byzantin, *by Theodore Uspenskij, published by Librarie Orientaliste Paul Geuthner, Paris, 1930.*

Fig. 123 Advertising piece for Link Aviation, using a venerable convention visualizing vocal emanations. Shapes are pure, with texture also communicating information. Courtesy Link Aviation.

Fig. 124 Sales promotion piece centering on the translation of a popular phrase. Courtesy CBS Television Film Sales, Inc.

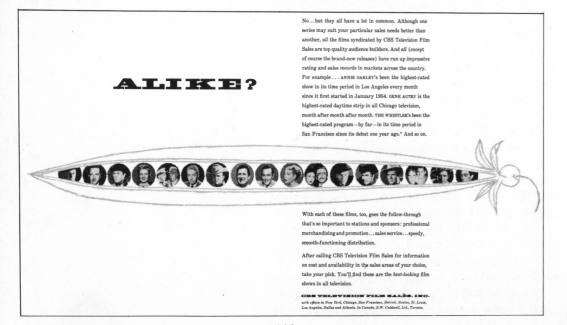

dience for which it was intended. This is an effective statement, again linking word and culturally evolved graphic device.

popular expressions If we were to pick at random a group of ten popular expressions out of the many thousands floating about in the culture, the list might look like this:

· In one ear and out the other
· Keep your fingers crossed
· He's behind the eight ball
· Two wrongs don't make a right
· Like a bull in a china shop
· The strength of Gibraltar
· Sharp as a tack
· Love of money is the root of all evil
· She's shooting up like a weed
· Cross my heart and hope to die

It is easily seen that the list draws from many areas of human experience. Not yet formally approved for use by any social institution, and ranging back into time, such expressions reflect both the permanent and changing aspects of a society's movement through time.

Every aspect of the environment is scrutinized for meaning: commerce, superstition, music, trades, professions, plant forms, ethics, and so on. Quite a number of these have been derived from parts of the human body: heart of stone, nose to the grindstone, sharp tongue, looking daggers—these could begin a list pages long. Animal behavior has been closely watched and furnishes us with meek as a lamb, eager beaver, free as a bird, and crazy like a fox.

How many of these can be translated into graphic form? When we examine the list of ten popular expressions, we see that the first is a good possibility, the third is fair, number five is all right, and number six has been used by an insurance company for many years. The others range from fair to impossible. This is a little better in terms of percentage than we should expect. In terms of landscape it is the special one percent that proves valuable to an artist—other areas of inspiration do no better.

Some phrases will translate weirdly—keeping an eye on the clock, and looking daggers, for example. Many which at first appear barren do well. We see one of these in Figure 124, a sales promotion piece for a television company. Projects and experiments based on popular phraseology will promote the inventive use of materials and the correlation of drawing and painting with other techniques.

the coded symbol When one of two people draws a mark in the mud and the other concurs in its meaning, the ground is laid for continuity of exchange of information. Because we can remember what we see and retain the essence of the agreement, communication through space and time is possible. Civilization depends upon this. Brains of animals can store such agreements up to a point, but the human brain can retain many thousands, permitting some individuals to read an entire orchestral score by scanning, for example. We invent simple coded systems to keep score in card games, to mark off days on a calendar, and to record counts of multiple units.

If we should have 100 different items to account for and made a symbol for each, based on the appearance of the object, we would have a pictographic language. The symbol is art in extreme abstraction. Chinese is such a language. It is wonderful to look at (see Fig. 7b, p. 10) but it is somewhat difficult to learn, in that there are many thousands of symbols. Such a system proliferates in direct proportion to complexity of the culture.

Our written language is based on a different system. The symbols are taken from old Semitic pictographic forms but stripped of their original meaning. Our "B" once stood for a house. Some of these pictographs were arbitrarily assigned to sounds. Thus we can string together symbols to represent the sounds in words. We really do not need 26 symbols, but the system is remarkably good. Our feline pet can be represented in two basic ways: in the arbitrary symbolic system CAT, and in the observation-based system, thus:

Numbers, of course, communicate information about certain aspects of the environment. We do not need this system to describe one cat, although where there is one there is bound to be another, and more to follow. Then we do need it. Arithmetic uses ten symbols, visually varied in form and therefore of interest to the designer. These can be maneuvered to express different qualities—perhaps to suggest regimentation. We see numbers in another connection in Figure 125. Here numbers communicate complexity. By contrast, the line of letters in

Fig. 125 *Institutional advertising piece using numbers. Formation of numbers communicates complexity, with the line of letters suggesting control. Courtesy Olivetti Corporation of America.*

imitation of a keyboard communicates control.

Higher mathematics uses the arithmetical symbols plus a great number of others. Musicians use a coded system which admits of vast permutation. This system must indicate scale and exceptions, rhythm, speed, pitch, duration, volume, inflection, and silence. The variations are visually interesting. When using these elements in the design process, one should try to reflect musical qualities—not an easy thing to do. Old scores, of course, communicate something of another time and place.

Similar coded systems are used in chemistry, in commercial and monetary transactions, in medicine, in timetables, in manuscript corrections, and in electrical systems. Almost every trade and profession uses the coded symbol in some way. In using these elements in

Roses have thorns
Violets are tender
You are you
And you are who
Is chosen for the own true love

of this unworthy sender

Fig. 126 St. Valentine's Day card by Joseph and Ruth Low. A traditional theme grown to cliché, the artists give it fresh and witty treatment in this hail of symbols. Courtesy the artists.

design one can communicate a general sense of subject area or exact information; it depends on the audience's knowledge of the forms. The designer should always know his audience, in order to shape his material fittingly. If one gathers enough of such material together, one can construct whole stories, with the aid of a few pictographic figures.

traditional mythology

Greek and Roman mythology presents a wondrous complex of human-god relationships. Some of this material filters down to us, becoming imbedded in the cultural strata and turning up like ancient sea shells in a gravel pit. We still speak of an Achilles heel, a bacchanal, Herculean strength. Through the lips of Oberon, Shakespeare speaks:

> Flower of this purple dye
> Hit with Cupid's archery

We still see Cupid on St. Valentine's day. This particular idea is given fresh expression by the designers Joseph and Ruth Low (Fig. 126). The heart, of course, is a traditional symbol of love. In wit the Lows remind us that the symbol is everywhere around us.

Then too, there are current references originating in Siren, Mars, Hades, Morpheus, Amazon, Adonis, Aphrodite, and Oedipus. Janus, the two-faced Roman divinity who could look forward and backward at the same time, is seen in appropriate if less exalted connotation in Figure 127. Such use is typical of the kind of changed application which traditional material may see. This is to be preferred over the dreary reconstruction of the scenes of mythology as practiced by sculptors between 1800 and 1850, even then living in a machine age. There are good ideas in classical mythology—the story of Icarus, for example. Picasso found in Greco-Roman mythology a source for some of his most imaginative work.

North Europe provides an elaborate mythology, as do most areas of the world. Those of ancient Egypt, India, China, and Mexico provide a wealth of fantastic imagery. Among the composers who found inspiration in myth are Gluck, Wagner, Stravinsky, Ravel, and Prokofieff.

religion

Each designer will find that his own religious tradition is rich in symbolism. This he should explore for himself. We see in such an expression as "He who lives by the sword shall die by the sword" evidence that these traditions spark contemporary debate. Is there justice here or shall we change our views? Shall we beat our swords into plowshares? This question, too, has meaning for us. So also will we find symbols for love, evil, cleanliness, betrayal, pride, and for whatever else, in the various religious traditions.

An example of continuity of symbolic meaning is the connection between the olive branch and peace. Other symbols, like the peacock, have their meaning changed. Once associated with immortality, the peacock is now connected with pride and vanity.

Job said, "Yet man is born unto trouble, as the sparks fly upward." Here, direct observation provides the material for an expression of inevitability. Perhaps the symbolism of the shepherd and the lamb is one which stems from experience. This kind of symbol carries its meaning better and has more impact than those in which image and imbued content are far apart. In "Guernica" Picasso's use of the bull and the horse, the latter a symbol of persecuted innocence, stems from the bullring and thus has fresh meaning. In contrast is the association between the owl and wisdom. The owl was the sacred bird of the Greek goddess Athena, who was associated with wisdom. On evidence, the association seems a bit shaky. A study of one's own religious tradition will reveal the symbols which have wide meaning for us today, as well as those in which image and meaning are too obscure or too far apart to be useful in communicating ideas.

special days   Usually there are some traditional symbols associated with our holidays. Mentioned before, St. Valentine's Day is one on which school children and family exchange affectionate cards featuring Cupids and hearts. St. Patrick's Day features the shamrock, the color green, and sentimental Irish songs. Good Friday and Easter have appropriate symbol objects, one of which is the white lily. Easter is also the day for new clothing. Memorial Day is accompanied by melancholy reminders, while May Day features May baskets and parades of workers. On Independence Day, one hears the crack of fireworks, the blare of brass, and the clamor of oratory. One sees the flags flying and rockets and Roman candles. Rosh Hashanah, the Jewish New Year, brings out the shofar, the colorful and ancient ram's horn. Hallowe'en features witches riding brooms, carved pumpkins, black cats, soaped windows, and a mummers' parade of small people. Thanksgiving opens on a panorama of turkey, cranberry sauce, cornucopias, and Pilgrims. Christmas Day sees the decorated tree, the hung stocking, Santa Claus with reindeer, and gifts. Heard in the background are songs of wassail and the yule log, of good King Wenceslas and the kings of Orient. Christmas is indeed the day of the mixed metaphor. New Year's Day follows with celebrations. New Year's Eve is elaborated with funny hats and noisemakers and the familiar image of the

Fig. 127   Two-headed locomotive engine named after the Roman deity Janus. Machine-age application of mythology. The engine dates from 1869. From Locomotive Engineering, *1900.*

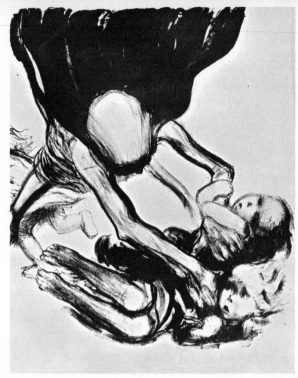

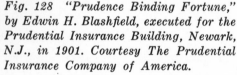

Fig. 128 "Prudence Binding Fortune," by Edwin H. Blashfield, executed for the Prudential Insurance Building, Newark, N.J., in 1901. Courtesy The Prudential Insurance Company of America.

Fig. 129 "Death Snatches the Children," a lithograph by the 20th-century German artist Käthe Kollwitz. Death is symbolized by a cadaverous figure with a cloak in dramatic black shape. From University of Wisconsin print collection.

old man and scythe, together with diapered baby. This Grim Reaper has been that for a long time, having appeared on old English gravestones. Shakespeare writes, "And nothing stands but for his scythe to mow."

Now it may seem at first glance that this kind of material is well worth shunning. It speaks cliché loudly. But this is part of the nature of symbols. When two or more people agree on the meaning of a solid or graphic form, communication is possible. This means that those in on the agreement have seen the form before. A personal symbol is like a secret proclamation, a sound wave with no ear. For this reason, we may have seen a symbol so many times in routine application that it doesn't register any more. Its impact dissolves then, and it is completely useless as a device of communication. And yet the advantage of a widely recognized symbol is obvious. This dilemma is laid directly in the designer's lap. He must give traditional material new life.

We see in Figure 128 a 19th-century manner of presenting symbolic material. Prudence, accompanied by a spinning wheel, is binding Fortune, represented by a gaming wheel. We have to agree that this wrestling match is a little silly. However, there is nothing silly about the symbolization of death in "Death Snatches the Children" (Fig. 129). The great Käthe Kollwitz gives old material new meaning. These contrasting images point up the fact that while symbolic material, like material from other areas of the environment, varies in suitability, the real difference lies in what the designer does with it.

symbolism in paraphernalia

The tools a man works with often come to symbolize his line of work. Thus a saw stands for the carpenter's trade and the transit for surveyors' work. Gavel and judge are in association, stethoscope and physician, trowel and mason, pointer and teacher, horn and player, palette and painter, glasses and oculist. Sometimes this kind of material is used on store fronts to designate the enterprise going forward inside. Occasionally an object designed to serve one purpose acquires a broader meaning. Glasses now signify the intellectual, as in Chinese culture. The lorgnette is seen as a symbol of snobbery, along with the monocle. And the eyepatch speaks of a man who has been around. Scales used in weighing are in long-standing association with justice. Hammer and sickle became the symbol of a political party and then took on graver overtones of meaning. An hour glass, an instrument of time measurement, comes to speak of aging and of impending demise. Some objects convey vivid impressions without benefit of cultural stamp. A tack, a mailed fist, a feather, the keen edge of a dagger, and the image of a pistol's muzzle trigger response.

Familiarity with materials often enables a designer to speak out effectively. We see an example of this in Figure 130, an announcement needing no verbal explanation. Here in punning arrangement a familiar functional device is utilized to carry its meaning to another level.

Brevity is the soul of wit, they say, and here we see the designer at his best in both. Designers would do well to equip themselves with the available flotsam of mechanized society. Experiment with arrangements of buttons, old coins, nails, nuts, washers, bolts, and hinges will often reveal communicative potential beyond the raw material. On the distaff side, hairpins are good, especially the old celluloid type in which the curves give helpful meaning. Bottle caps, matches, toothpicks, tacks, pen points, paper clips, gears, and string suggest the unlimited range of useful materials.

correlating symbols and words

When we look at a pair of dice we see two cubes with little black dots. This is its cold plastic communication. Human experience and attitudes enable the dice to speak on other levels. They may stand for gambling as a generic entity; they may talk of bad luck or good fortune. They may stand for such good qualities in man as his willingness to take a chance

Fig. 130   Announcement by designer Al Sherman.

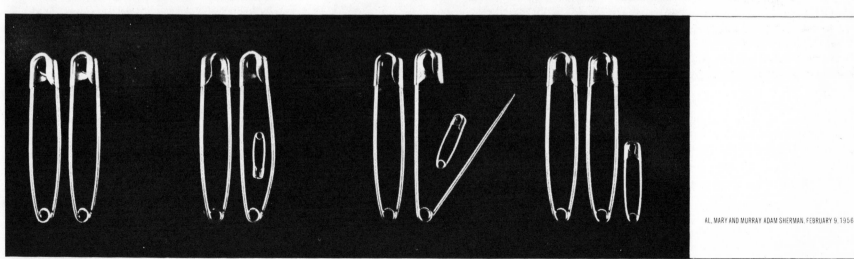

AL, MARY AND MURRAY ADAM SHERMAN, FEBRUARY 9, 1956

115

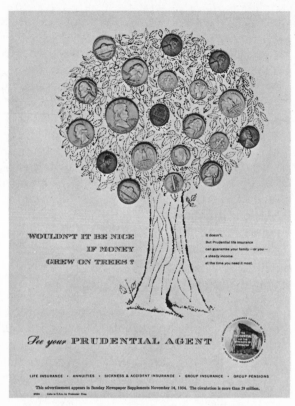

Fig. 131 *The vocal phrase turned visual. Copy helps to fix specific meaning. Courtesy The Prudential Insurance Company of America.*

Fig. 132 *Rebus study, or ideogram. Drawn or pasted images substitute for words or parts of words. From a University of Wisconsin studio.*

instead of waiting for security. To some, dice may represent the laws of probability; to others they may speak of fate, excitement, or ruin. Dice may also be symbols of evil. Thus we observe that our experience invests some objects with the potential of communicating various shades of meaning. In order to pin down the meaning to the one intended, screening out other possibilities, the designer often uses words. Figure 131 uses a popular phrase which creates a dream of idleness, a vision of life without work. The small print brings us back to reality. Words in Figure 124 stress variety.

Thus in symbol, graphic image and verbal image may reinforce or clarify the intended meaning. This idea is the basis for most good

116

advertising. But there is scarcely any firm design tradition which relates word and picture clearly. For beginners, designing ads is actually an inhibiting practice, bringing on superficial imitation. Rebus diagrams (Fig. 132) are helpful here. In a rebus an image is substituted for a word or part of a word wherever possible. Words and letters can be cut out of magazines and newspapers or rendered simply, pictures should be as simple as possible, but variation in style of presentation is good. Various materials can be introduced as needed. In Figure 132 the project called for handwork all the way. Such hieroglyphic studies are not new, Benjamin Franklin having produced an eight-page book in this manner, entitled "The Art of Making Money Plenty, in every Man's Pocket." Another simple project involves the translation of a popular phrase with one word to give directional meaning. Thus "needle in a haystack" can be composed of materials, with one cut and pasted word pinpointing the idea.

symbols and repetition

Although arbitrary forms can be established as coded symbols through the repeated showing of form and meaning together, we are not yet certain that the repeated dose of masses of material is the correct teaching procedure. A single presentation of a limited amount of information has proved highly effective. Shapes with irregularities arrest the attention and are easily remembered. Thus the thick-and-thin old-style Roman lower-case letter provides more differences in shape and is easier to remember than single-line Greek-style capitals. Referring to highway signs, William Elliot, a research engineer of the United States Bureau of Public Roads, states: "It is possible by mass indoctrination to make any symbol mean what we want it to." Thus to some extent symbols become established by institutions in our society that want them established. At times they creep into the culture by common consent. A trademark can be established merely by persistence. It does not have to be particularly apt. One company who manufactures ale uses the old symbol for the Trinity. And how inappropriate is the old static symbol of the atom. Those symbols which arise spontaneously in the culture only remain there by agreement on aptness. Thus individuals hear a remark, repeat it, and pass it on if it seems to suit the occasion. For this reason the old saw or adage and the slang expression may contain exactly what we need to solve a particular design problem.

The symbol comes from many sources. Cigarette manufacturers use color photographs of green woods and flowing brooks to convey the quality of coolness. Automobile manufacturers appeal to status longings by showing the admirable class of people who use their products. Softness in a tissue is shown with a baby cuddling a small furry animal. The tattoo stirs the imagination, while an umbrella speaks of the dry quality in gin.

Wherever they come from, symbols are by definition repeating entities. Paul Rand, the distinguished American designer, reminds us of this fact in Figure 133. Here he uses four different sources in theme repetition: the asterisk (a device from publishing), the schoolroom exercise, the old belief about the elephant's memory, and the memory-jogging string around the finger. This study demonstrates that good designers possess knowledge beyond that of the techniques of imagery.

summary

We live surrounded by symbols, and much of the world's work goes forward with their aid. Through coded symbols, where forms are attached to pre-assigned values, we learn language, mathematics, and music. They are widely used in a great many professions and trades.

The cultural symbol derives from our desire to preserve in concise imagery past events of special significance. It is this concise image which preserves the past and rivets belief. Sources for the designer include literature, mythology, religions, holidays, man-made articles, and the natural environment. Many useful symbols are imbedded in popular speech.

Symbols remain in the culture through repeated use. We learn coded symbols and use them all through life. Some symbolic material remains in the culture through stress by interested institutions, while popular imagery remains by virtue of acceptance through aptness. Symbol repetition creates habit patterns in belief and action which stabilize society. It is important, therefore, that the designer learn something of the symbol and how it is used to control or influence human behavior.

Fig. 133 Car card using four culture-derived ideas associated with memory. Basic shapes are also repeated. Courtesy Paul Rand and the New York Subways Advertising Company.

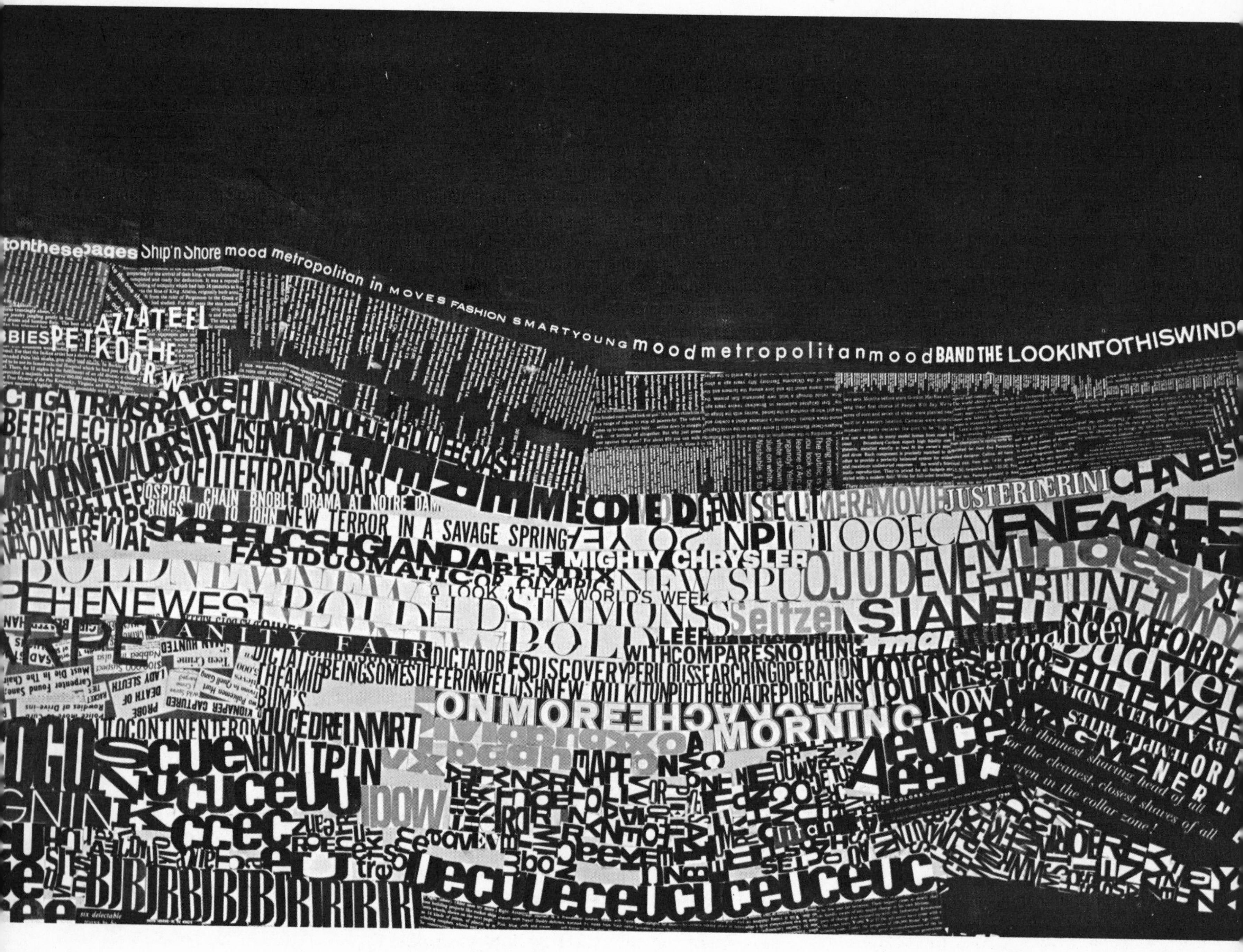
tonthesepages Ship'n Shore mood metropolitan in MOVES FASHION SMARTYOUNG moodmetropolitanmood BAND THE LOOKINTOTHISWIND
NEW TERROR IN A SAVAGE SPRING
MIGHTY CHRYSLER
A LOOK AT THE WORLD'S WEEK
VANITY FAIR
WITHCOMPARESNOTHING
MORNING
the thinnest shaving head of all
for the cleanest, closest shaves of all
even in the collar zone!

10 *the function of texture*

We use the word texture in reference to the composition of a substance—in particular, reference to its surface quality, since this is visually most important. Information about surfaces comes to us primarily in one of two ways: surfaces are seen or they are felt. Obtaining knowledge about a material through the sense of touch is called a tactile experience. Until we get our hands on an object, however, we have to trust our eyes to tell us what materials are like.

Scale plays a part in our terminology. If a leaf is held at arm's length it registers as a shape. If it is turned to the light and brought closer, the linear mosaic can be seen, and shape is forgotten. If it is seen through a microscope, the resulting image would be described in terms of line or shape but not of texture. If the leaf is seen along with others at a distance of 50 yards, individual shape disappears and the resulting variations are called a texture. Figure 134 features a rich textural play; if we imagine the work enlarged ten times, we would be aware of variations in light and dark shape. Texture refers to minute variations in form.

The world swims in texture, since everything has it. We pick up a rock and find its surface pitted. A piece of velvet reflects light in a manner different from burlap, silk, or tweed. The wood of various trees shows distinctive grain. Sand, waves, marble, granite, skin, wheat fields, brass, paper, and insect wings possess individual qualities of texture by which each can be told from the other. In this way texture communicates identity through learned cues.

the constitution of texture

What are the sources of texture? What are its causes? There are four principal factors in the formation of textures, and they are usually seen in combination.

1. Reflection and absorption of light in varying degree by different materials, with a mixture of such materials being perceived as one kind of texture.
2. Differences in light and dark due to the light-scattering and stenciling properties of physically broken surfaces.
3. Differences in color caused by selective absorption and reflection of the various wavelength components of light.
4. Differences in opaqueness, translucency, or transparency of a material, caused by absorption and reflection of light at varying depths through the material.

It will be noticed that each of the four have in common a light source and variation; whenever these occur, an information potential is present with light the carrier and physical structure the stencil. Figure 134 illustrates the first listed principle. Here some parts absorb most of the light, some relieve the light source of half its energy, while other sections reflect most of the light waves. The latter condition results in the excitation of more retinal cells; materials seen as gray excite a lesser number, and black excite fewer still.

In Figure 135, a photograph of a section of the moon, we see materials that all absorb at about the same rate, with variation caused by angular contour reflecting light in another direction than ours and stopping light from

Fig. 134 Student type collage, featuring a rich play of texture depending on the ability of materials to reflect or absorb light at varying rates. Courtesy Raymond Dowden, Head, Department of Design, and Neil Welliver, Instructor, Cooper Union Art School.

119

When light energy is screened at the surface of an object, that energy which is not reflected back into the eyes of the observer is translated into heat. Black garments, absorbing almost all light energy and reflecting little, turn hotter and are to be avoided in summer time. But some materials do not absorb or reflect light energy at the surface but rather at varying points in the interior of the substance. Thus some materials reflect or absorb at varying degrees of *depth* both strength and frequency. This is a fourth method of variation, providing a fourth information potential and revealed to us in the degrees between opaque and completely transparent. Windows let the heat in.

Thus light, materials, and our organs of reception use four screens or stencils which provide different kinds of information: intensity of light energy, by absorbing rate at the surface of the material; intensity of light reflected at the surface, governed by contour (a copy of which provides the illusion of three dimensions); selection of wavelengths at the surface; and selection of intensity and wavelength by depth factor. This last is seen in translucent and transparent phenomena. All these in mixtures provide us with all of our visual information on surfaces.

Fig. 135   Part of the moon seen in the last quarter. Material absorbs light at an even rate; variations are provided by changes in physical contour. Contour stops out light, which on the moon (lacking atmosphere) is seen as dead black, with felt tactile qualities enhanced. Courtesy Mount Wilson and Palomar Observatories.

Fig. 136   Curlew. Organic evolution produces textures which match environment and disrupt distinguishing contour. Texture of terrain determines foot structure. From Ornithologie, *by M. J. Brisson, Paris, 1760.*

reaching the surface at all. On earth, dust and moisture particles reflect light back into a shadow, so that the conformation of the form on which it is cast can often be determined. On the moon, atmosphere is absent, and cast shadows result in a complete blank, heightening tactile sensation even in a flat image. This weird phenomenon can be reproduced with the aid of a darkened room and very strong light.

The third factor, color, depends partly on the strength of light energy absorbed or reflected by various materials, but primarily on their selective ability to absorb or reflect *long* or *short* wavelengths of light energy. Some cells in the retina are activated by *wavelength* rather than numbers. Thus surfaces seen as red reflect the longest wavelengths, absorbing the rest. This selective screening of light waves provides the third method of securing the variation needed in information potential. What we see are tiny spots of various colors making up the texture.

120

the importance of texture

Animals and man have developed physical features enabling them to operate in special textural environments. Textures sometimes evolve to conceal animals from their enemies (Fig. 136). Feet are adapted to the textural environment—flies can remain on glass upside down. Our own feet contain nerve endings enabling us to tread the ground and make quick changes in leverage and weight distribution. We are able to walk on polished marble with bare feet. With shoes on, we find it difficult, but at least we have read the textural clues and are for the most part ready for it.

We examine the textural environment for information and pleasure. We seem to require variations in the field for our own well-being. How much our physiological and psychological structure depends on the changing field is hard to assay, but we can imagine a world of identical surface as some kind of torture. As presently constituted we might not be able to exist in such a world.

the sources of texture

An examination of section 4 will remind us that the natural environment is an endless source of rich textures. Microscopic studies reveal the minute cell structure of organic material. Any laboratory dealing with cell structure can furnish wonderful material. Researchers are helpful; they appreciate the small variations too. On a larger scale, shelled creatures, fish, snakes, and lizards reveal elegant textural patterns dictated by structure or concealment. Many insects, as we know, reveal a labyrinth of wing structure; others possess bodies intricately delineated.

Vegetation produces a richness of texture. Microscopic studies of cross sections of plant stems are especially fascinating. Lichens present a marvelously involved surface, and the corky inner lining of some trees shows a fine structure of tiny round forms punctuated by round dark spots. Angle-cut sections of trees are fantastic in their flow of texture. Everyone has seen the interesting textural development of maple veneer.

Geology furnishes endless variations in surface elaboration. Photographic techniques permit us to see the faceted structure of crystal materials, the curious twisting in the growth of metal whiskers, and the odd maps of polished steel. Conglomerates of gravel, crystals, and ancient shells are richly varied in surface. Veining in translucent stones is a study in subtlety, as are the color flashes in an opal. Granite and marble also possess rich surfaces.

As we have seen, weathering action on metals and painted surfaces produces sharply etched textures. Without esthetic intention, man produces many variegated surfaces. Pebble and asphalt streets form fine mosaics with subtle colors against a dark ground. The abrasive action of sandy shoes on varnished wood produces a sharp intaglio net. Sometimes the textures appearing on school desks through cutting and scraping actions are as good as those we produce intentionally.

Then there are the curious tracery of old grillwork, the quaint surfaces of old tin ceilings and poor wallpaper. Man produces a mass of rigid textures. The familiar corrugated board, screens, nets, and pegboards are among them. Brick walls, wood siding, and parquet floors are textures found around and in the home.

Man also produces interesting textures out of coded symbols. In Figure 137 we see an example of cuneiform writing. The sharp, angular strokes used to form the characters create an active surface rich in variation. Manu-

Fig. 137 Cuneiform characters. Man's use of coded symbols often produces rich textures. From Babylonian Boundary Stones and Memorial Tablets in the British Museum, *edited by L. W. King, 1912. Courtesy Trustees of the British Museum, London.*

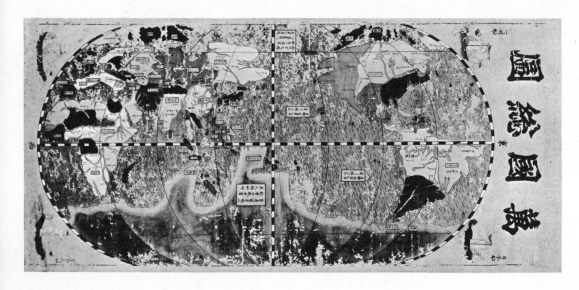

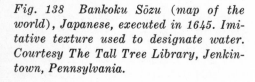

Fig. 138 Bankoku Sōzu (map of the world), Japanese, executed in 1645. Imitative texture used to designate water. Courtesy The Tall Tree Library, Jenkintown, Pennsylvania.

Fig. 139 "Wood," a drawing by Peter Takal. Aside from the large shape, texture alone tells of the strength of wood, indestructible through time. Courtesy of the artist.

scripts in Chinese, Arabic, German Black Letter, and Hebrew are among the most interesting examples of texture in writing. Newspapers and magazines provide fine textures for collage purposes, as the opening illustration of this section demonstrates.

Textures, then, are available in every form and description. They not only serve to give us required information but add variety to the visible panorama. Some are fascinating in their own right and may also help us in our work.

texture and the designer

The simplest use of texture is found in technical drawings and maps. In the former, texture makes up coded symbols for such materials as steel, slate, zinc, water, and electric windings. In maps, highly abstract textures are used to designate swamps, mountains, water, and wooded areas. These techniques of abstrac-

tion are used in maps which go beyond providing basic information. We see one of these in Figure 138, a Japanese map of the world. Imitative texture, executed with great sensitivity, is used to designate water area. Also notable here are the elegant flowing contour and sudden contrast—strong features in Japanese art. Thus the role of texture in art parallels its role in the environment—providing information, sometimes with elegance.

Just as a child will pick up a stone of striated texture, moisten it, and admire it for its own sake, perhaps taking it home, so do artists admire textured forms. Such forms may join other studio bric-a-brac kept about for its instructive value and may at times be used in studies. For Figure 139, Peter Takal executed a careful drawing of a piece of wood. With tender regard for the subtleties of texture, he implied the timeless, indestructible quality of the material, thus creating a poetic image.

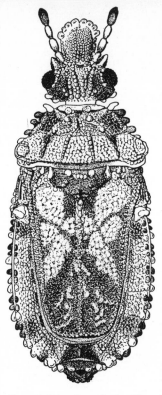

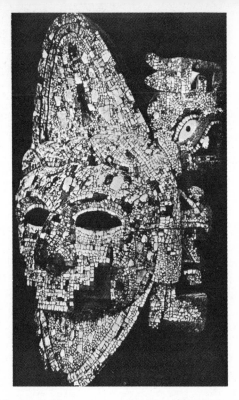

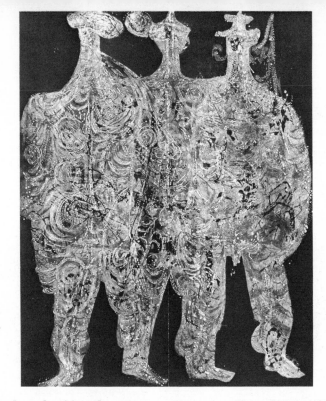

Careful textural studies should be a studio pursuit, since they provide excellent training for both hand and eye. Copying the object exactly gives the best practice.

Occasionally a work of art exploits texture for all it is worth. As natural processes may evolve a creature which is a moving texture (Fig. 140a), so artists may strive to achieve glittering configurations which communicate splendor. The mask in Figure 140b is one of these. An Aztec Mexican work, possibly representing Quetzalcoatl, it no doubt fulfilled its functions in its particular culture, giving stature to a deity. Contemporary artists working in two dimensions exploit texture when the occasion arises. A historical example is provided in Figure 6 (p. 8), where purpose lay in weaving an enigmatic texture signifying mystery. In Figure 140c, texture is exploited by Misch Kohn in an intaglio study, "Three Kings." Here intricate swirls of white and

punctuating dots of black embroider the combined shapes to reflect what might have been: the oriental potentate, then impressive, now heavy with decorative trappings.

As the natural landscape exhibits variety of texture in meadow, wood, and sky, so artists use texture as a change of pace in the total fabric of the work. Since texture involves value, it serves double or triple duty. Textural play may define a shape, as Figure 140c demonstrates; it is used in modeling the illusion of three dimensions, as Figures 110 and 111 (p. 101) show. Thus texture adds a change of pace while defining space and shape. In painting, pigment is often applied thickly, creating a surface physically changing. Light play upon such surfaces appeals to both visual and tactile senses. Potters sometimes create rough and pigmented surfaces. A painter may introduce solid particles, such as sand or asbestos fiber, into his pigments to get a physical

Fig. 140 a. Bug, Calisius dilaticeps. Natural processes may evolve a living texture. Courtesy of Bernice P. Bishop Museum, Honolulu, sponsor of an article on the insects of Guam by Robert L. Usinger. b. Aztec (Mexican Indian) mask. Texture pushed to its maximum in giving an important cultural symbol eminent stature through plastic means. Courtesy Prehistoric and Ethnographic Museum, Rome. c. "Three Kings," by contemporary printmaker Misch Kohn. Texture exploited to simulate the splendid aspect of Oriental potentates bogged down in the trappings of office. Courtesy the artist.

change in surface. In mosaic work, individual tessera are tipped at different angles to reflect light in a variety of ways. This adds to the richness of the imagery. Weavers, who deal with texture constantly, often combine two materials which handle light differently. Thus a metallic thread adds brilliance to a series of linen threads.

In two-dimensional design, texture generally follows the over-all form concept of the work in which it plays a part. It may be imitative of specific materials—cloth, grass, and so on. Textures may also be presented in the entire range of abstraction, to the point where they do not communicate identity. At this point texture becomes an arbitrary invention. In any case its general function is still to give life, variety, and richness to the work.

On imitative texture in design concept, we have two considerations. We can paint the texture in imitation, or we can use the actual texture, pasting or otherwise fastening it to the surface. The medieval manuscript illuminators found that painted gold was not so good as the real thing, since pigment and metal reflect light differently, so they glued gold leaf in where needed. Similarly, Braque, Picasso, Gris, and others used actual textures in their paintings. In certain paintings textures were wholly imitated (see Fig. 116, p. 104). Braque early in his career had been a house painter and decorator and had learned to imitate with pigment all kinds of surfaces. Some of the paintings he did around 1913 combines both methods of texture presentation, painted and pasted. Still other works feature the collage method entirely, with no brushwork. Thus newspaper columns and ads, wallpaper, stamps, certificates, licenses, charts, graph paper, embroidery, menus, metal foil, packages, photographs, hair—all are used in exercises which can range from formal experi-

124

ments in shape and texture to communications of specific ideas with powerful emotional quality.

Since found textures may possess identity and symbol content, stemming from their source, they have good range and potential for the designer. For examples, see the section on Images out of Order, pages 212 and 213. Collage is particularly helpful to those beginners who have good ideas but are still untrained in brush and pen skills.

Figure 141a shows texture used in effective abstraction. The dust texture on Alvin Lustig's book jacket is obtainable by putting wet paint on such a surface as burlap and printing it on paper. Serving as a foil to the high abstraction and simplicity of the other elements, the dust texture performs the function of identity as well as variety. In contrast to such a do-it-yourself method, Figure 141b shows actual textures and materials used to create an image. The textures act out their environmental role, while found objects substitute for limbs.

texture using artists' materials

In looking at two-dimensional art and in studio practice, we find that the various surfaces carrying images impart a character to the final work. Canvas not only serves to drag paint from the brush but may texture the work as well. Rough water-color paper gives the brush stroke a broken edge, and scratchboard permits a fine white line. We can work on many different kinds of surfaces, each one capable of performing a service to the designer if properly exploited. It is for this reason that we must investigate these many surfaces, find out what they can and cannot do, and file the information away in cabinet or memory so it will be on call in case of need. To accomplish these ends the beginning de-

a handful of dust

evelyn waugh

leggeri più di prima

Giovinezza nuvole
sogni e membra leggere.
Gaiezza. Oh età di prima!
Ancora età di prima

con Margarina Flavina

Fig. 141 a. Book jacket by Alvin Lustig. Texture communicates identity and serves as relief for forms in severe abstraction. Courtesy New Directions, New York. b. Italian ad for margarine, one of a series using actual textures in clever arrangement. Courtesy AGIP Publicity Service, Rome.

signer can make a collection of papers, neglecting none, to see the effect on each of the various ways of applying the many different pigments available.

As has been mentioned, textures can be copied from the environment with brush or pencil. Textures can also be created by a rubbing technique. Here thin tough paper is used. It is placed on the textured surface and then rubbed with wax crayon, lithograph crayon, chalk, or graphite stick. The texture will be revealed in reverse value. Scored floors, pitted bricks, and cloth book-covers are suited to this treatment. This is an old technique, often used by archeological researchers who obtain rubbings from ancient inscriptions for later study.

Textures can also be taken from objects through simple printing techniques. A surface is covered with pigment, using brush or roller, and the pigment is then transferred to absorbent paper with the aid of pressure. The texture image of cloth, crazed varnish, or cement can thus be caught. Shapes, too, may be printed in the same way. Even a fragile leaf can be rolled up with ink and printed.

Spatter work with an old toothbrush can also reveal images. A pattern of string laid on the paper acts as a stencil and shows up after spattering the pigment. Screens and perforated surfaces, such as erasure shields, work well here. The contour of tools and other objects may be obtained in the same way.

Resist techniques offer good possibilities for textural studies. Rubber cement acts as a stencil with water-soluble pigments. Wax rubbed on toothed paper will stick to the raised parts and prevent pigment from adhering to them. The indented parts may be in one value or color while another is applied to the waxed raised parts with a printing roller.

Any part of work which is raised above the surface may be rolled up with ink. Thus string,

rubber-cement lines, wood veneer, and cut-out cardboard shapes can be rolled up with water-resistant pigment. Water-soluble pigment can then be applied to the indented parts.

These are a few of many possibilities. To demonstrate what can be done with a pencil, brush, razor blade, adhesive, and ingenuity, examine Figure 142, a fine study by I. Rice Pereira. Here she has combined drawn textures, rubbings, painted and cut-out shapes in a kaleidoscopic arrangement. Studies of this kind will instruct the student on textures—where they are, how to obtain them, and, finally, how to make use of them in the design process.

recapitulation

The manner in which various substances handle light creates environmental texture. Four factors are at work here to originate small surface variations:

1. Reflection and absorption of light in varying degree by different materials, with a mixture of such materials being perceived as one kind of texture.
2. Differences in light and dark due to the light-scattering and stenciling properties of physically broken surfaces.
3. Differences in color caused by selective absorption and reflection of the various wavelength components of light.
4. Differences in opaqueness, translucency, or transparency of a material, caused by absorption and reflection of light at varying depths through the material.

Textures of materials play a part in dictating the form of living creatures. Many interesting textures in the natural environment are caused by the need for concealment. Man reads the texture content of materials, calculating

how to walk on or grip the various surfaces he encounters.

Textures are seen in all corners of the environment: natural ones in snakes, birds, lichens; man-made ones in brick, corrugated board, printed page and lettered manuscript; with physical and chemical forces helping, to form rust, stains, and cracked paint.

The artist uses textures in design as man uses environmental texture—to inform and to provide needed variation. Texture fits concept, and may range from careful imitation through abstraction to pure invention. Actual textures are sometimes substituted for imitation. Surface, pigment, and applicator are all involved in the creation of textures. The permutations are almost endless. Studio practice should be devoted to study of this important device.

Fig. 142 "Exploration with a Pencil," by Irene Rice Pereira, 1940. A study in gouache and pencil. Many textures are created with limited means. Courtesy Museum of Modern Art, Gift of Mrs. Marjorie Falk.

127

11 *the point of view*

"All this time the Guard was looking at her, first through a telescope, then through a microscope, and then through an opera glass. At last he said 'You're traveling the wrong way,' and shut up the window and went away."

These curious lines from Lewis Carroll's *Through the Looking Glass* serve as a reminder that there are a number of ways to look at the world of forms (Fig. 143). The way we represent these forms in two dimensions depends entirely upon our point of view.

We obtain information about the environment in a variety of ways. We see, certainly, but we also have other means of translating information potential. Variation in heat is registered through nerve endings. Speech is invisible (except, as we have seen, through electronic alteration) and is focused and made ready for the sensation process by the complicated mechanism of the inner ear. Position plays a part here. Volume depends on distance, and two-dimensional sound depends on sound waves reaching our ears. Odors, too, vary as the distance. Taste depends on quantity of stimulus and proximity to selective receptor organisms in the tongue.

Nerve endings in the stomach translate contact with acid to sensations of pain. Too close approach to a feeding dog may result in another kind of pain. Is the pain of love accentuated by proximity? A fear of cats may be somewhat reduced by avoiding the sight of them.

Thus on all levels of experience, initiating stimulus and consequent reaction are variable, with many factors involved. When we see an interesting rock in an old creek bed we can take it up and examine it closely, turning it this way and that, feeling its contours, and placing it on different backgrounds. In a lapidary workshop the rock can be cut, etched, polished, and examined with a microscope to make it reveal new information. It can be analyzed for specific gravity, physical mixtures, crystal alignment, and molecular structure. Most of these aspects can be put in visual form and thus are of interest to a designer.

varying aspects

We tend to form stereotyped concepts about our environment, brushing aside individual differences and cutting visual aspects down to one. For example, we learn as children to associate thus: TREE = 🌳 . These stereotyped images remain with us. They are quite necessary for learning and conducting the ordinary business of society. They are not good enough for scientists and scholars, however, and they are not good enough for designers. In art, stereotyped ways of representing form may stem from viewing the environment from a point five or six feet above the ground. This one-position view in representation has been greatly reinforced by painting since the Renaissance. Only in the last 50 years have artists shown any inclination to depart from it. It is imperative that we attain more flexibility in the consideration of communicative aspects of objects. We should consider the many different aspects of various subjects in order to choose that which is most expressive.

Figure 144 shows a panorama of the visual aspects of one subject: the tree. First, we have the typical tree image, familiar alike in the environment and in art. In 144b, the com-

Fig. 143 *One of John Tenniel's brilliant illustrations for* Through the Looking Glass *by Lewis Carroll.*

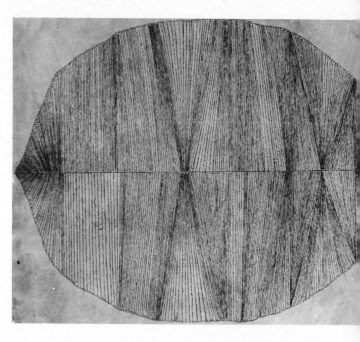

plex root system is shown, a possible symbol of ideas centering on the complexity of society —the number of people involved in putting food on the table and so on. A familiar aspect is again seen in 144c, tree sans leaves, which scores over 144a in dramatics and elegance. Vin Giuliani's drawing of a leaf makes use of the structural elements, building up alternate areas of tension and relaxation in a fine study of symmetry. Now, skipping the seed with its symbolic content, interesting form variation, and method of dissemination by propeller and bird, we turn to a cross section of a young branch of the Douglas fir. Here the intricate changes in cell structure make a rich ornamentation. Cross sections of large trees with annual ring growth are well known. In 144f we have the tangential view of secondary phloem of jack-pine bark, giving several shapes in interesting variation. This aspect, enlarged, is

130

seen in 114g, where finely grained texture alternates with larger circular forms. Figure 144h presents a photomicrograph of the inner bark of Noble fir. Here the twisting pattern of growth becomes an image of fantasy.

A complete survey of the visual potential of this one subject would fill several volumes, but this brief exhibition shows the possibilities beneath the surface of many familiar objects in the environment. The good designer looks into all possible aspects of his subject in the search for the one rewarding image which suits his purpose best. This involves research, with attendant disappointments. There are wrong hunches, good leads turned bad, distracting side issues and so on, but a day that fails to produce the fitting image for the occasion often turns up material which can be used in another connection. Libraries, museums, art galleries, and laboratories usually have what

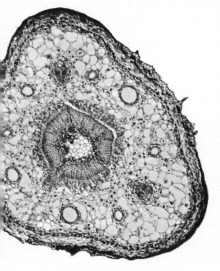
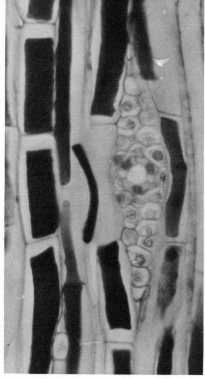

is needed, and trained personnel to aid in the search. The reward is in finding the one image that fits the need.

A theoretical problem shows up the research need. Let us say we have to design a page that has to do with piano music in general. (For a specific composition, we should hear the music itself.) We find a grand piano and walk around it, looking for something to use, and see nothing. We put the lid up and it's no better—the shape is clumsy and offers little in the way of variation. The designer who used this aspect would have to be very inventive. What about the polished mahogany? Very difficult, since it's all black, but we register this as a remote possibility. Then we see the keyboard. Very good. Strong, with interesting regular repeats of pattern, it speaks piano. With repetition we could communicate virtuosity. Two problems arise, however. It is a

symbol very much overused, and its very rigidity might not fit the mood we seek to communicate. But we go on and ask ourselves about the connection between the keys and strings. A padded hammer strikes the strings to set them in vibration. This, one of the key points in the mechanism, is a good possibility. Could it be repeated with a variation in size? Very possibly. In looking at the piano from the top we see something like the image in Figure 145. This is interesting, no doubt about it. Perhaps it will do in combination with other elements to soften the severe geometry. Now, how do the strings vibrate? Is there anything visual in it? Well, here we can go to the library and get a book dealing with the subject in detail, and it turns out that we can indeed show strings in vibration. Pitch and frequency too can be expressed visually, and electronic equipment shows us the sound wave. Depending on

Fig. 144 a. Typical aspect of a tree. Old engraving, author's collection. b. Root system, author's sketch. c. Part of a painting by an untutored hospital patient, author's collection. d. "Leaf," ink drawing by American artist Vin Giuliani. Collection, World House Galleries, New York. e. Cross section of a young branch of Douglas fir. Courtesy Forest Products Laboratory, Madison, Wis. f. Tangential view of secondary phloem of jack-pine bark. Forest Products Laboratory. g. Annual ring structure of white ash. Forest Products Laboratory. h. Photomicrograph of inner bark of Noble fir. Forest Products Laboratory.

Fig. 145 Top view of a keyboard instrument. One of several expressive aspects of the piano. From Gallon Planches, *op. cit.*

Fig. 146 Bamboo engraving of a fishing scene. Lake and turtles are seen from the top, fish from the side, and men from the front folded out from the lake. From L'Art Néo-Calédonien, *op. cit.*

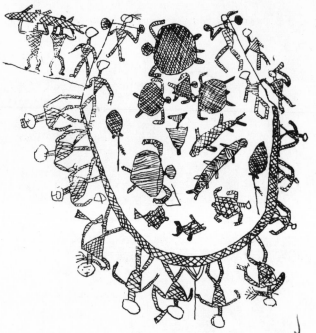

the particular subject, more material might be needed. We might go to original scores, program notes, portraits of the composer, or look for symbols to express mood. But certainly we would have enough material to begin constructing ideas in sketch form. With this approach we do not have to start with pencil in hand and a blank piece of paper staring back. We have something to work with and that's what makes designing fun.

combining different views

In preparing house plans for presentation, three views—top, front, and side—are drawn on the same piece of paper. They are drawn in the same scale with connecting lines of dimension, so that two views are linked in image. Top and front views are seen in two connected aspects. This procedure in representation is typical of much pre-Renaissance art. A lake

132

seen on edge is a line. From above, the lake reveals its form but fishermen on it do not. In Figure 146 both lake and fishermen reveal meaningful contours. Similarly, medieval works show King Arthur's Round Table from the top, knights folded back in front view like cut-out dolls. Chinese illustrators picture a courtyard from the top with buildings folded out in the four principal compass directions. In Figure 147, human figures are expressed in front view. The halo is shown tipped back flat, while containers are shown in profile with the plate tipped toward us. Thus the halo and plate are oriented at 180 degrees in relation to each other. Coincidental folds of cloth in garment and table add interest to this work. Thus both the primitive artist and the mechanical draftsman combine views with utter frankness when even the cubists quibble a little.

We have already seen the progressive layer view in one example, Figure 106f (p. 99), wherein the artist peels off the skin to reveal underlying structure. We see this method used in the fine study of a horse in Figure 148. To show complication in depth, industrial artists place images on transparent acetate so one can see through one layer to another. In section views, the draftsman reveals a form as if it had been cut in two with a saw. This idea is valuable to the designer because the containers or shells of organic and man-made solids often hide important and visually eventful substructures. Thus the section view of a water-cooled gasoline engine or a cabbage is in many ways more expressive of function or pattern of growth than an exterior view. We see in Figure 149 how effectively H. Douglas Pickering makes use of the decorated convolutions of a pomegranate's interior. In this view contour shape is retained, augmented by other information. Many fruits and vegetables are interesting in this view, especially with color.

The draftsman also uses exploded views of machinery. In this method the mechanism is shown in complete disassembly, with the parts oriented in sequence and direction of assembly. In representing the human in illusion, this view is seldom used except in scientific studies of articulation.

Phantom views are also used in showing part relationships in machinery. Here exterior shells are not cut away but revealed faintly, so that one can in effect look through the machine. We have already seen some applications of transparency. More will be shown later on.

movement and extension of vision

When we pick up a stone, we are able to rotate it in any direction in order to see all its possible aspects. At times we do not move, but an object moves. Thus a bird hopping, flitting, and flying, can in a few minutes reveal

Fig. 147 "Supper at Emmaus," from an 11th-century reliquary in Hildesheim Cathedral, Germany. The design is engraved on metal. Some objects are shown in profile while others are seen from the top. Plate and halos are turned 180 degrees in reference to each other. Stoedtner photograph.

Fig. 148 Engraving of a horse. Outer structure is removed, in a method of representation used by mechanical draftsmen. From The Anatomy of the Horse, *by George Stubbs, London, 1853.*

Fig. 149 "Pomegranate," a drawing by H. Douglas Pickering. The section view in art. Courtesy the artist, Art Department, Allegheny College.

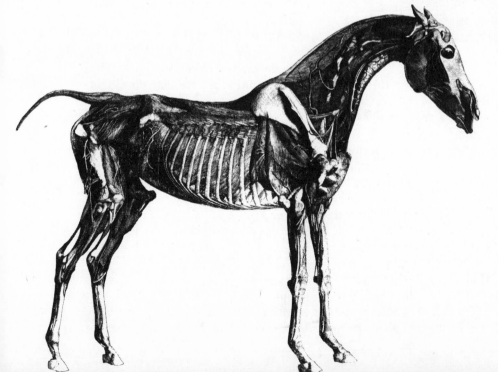

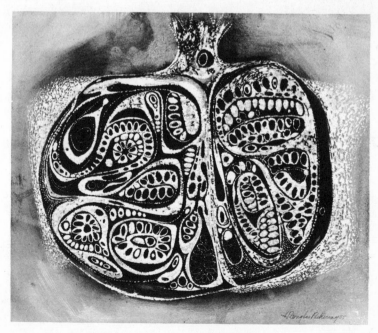

133

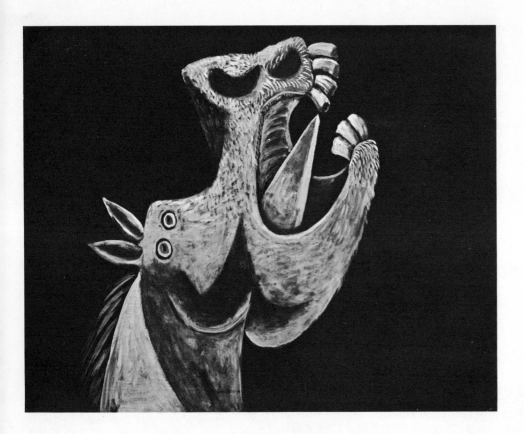

position relative to it, but rather it is the result of an intuitive grasp of the possibilities. Obviously expressive force is gained.

When a group of objects is in motion, many aspects of the subject are revealed. Thus in Figure 151, a rock painting from the South African region, not only are individual figures seen in action but groups are very nearly sequentially arranged. This enhances the suggestion of movement; if a few figures were added to fill in gaps, we would pass from static imagery into the dynamic like a stroboscopic photograph. This effect we will examine later.

Similar to our moving a stone closer or farther from the eye, we have devices which augment this way of examining form. Figure 135 (p. 120) gives a demonstration of what a telescope can do that our eyes cannot. Several studies in earlier parts of the book required the use of the microscope. Our range of vision is thus extended, revealing environmental forms equal in visual interest to those more familiar. Thanks to enlarging techniques in photography, we can study media such as intaglio and newspaper cuts (see Fig. 29, p. 38) to become better informed on method. For designing purposes we can obtain an image of a thumb print as big as this page or one of a boxcar as small as a thumbnail. We can see a form in exaggerated perspective, as fish are enlarged in photography. Size of image is important in communicating ideas. With it we can make a man squeak like a mouse or trumpet like an elephant.

Our vision is also extended by the airplane and by devices which go deep underground and far under the sea. Certainly the airplane provides a startling change in point of view. Because of gravity and attendant problems of support, many objects in our environment stand upright and we are used to seeing them that way. It is quite odd, then, to see them

itself in many aspects. In examining the stone we can move it farther away or nearer to us, and again at times we can remain still while the object moves toward us. Our vision is blurred on both extremely near and extremely far views. Motion back and forth and rotation may be taking place at the same time, of course, which complicates the illusion problem. All of these view possibilities imply *movement* on the part of either the viewer or the subject.

The kind of image obtained by rotating an object or moving about it, combining significant bits of information from the several aspects, is seen in Figure 150. This horse's head by Picasso is not plotted out as one might plot out the various images of a cube as one changes

from a distance, with the viewer rotated 90 degrees relative to the earth's plane. With all familiar landmarks gone, the landscape seems as endless as death. From the air a city at night is an unforgettable visual experience defying verbal description. Two such views are presented in Figures 152a and 152b, one a view of land and the other a view of New York City. In Figure 152a we see the geometry of man superimposed on the amorphous form of the terrain. The companion piece presents a dramatic image of perhaps the most complex thing that gregarious man has created.

invisible entities It is apparent that much of our study on aspect possibilities centers on making invisible forms visible. The halo on end is nothing, the men seen fishing in top view reveal nothing, a table top hides the legs, the shell hides the embryo, profiles blot out one eye, inadequate vision blurs the detail, skin covers muscles and bones, the face conceals emotion, doors shield the smoke-filled room, and rugs cover the dirt. And so on and on. Here scientists, artists, and writers share common pursuits. They all want to see more, reveal more. Writers have their own ways and can go through walls with a word. Artists, scientists, and special investigators have more difficulty, in that they must prove the case. Seeing is believing. In art we can reveal what is going on in the various rooms of an apart-

135

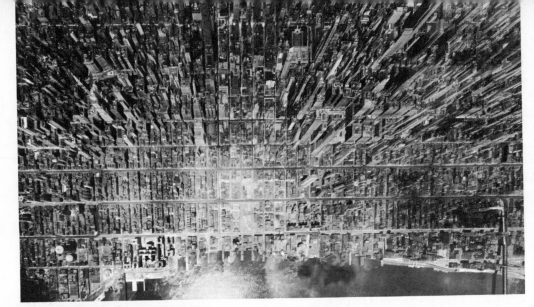

Fig. 152 a. Aerial view of earth. Courtesy Scamahorn Air Photo, Coleville, Washington. b. Aerial view of New York City. Courtesy U.S. Coast and Geodetic Survey.

ment building by removing the façade, as is sometimes done in the theater. If we want to show all sides of a house at once we can build a house model of cardboard and flatten it out, with internal configuration drawn on the various façades. Front and back aspects of the human form can be cut out of paper in twin image with appropriate markings. Any congress of human elements can be described in this way. Cut-out faces can reveal two facets of personality. Cutaway views can reveal personality through plastic invention and symbol. In one of Paul Klee's works the image of a bird is imbedded in a cat's forehead. Speech and thought, as we have seen, can be made visible through the comic-strip device. Coded symbols are available for the language. Ghosts, spirits, and demons are made visible in many cultures.

Scientists photograph the shock waves of bullets, make sounds visible, reveal objects through clouds and darkness, invent devices that see through solid matter, make visible records of brain and body activity, and photograph the emanations of a rose petal. Taste and touch can be suggested through empathic response to appropriate image, such as the image of broken glass. Hot and cold, too, can be made to seem visible by color, word, and symbol.

We see a few of these devices used in Figure 153, a good-natured study by James Flora. In this we see the freedom of the designer to use any device or manner of presentation which suits his purpose. Along with this freedom, however, we do expect unity of style and effect. If the beginning designer concentrates on finding ways of making visible that which needs to be visible, he will be learning the devices of iconography in a natural way. Perhaps we can follow the suggestion in Figure 153 and not take too serious an attitude the first time we try to handle this material. Perhaps in this way experimentation will go forward in an atmosphere of freedom.

review

The quality and strength of a visual stimulus depends upon its position relative to us and its distance from us. Nonvisual information is variable in a similar manner. We tend to form and hold stereotyped impressions of many objects familiar in the environment, thus blocking out other possible aspects. This handicap to the designer may be corrected by looking at an object from every possible point of view and pursuing promising leads through the aids of science. This means that research constitutes a part of every designer's duties.

Engineering drawing has developed some of the same methods of representation as has art. The simultaneous presentation of two views, the cutaway view, the section view, and the phantom view are all found in world art.

Obtaining a comparison of views on any subject depends on movement. Either the object under study moves, or the viewer moves. The object can be either rotated or moved

closer to or farther from the viewer. Since our processes of perception have limits, the telescope and the microscope serve to extend them. The airplane also provides mobility and enables us to look at the earth from a relatively new position.

Presentation conventions should be thought of as means in making hidden forms visible. These conventions may be practiced in the studio with the aid of simple materials.

Fig. 153 Album cover by James Flora. The cutaway view and other conventions of illusion in a witty play of forms. Courtesy RCA Victor Records.

137

12 *materials and techniques*

The reproduction on the left presents a work by a fifth-grade student in one of our public schools. It tells a fine human story of carefree play, with teacher slightly removed from the action, too old or too encumbered by the weight of office to join in. In the flow of shapes and in the reciprocating action of positive and negative space, it is quite a remarkable work. Heads start out simply but break into suggestions of features, and curves are countered with straight lines and geometric variations, true in life and good in design principle. When we are through contemplating the iconography and analyze the work in terms of means, we see that they consist of a piece of toned paper, a page of want ads, a sharp edge, and paste. This is indeed something to ponder, for it is evidence that communication depends more on human intelligence than on medium. The great application of brain power and ingenuity used in constructing communication systems, both symbol and carrier, should not be underestimated, but communication means variation, and the cave artist has created variations with no more than fingers in damp mud. There is considerable merit in having few things to work with. It forces the designer to think of ways to make a medium clearly expressive, to make ingenuity cover a medium's weaknesses, to learn a medium so thoroughly that it becomes a part of him, letting expression flow naturally without trickery in the graphic content.

If a designer were by some accident cut off from an art materials store and confined to his home, he would shortly be in business again with materials found around the house. He would soon make a pen out of a stick, a piece of a reed curtain, a bamboo fishing pole, or a feather. Brush materials are plentiful around a house; crude brushes could be made from yarn or cat hair. For pigment we have charcoal, saffron, instant coffee, chocolate, beet juice, blueberry preserves, and bluing. Eggs, gelatine, cornstarch, and flour provide glues, some unexcelled. Delicate mosaics can be made with black pepper, paprika, mace, cardamon, savory, and cinnamon, or with plant seeds—lettuce, cress, turnip, and radish, with wild columbine or basil for black. For larger-scaled work, beans, peas, and pasta would serve. Facial tissue and paper toweling are excellent drawing papers. Wax paper provides a unique line, with metal foil available for representations of metal objects. Plenty of color is available in magazines, food containers, and scrap clothing. Candles are available for resist work and tapes for stenciling. If there happened to be a typewriter in the house the designer could make his images on that instrument. Invoices often contain good typewritten textures, and coded instructions which enable one to render the portrait of Abraham Lincoln are available—not creative but a demonstration of potential.

Men and women everywhere through time have made use of what was available. The cave artists were limited in choice of colors and their brushes were poor but they produced impressive images. Not up to that standard, but illustrating the point, is the camel saddle blanket in Figure 155a, a work from French West Africa. The blanket is decorated with seashells. Notice the typical geometry varying from the rigid repeat with the X sometimes doubled, at other times single.

Fig. 154 Collage by fifth-grade student, a lesson in economy of means. Courtesy Racine Public Schools, Racine, Wis.

139

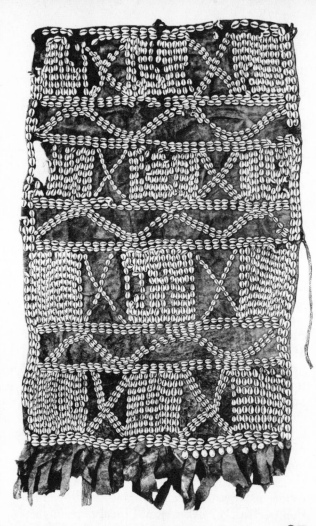

Typically, as soon as beads are introduced into a culture, the recipients make use of them. The beaded figure in 155b is a representation of a deer and is dedicated to the sun. Beads are stuck on the wooden form with beeswax. With its simple basic form and complex variations, the original must have presented a rich visual and tactile experience. This image also serves to show how unfortunate it is that for various reasons prejudice prevents the use of perfectly useful materials. Thus beads may be associated with women's busy work, and some designers may eschew the colorful Indian corn because of its bucolic connection. Any material should be judged on its plastic countenance, with special consideration given those which please the frugal.

Since it is possible to execute good pieces with a minimum of equipment, why do we encourage wide exploration in materials and techniques? First, the beginning designer who did not explore widely might miss the medium especially suited to his own temperament. Then too, different commissions call for different techniques; different kinds of ideas require special treatment, and the designer must feel at ease in fitting idea to plastic image. To do this, he must be learned in the paraphernalia of visual expression. Lastly, wide knowledge of media gives an artist perspective. With it he is better able to judge his own place in the flux and to know when he is in danger of violating a medium.

Fig. 155 a. A camel-saddle blanket from French West Africa, decorated with an available material, seashells. From Tissus Négres, Librairie des Arts Décoratifs, Paris, 1931. Photo by A. Calavas, from the original in the Musée Ethnographique du Trocadéro, Paris. b. Wooden deer decorated with beads brought into the Mexican Indian culture by white men. From Lumholtz' "Symbolism of the Huichol Indians," op. cit.

notes on two-dimensional media

Wherever possible the beginning designer should visit places where commissions are being executed, the studios of established people in all fields, museums, and art monuments. The kind of experience gained by this means is obviously superior to verbal explanation.

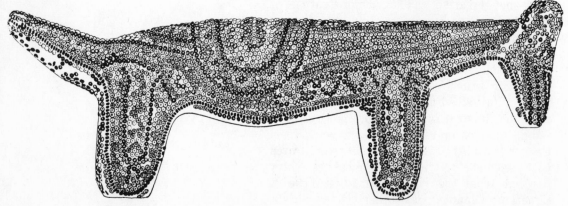

This briefing is a reminder of some of the media artists have used and may be supplemented by the good books available which give thorough coverage.

encaustic Cave artists probably used animal fat and bone marrow to make their earth pigments stick. Later, first supposedly in classical Greece, beeswax was used as pigment carrier. This medium preceded oil and is now called encaustic. Turpentine and heat are used to make the wax more pliant. A few pieces of equipment are necessary for work with encaustic—a heating unit, a muffin pan, blowtorch, and palette knife are minimal. The wax worked this way gives a wonderfully transparent effect.

oil and lacquer Oil has been in wide use as a medium for 300 years. It is based on the fact that a drying oil changes to a kind of varnish. Oil is a very flexible medium and colors remain clear, but it is difficult for beginners because of its slow drying time. Auto lacquers have been used by artists for about 20 years. This medium is a cellulose acetate and it dries very quickly, but its fumes are somewhat toxic. Vinyl acetates are good but suffer from the same defect. Promising for studio use is the white glue found in drug and hardware stores. It is a fine glue for paste work, drying quickly and invisibly, and it can be mixed with dry color, water color or tempera. These glues are a polymer emulsion, which means that a molecule of the substance consists of one long chain with side chains branching off. On drying, the chains interlock and form a permanent surface. Quite rapid drying is one of its merits. Casein, a milk-derived polymer in suspension, is good but it is more readily dissolved and gives a somewhat dead appearance to the pigment when dry.

tempera and fresco Egg tempera, now in eclipse, had its start during the medieval period, found wide acceptance during the Renaissance, and has been almost totally neglected since 1600. The yolk of the egg is a very good adhesive and produces excellent transparent films. Egg white, a colloidal solution of albumen, was used in manuscript illumination. Water-color media use gum arabic, glycerine, and glucose. Since paper is used to hold the pigment, one can take advantage of the flexible properties of the medium. Dye colors can also be used on paper and they are very powerful. Bleaches can be used to remove these dye films. Water colors and dyes are very transparent and high in luminosity.

In fresco painting, pigments are dissolved in water and applied to wet lime plaster. Fine examples of fresco painting dating from around 1600 B.C. have been found on the island of Crete. Fresco is the method of Giotto, Francesca, and Orozco in mural painting, and it puts heavy demands on the artist. Less demanding is a recently developed method of applying pigment to dry cement. The adhesives here are compounds of silicon which form gels that grasp small particles of the ground firmly when completely dry. Vinyl acetates are sometimes used for outdoor murals, where fumes readily escape. New thermosetting plastics using a catalyst are promising. In these the molecular structure is permanently locked. Thin objects, colored film, film negatives, paper, leaves, and so on can be imbedded in such plastic sheets. It makes possible the effects of stained glass within the range of studio practice.

stained glass Stained glass involves fusing metal-based color into liquid molten glass. Various pieces of colored glass are held together with lead strips, with the whole sup-

141

ported by an iron frame. Chiefly used in church architecture, with notable examples in Gothic cathedrals, stained glass, through its transparency, colors light, thus furnishing an impressive spectacle. Small windows of stained glass were included in some American houses built as recently as 50 years ago, a remnant of a Gothic revival. Stained glass needs another revival now, and will probably be taught in some college laboratories within the next ten years. If a student has an opportunity to visit a commercial establishment he should go. Designers in this medium are needed from time to time, and those with appropriate religious conviction could find in stained glass a satisfying way of life.

mosaic The mosaic technique reached high points in the Early Christian and Byzantine periods. Figure 30a shows the technique, that of placing small pieces of colored marble in cement. In the Byzantine mosaics gold leaf is fused into glass for some of the tesserae, while others are a kind of colored porcelain called *smalti*. As mentioned previously, these tesserae are placed at slight angles to one another to increase the play of reflected light. Both stained glass and mosaic force strong simplification of form. Design laboratory projects in mosaic can make use of broken pottery, broken glass, sawed-up metal, stones, broken brick, assorted bottle caps—anything which can be imbedded in cement. The cement can also be scored, carved and painted, or mixed with pigment. Mosaic is experiencing a strong revival in this country at the present time and the reader may be able to find examples near at hand.

enamel Enameling is a process of fusing colored glass to metal. Since such colors can be transparent, light penetrates to the metal and

is reflected out. The result is elegantly luminous. Powdered enamel is applied to copper, dry or wet, and fired in a kiln. The process is usually repeated a number of times to develop the image. One contemporary worker, June Schwarcz, creates an intaglio image before adding the color. Inspired by natural formations, she hammers, scratches, scrapes, solders, digs, and etches the surface with acids until it contains the shapes and textures which suit her. With such a rich development of surface, her colors tend to be subdued. Beginners will find enamel work fascinating, and the equipment is not difficult to obtain. Small portable kilns take care of small work. Industrial equipment makes it possible to consider large units which could be joined to form whole walls.

print media

All print media require a plate, ink, paper, and some means of applying pressure. Printmakers create the image on the plate; and after the plate is inked, the image is transferred to paper, after which the plate is inked again, another image obtained, and so on. The print media derive their generic titles and graphic characteristics from the way the ink is carried by the plate.

relief printing In relief printing, parts of the plate which are to be white in the final image are cut away with carving tools. Greasy ink is then rolled onto the raised parts of the plate. Paper is placed on the plate and it is run through a flatbed press to apply pressure, which transfers the image from plate to paper. Linoleum, wood, and sometimes hard rubber, are popularly used for plate material in this method. Figure 92b (p. 83) shows the woodcut technique. A visit to a print studio will

142

prove informative. The work of Antonio Frasconi is especially noteworthy.

Since a beginner will not be as interested in obtaining multiple copies as in single-copy applications, he can use many materials in applying the relief principle. Almost any material which has a broken surface or can be given a broken surface can be rolled up with ink and printed with the aid of body push. If the working surface is raised, this will retain the ink, available in many colors. It is not even absolutely necessary to use printing ink. Water color and tempera can be used. If absorbent paper is used (rice paper, blotters, or damp water-color paper), figures may be cut out of light cardboard, painted and printed, painted and printed again. In Figure 156 a paper shape is cut out, placed on an ink-laden glass where it picks up pigment, after which the shape is placed on the working surface and covered with a paper. The image is transferred by rubbing the covered shape with a spoon. Hard illustration board can be incised with a sharp tool and rolled up—another approach.

Paper and tape stencils can be used to keep the ink roller from touching places where it is unwanted. Raised papers, like charcoal paper, can be pasted into the working surface to reveal an accentuated texture when rolled up. Sponges, folded tissue, and cloth can be dipped in paint to reveal their textures when printed. Small figures can be cut out of rubber erasers and printed; found objects similarly leave their profile. If they can be obtained, publication relief engravings can be rolled up and printed for variety of image. Cloth too can be used as the working surface. Large pieces of cloth can be placed on the floor and various forms printed thereon. Found objects can be used here too, with pressure furnished by body weight. Colorfast pigments should be used for cloth printing.

intaglio printing In the intaglio process, the parts which are to print are cut below the surface of the plate. Copper is most often the plate material in this method, but plastic and other materials are used. When copper is used, the designer obtains the lowered surface through the use of cutting tools, burin, sharp needle, and acid. Various acid-resistant materials are used to form stencils to keep the acid from reaching the wrong places. When the plate work is finished, ink of a consistency from watery to thick is forced into the recessed image, after which the surface of the plate is wiped clean by hand work. Absorbent paper is placed on the plate and the two are run through a press, which performs the service implied in the name. Image is transferred to paper by pressure and absorbency. Other impressions can then be taken.

With a vague history reaching back into medieval times in engraved armor, intaglio reached high development in the 15th century, with Mantegna in Italy and Dürer in Germany

Fig. 156 Cut-paper print by a research student of Norman Gorbaty, Design Center of Yale University, 1956. Courtesy Print magazine.

143

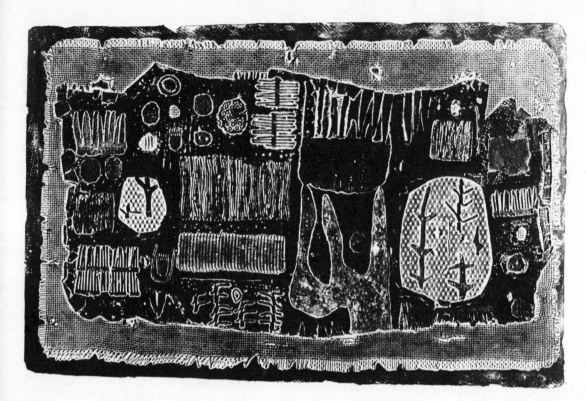

Fig. 157 "Once Upon a Mountain," by Michael Ponce de Leon, illustrating the experimentation taking place in the intaglio medium. Found objects are used to obtain the braille surface desired. Courtesy the artist.

press fitted with springs to ensure faithful impression. We see one of these prints in Figure 157. Techniques have been developed to print several colors at one time, and very soon whole murals may be executed in intaglio. Intaglio currently enjoys and suffers an over-concern with technique at the expense of content. Exploration is valid at all times and places, and it is the sacred touchstone of science, but art is different in that what one expects to be delivered is not research but the artist himself, in comment on himself, his environment, and his fellow creatures. The two are intermingled, of course, but let the designer ponder this problem from the outset. The human being is to be heard through the technique and not the other way around.

The softground method can be duplicated by using a hard-surface illustration board coated with paraffin—a candle will do. A needle or a razor blade can cut through the wax and into the paper surface. Ink or tempera can be floated into these recessed parts, after which the wax can be scraped off, leaving a linear image. This process can be repeated with different colors. Single-copy intaglio objects can be produced on any surface which can be wiped clean after the application of pigment, as in the bamboo etchings seen earlier. A pen line can be forced through a lightly waxed surface to give an intaglio effect, or small prints may be pulled from scratched tin.

planographic printing In planographic print processes the ink lies on a plate surface that is neither raised nor lowered. Lithography uses flat pieces of Bavarian limestone for plate material. The print maker creates the image with grease pencils and with brushes charged with a greasy liquid called tusche. These markings are to print. Those areas which are to remain white in the final print are left un-

executing particularly fine pieces. (The latter also worked impressively in relief.) In the 17th century, Rembrandt, using the softground method (cutting through an amalgam of wax, gum, and rosin to expose the plate to acid), produced many works inspired by peasant life. Since then, intaglio has been used for illustration, with invention and power declining. In the last 25 years the intaglio process has seen a vigorous rebirth. With Stanley William Hayter in Paris and Mauricio Lasansky of the University of Iowa leading research and inquiry, intaglio presently has a status almost equal to that of oil painting. Roland Ginzel from the Iowa atelier, now at the University of Illinois, Chicago, works with cardboard plates. Michael Ponce de Leon uses a metal collage technique featuring found material, with a touched. The greasy materials leave in the stone an impression which is strengthened by chemicals to insure that it will subsequently exhibit a special affinity for the greasy ink with which the roller is charged. The plate material itself is hydroscopic, that is to say, it holds water, and its surface is moistened before the image is rolled up with ink. Greasy ink cannot penetrate these wet areas and the water cannot penetrate the greasy image, which readily accepts the roller's ink. In printing, the plate is always kept wet. Paper is placed on the stone. The two are run through a press and an impression taken off on the paper. Figures 34 and 129 (pp. 42, 114) represent two approaches to lithography. In the 19th century much fine pictorial work was executed on stone. Commercial lithography then used stone exclusively. The famous colored prints produced by Nathaniel Currier and J. Meritt Ives in New York after 1857, fine pieces of Americana recording 19th-century manners, customs, and famous men and events, were lithographed. Goya, Daumier, and Toulouse-Lautrec are also especially noteworthy among those who produced fine lithographs. Lithography has no direct classroom application except in texts—this book, for example, is produced by a lithographic process using metal plates instead of stones.

In serigraphy the artist creates the image on a sheet of fine woven silk stretched flat on a wooden frame. In printing, the screen is in direct contact with the paper. Semiliquid paint is poured on the screen and forced through the screen and onto the paper by use of a rubber squeegee. Image creation involves making a stencil of the screen to prevent paint from reaching those parts which by design are to remain white. Although the theory is old, serigraphy was used in commercial practice only until re-examined by Anthony Velonis and a group on the New York WPA Art Project during the late 1930's. In Figure 158 we see a serigraph by Robert Gwathmey, executed in 1945, some years after the work of the New York group. Developed in rather strong, flat planes, this work well demonstrates the stencillike nature of the serigraph process.

In the pioneer days of art serigraphy, stencils were made with cut paper and film, and areas tended to be unbroken and flat, as Figure 158 demonstrates. As time went on, artists developed stencil methods involving adhesives

Fig. 158 Serigraph by Robert Gwathmey, "Children Dancing," executed in 1945. This work follows closely on the experiments performed by a WPA art group in New York City. Their purpose was to exploit the serigraph printing technique for personal expression. Gwathmey's print demonstrates clearly that serigraphy is a stencil process. Courtesy the artist.

which could be drawn or painted on the screen; the paint solvents could not touch the adhesives, which could later be removed from the screen. Pigment quality ranges from thick and opaque to thin and transparent, from mat to glossy. Metallic and highly luminous pigments may be used. With research by individuals like Dean Meeker of the University of Wisconsin, Howard Bradford in Southern California, and Edward Landon in New York, the medium now rivals any in potential richness. Through the silk-screen process, images may be printed on cloth. Transparent lacquers can be printed on glass or plastic with stained-glass effect. Images can be transferred to metal and to practically any kind of surface except water. Thus it is a versatile print medium, and the small cost of the basic plant puts it within reach of anyone. Simple stencil methods force methods of simplification of form which will prove most valuable.

Planographic print methods involving gelatin plates as in mimeograph reproduction and collotype, which is used in reproducing paintings, have generally been ignored by artists and designers and probably need investigation.

commercial printing processes All of the multiple-copy media have their commercial counterparts. Here are the generic designations together with the titles used in the printing industry.

· relief—letterpress
· intaglio—gravure, rotogravure
· planographic
    lithography—offset lithography, or
        photo-offset
    serigraphy—silk screen

In these methods of reproduction the plate is covered with a light-sensitive gelatin having the property of becoming hard and insoluble when struck by light. Photographic negatives then act as a light stencil. Where transparent, they let light through and where opaque they stop light. The soluble parts are washed away and the plate is thus imbedded with the information potential brought to fruition by several different procedures of chemistry. Those who intend to design for commercial printing must of necessity learn all about these methods of reproduction. Beginners in the field can visit printing establishments. In offset lithography, where metal plates are now used, in silk screen, and in gravure, the entire operation may be followed in one plant. In letterpress, photoengravings are usually made in one commercial establishment and type is set in another. The latter plant usually combines the two kinds of relief design and prints them. The various plates and negatives used are interesting to see, and the many different papers used may inspire ideas. There are possibilities in combining the light-stenciled image with those done by hand, but this area remains unexplored. Advanced technical ability is required here.

photography

Since its establishment in the third decade of the 19th century, photography has played a major role in communication. Until the latter half of the 19th century all single- and multiple-copy images were the product of eye and hand. The mechanical-physical-chemical processes of photography (still under scientific scrutiny) provided society with a new tool for examining its members and their environment. It provided a new test as to whether artists were escaping into pure nonsense (see Figure 13) or pursuing pure form as in the Mondrian studies. Photography was and is a weapon of belief and action. Mathew Brady's Civil War

146

photographs made inroads (albeit slight) on the romantic notions about war. It also catches and records moments of poignancy so subtle in origin as to defy the sharp eye of the artist (Fig. 106c). Photography provided a new tool for studying the human body. Eadweard Muybridge's studies of the human figure in action, first published in 1887, are still the finest of their kind. The photograph as documentation is too well known to require comment here. Its role in communication is very important. Every image in this book, for example, has been photographed at least once. Without photography in the reproduction processes, we should have to return to the hand-drawn image. As art, photography has its great moments, although much of salon photography has run to cliché. For a fine example of the photographer's art see Figure 82, page 76.

The designer's first practical laboratory experience with photography may well be through the photogram. Here objects are placed on sensitized paper and exposed to light, leaving a direct image on the paper. Experimental work by Man Ray, Moholy-Nagy, and others introduced the photogram to American design. An example of this kind of experimentation is seen in Figure 159, a rich thematic texture. Apparatus is not very expensive.

threads

Weaving is a process of positioning threads in a tight over-and-under web which is held together by the mutual friction of the material. In its simplest form a set of stretched threads called the warp is separated into two levels with alternate threads up and down. A weft thread is run crosswise through the gap between the two sets of warp threads, after which the position of the warp threads is reversed, trapping the weft. This process con-

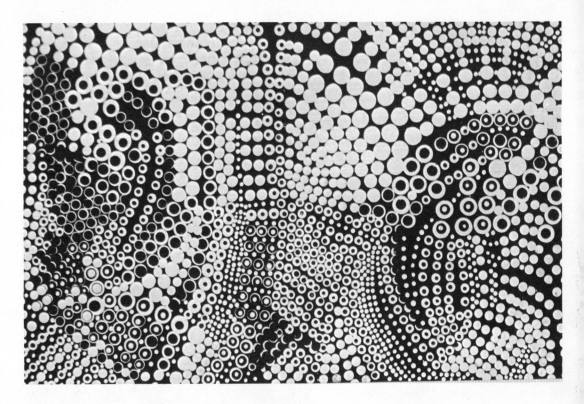

tinues and is called tabby weaving. The earliest use of weaving is lost in the far reaches of prehistoric time, for the materials used are fragile. Primitive and sophisticated cultures alike use weaving for utility and as personal expression. The many different kinds of animal hairs, vegetable fibers, insect cocoons, metal, and synthetic materials from which threads are derived make rich variety possible. These various threads may be gently colored by natural dyes or given brilliant hues with synthetic ones. In ikat dyeing the warp or the weft threads are colored in an interrupted pattern before weaving. The raising and lowering of groups of warp threads by mechanical means makes it possible to achieve an almost endless variety of patterns in the cloth. Various threads may be woven back and forth

Fig. 159 Student photographic project. Courtesy Raymond Dowden, Head, Department of Design, Cooper Union Art School, and Hannes Beckman, instructor in photography.

147

through a limited section of the warp. We see an example of this technique in Figure 160, a rich wall hanging by Mary Balzer Buskirk, giving an idea of the potential of weaving as personal expression.

Tapestry art consists in using a number of different segments of thread in each line of weaving across the warp. These segments may vary in length, color, value, or texture, thus making it possible to build up complex images in the cloth. Many impressive works in this technique were executed during the late medieval period. Recent work in France includes the romantic imagery of designer Jean Lurçat. The Scandinavian countries are especially noted for their fine tapestry designer-weavers, and in our country Jan Yoors and his family working in New York execute impressive tapestries of architectural dimensions.

Embroidery consists of sewing threads onto an already woven piece of cloth. It was widely practiced in the late medieval and early Renaissance periods. Several fine 14th-century works feature the legends of King Arthur, with dragons and jousting scenes enlivening the proceedings. The Bayeux Tapestry, previously mentioned, is really an embroidery and not a tapestry. Fine embroidery was produced by the Copts in 4th-century Egypt, and fine embroidery is produced today in the Orient and in the Philippine Islands, with that from East Pakistan especially well known. We have seen examples of embroidery in Figures 102 and 122 (pp. 94, 108). The late Mariska Karaz

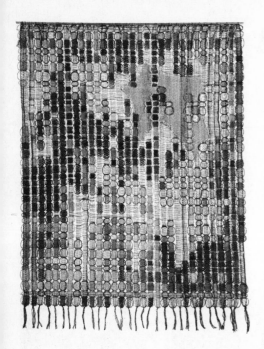

Fig. 160   Woven piece by Mary Balzer Buskirk, illustrating weaving as a means of personal expression. Courtesy the artist.

Fig. 161   Cotton cushion cover, a 17th-century piece from India. It combines mordant dyeing, resist dyeing, and direct painting. Courtesy The Metropolitan Museum of Art, Rogers Fund, 1928.

is perhaps the best known of those currently working in this medium in the United States.

The famous Persian carpets were made by knotting rows of short lengths of colored wool between lines of weft thread. Weavers selected and inserted the proper color of yarn as they went along. In the process the colors were massed to build up shapes meaningful to the culture and rich in visual effect. The individually knotted strands might run several hundred to the square inch. After the weaving was completed, the uneven tips were cut off, leaving an even pile. Though magnificent in appearance, the tedious handwork involved makes the technique a formidable one. At present, the V'Soske brothers of Grand Rapids, among others, execute fine hand-knotted rugs using somewhat heavier yarns and a smaller number of knots to the inch.

As noted previously, relief-cut images may be printed on fabric. Cloth also may receive images through direct painting with specially designed pigment carriers. Dyeing is another method of applying color. In mordant dyeing, a substance is added to the dye which makes the color permanent in the cloth. Resist dyeing involves putting wax on those parts of the cloth which are not to receive the dye. After dyeing, the wax is removed by boiling. Figure 161 is a reproduction of a 17th-century Indian cotton cushion cover. The piece combines mordant dyeing, resist dyeing, and direct painting. Resist dyeing, an old Eastern technique, is quite popular in this country.

Lace and crocheted and knitted fabrics are made by looping and/or twisting one thread around another. In netting, the thread is knotted to keep it in place. Such fabrics are useful where transparency is desired. In braiding, strands of material are twisted around one another in a fixed sequence. Appliqué is a method of decorating cloth; small pieces of fabric of different colors are sewed onto the ground fabric to produce a pattern. These are a few of the methods used in giving cloth expressive imagery.

This discussion has commented on some of the materials and techniques used in important personal expression. While some are clearly advanced and complex, it is important that we touch upon them so that beginners in the design field may see directions at the end of their studies, so that they may begin to formulate personal preferences for one of the many media of expression.

investigating materials and techniques

The beginning designer should budget his time so as to conduct a systematic investigation of materials which offer a potential in communicative imagery. This process broadens resources and leads to new ways of solving design problems. In such a survey we are chiefly concerned with material under three main headings:

· pigments
· surfaces
· tools of application

Under each of these headings a listing can be made of the several different items to be considered. The following discussion contains a number of suggested procedures.

pigments Combinations of pigments with different carriers often produce interesting effects. These may be caused by the two carriers having different values in surface tension or possessing incompatible chemical structures. The marbling seen in the end papers of old books was done by floating oil-based pigment on water and picking up the surface pat-

Fig. 162 Pigmented oil drops, water color, and India ink rolled around a piece of acetate. Author's sketch.

Fig. 163 a. Collage on the theme of travel, making use of airline tickets. Designed by Norman Harris and Arthur Paul. Courtesy Playboy Magazine. *b. "Imbroglio," collage by David Pease, in which he uses pieces of official records to recreate a phase of military experience. Courtesy the artist, collection of Italo P. B. Scanga.*

tern with a piece of paper. The pigment used to feed felt pens is suitable for this technique and can produce patterns of many colors. In Figure 162 drops of pigmented oil, water, and India ink were maneuvered on a piece of acetate. Here we see echoes of organic structure, with one form running through another in a flux of curved forms. India ink on water produces an interesting textural flow.

Experimentation with resists may provide some useful results. Drawing with India ink on wax paper produces an interesting broken line. If wax paper is placed wax side down on a piece of drawing paper and drawn on with a pointed instrument, a waxed line will adhere to the drawing paper. When the paper is covered with dark pigment the line shows up. Similar linear work can be done with wax crayon, liquid rubber, or rubber cement. Combinations of crayon and water color or dye make possible a red crayon texture on the top ridges of toothed paper with a green transparency on the bottom. Such vivid textures are hard to achieve otherwise. Brilliant colors can be applied to parts of a surface, covered in part with crayons, covered in turn with India ink, and washed off for a study in luminosity. Oil colors and printing inks are resistant to water-based pigments and the combination sometimes produces good results.

surfaces Collage techniques involve pasting found or prepared material onto the working surface. Good textural studies are executed in this way. The purpose here is the examination and comparison of the visual properties of various kinds of surfaces. If the correct material is obtained, thematic content can be communicated. An example of this is seen in Figure 163a, a feature piece for a men's magazine. Here tickets make a varied pattern while suggesting travel, the subject of the page. In Figure 163b the artist uses pieces of military orders, records, training manuals and other documents to recreate in one image the rather stiff and restrictive aspects of army experience. A hint of a rigid human figure can be discerned, with the line helping to define the form. The square head has been located near the exact center of the rectangular surface. Maps, stamps, and labels can be used in similar application. Various materials in combination with the human figure can suggest profession, personality, or attitude. How about bottle caps for the overdecorated dictator? Sometimes found images make comment with very little aid. One image in Figure 164 represents a 19th-century dress cutting invention, while the other was taken from an old book on phrenology, a wonderfully fraudulent discipline. As we can see, the juxtaposition of these two images suggests a pinball machine and operator. The reader is encouraged to complete the image thus presented with appropriate drawing and colored light, noise, coin, and action symbology.

Adhesive materials are useful for stencil purposes. Rubber cement can be used for backing cut-out shapes, which can be glued to the working surface and removed after paint application, brushed, blown, or stippled. Various tapes can be used in the same way; since they are available in color and value they can even be kept as a permanent part of the working surface. Colored plastic tapes used in map-making are available in near-line widths and are especially useful. Black cloth tape furnishes the image material in the study for an album cover seen in Figure 165. The vertical pipe organ shapes make an interesting pattern, suggesting the specific content of the music and its quality of dignity. Paint and brush, tape, and a razor blade are the raw materials. In using music as inspiration for graphic pieces, it is better to derive ideas from the music than from titles and program notes. Thus sound rather than literature suggests the graphic form, a difficult problem since it involves a new kind of translation for most beginners. It is a good problem, since value, color, shape, and line may all play a part in creating the appropriate surface activity.

Papers, as has been suggested, take pigment in various ways. Some take pigment instantly —clay-coated surfaces for example—and set it permanently; others allow for manipulation. Thin papers cannot absorb much water, while heavy water-color papers absorb great quantities of paint without becoming saturated, especially in high humidity when the atmosphere takes out medium as fast as it is put on the surface. Other papers resist the action of pigment, giving a soft line where receptive papers give hard, sharp effects. Waxed surfaces absorb little. Brilliance in color varies with the ab-

Fig. 164 *Juxtaposition of two found images suggests pinball machine and operator with completion left to reader. Propach's Indicator, a dress-cutting invention, from* Harper's Bazaar, *1886. Head from* Phrenology, or the Doctrine of the Mental, *by J. G. Spurzheim, M.D., 1833.*

sorbency rate. Coated or high-finish smooth papers which absorb instantly, leaving no time for maneuvering and forcing the direct-action statement, exhibit color in its most brilliant state. On papers which absorb slowly, color is dulled. These facts can only be discovered through experimentation.

tools

For linear problems a large variety of metal pens are available, starting with the crow quill point for fine work and ranging through variously formed lettering pens up to those making a strike ⅜ of an inch wide. Pens are available which make double lines; those which musical arrangers use to delineate the staff draw five lines at once.

Felt pad pens are helpful in sketching, although their square-edged strokes intrude on personal style until worn down. Drafting pens provide the straight line; contour pens swivel and furnish the curve. So-called railroad pens make a double line.

Fortunately, it is also possible to make pens in the studio. These may be cut from bamboo or other reeds with the nib designed to fit the need, and ink holders may be made from thin, springy metal. India ink fountain pens are available and well suited to projects which involve continuity of line.

There is a brush made to suit almost any design need. These range in size from brushes of gauge 000 with only a few hairs to Japanese watercolor brushes several inches wide. House painting brushes made of stiffer bristles are good for rough work. The so-called red sable brushes are best for fine work and are relatively expensive. Brushes made of squirrel, camel, or ox hair are of lesser quality but useful. Stiff bristle brushes are best with thicker pigments, and the inexpensive stencil brush can be very useful since its hairs may be shaved to provide a rounder mark without jeopardizing a heavy investment.

Air brushes are useful to have around a design studio, and several can be hooked up to the same "air" tank or compressor. The tank has the advantage of being silent.

There are many devices in which pigment and applicating tool are combined. Pencils are in this category and are available in great variety; they include not only graphite in various degrees of hardness and size but also many other materials. Charcoal, carbon, and lithograph pencils leave different kinds of marks. Several kinds of colored pencils are manufactured, as are those leaving a metallic deposit. Wax and oil crayons are very useful and relatively inexpensive. Chalks, colored and gray pastels, furnish unique qualities. Conté crayons, lithograph crayons, and charcoal sticks are also useful.

These are but a few of the tools which can be used to manipulate pigment on a surface. To set up an experimental situation in a classroom it might be well to prepare longer lists of useful materials. Since each student could hardly afford the entire range of possible materials, each could acquire a few of the items. In this way, through observation and mutual borrowing, an entire class could over a period of time learn something of the wide range of the materials of design.

review

Man everywhere makes use of whatever comes to hand to fashion his graphic and plastic modes of expression. Some of these materials have become established in tradition; beeswax, oils, gums, resins, eggs, and synthetic plastics all have been used to bind pigment. Ivory, bamboo, skins, paper, plaster, and cloth are some of the materials which receive images. Among great media are mosaic, stained glass, and fresco.

Multiple-print media include relief processes, with ink on a raised surface; intaglio processes, with ink on a lowered surface; planographic processes, lithography, with ink lying on the plane of the plate, and serigraphy, wherein pigment is forced through the stenciled plane of a silk screen. Commercial counterparts of the four print methods use photography in plate making. The original is photographed and a transparent negative or positive serves as a stencil between a light source and a plate surfaced with a light-sensitive gelatin. Photography is also widely used as a device for recording and expression. One introduction to photography is the photogram.

Important expressive methods involving threads and cloth are weaving, tapestry, embroidery, and rug-making. Impressive examples rival any medium of expression in richness of imagery.

Research centers around three areas: pigments, applicators, and surfaces, with each contributing significantly to any finished work.

Fig. 165 Album cover, using black cloth tape. By a student at the University of Wisconsin.

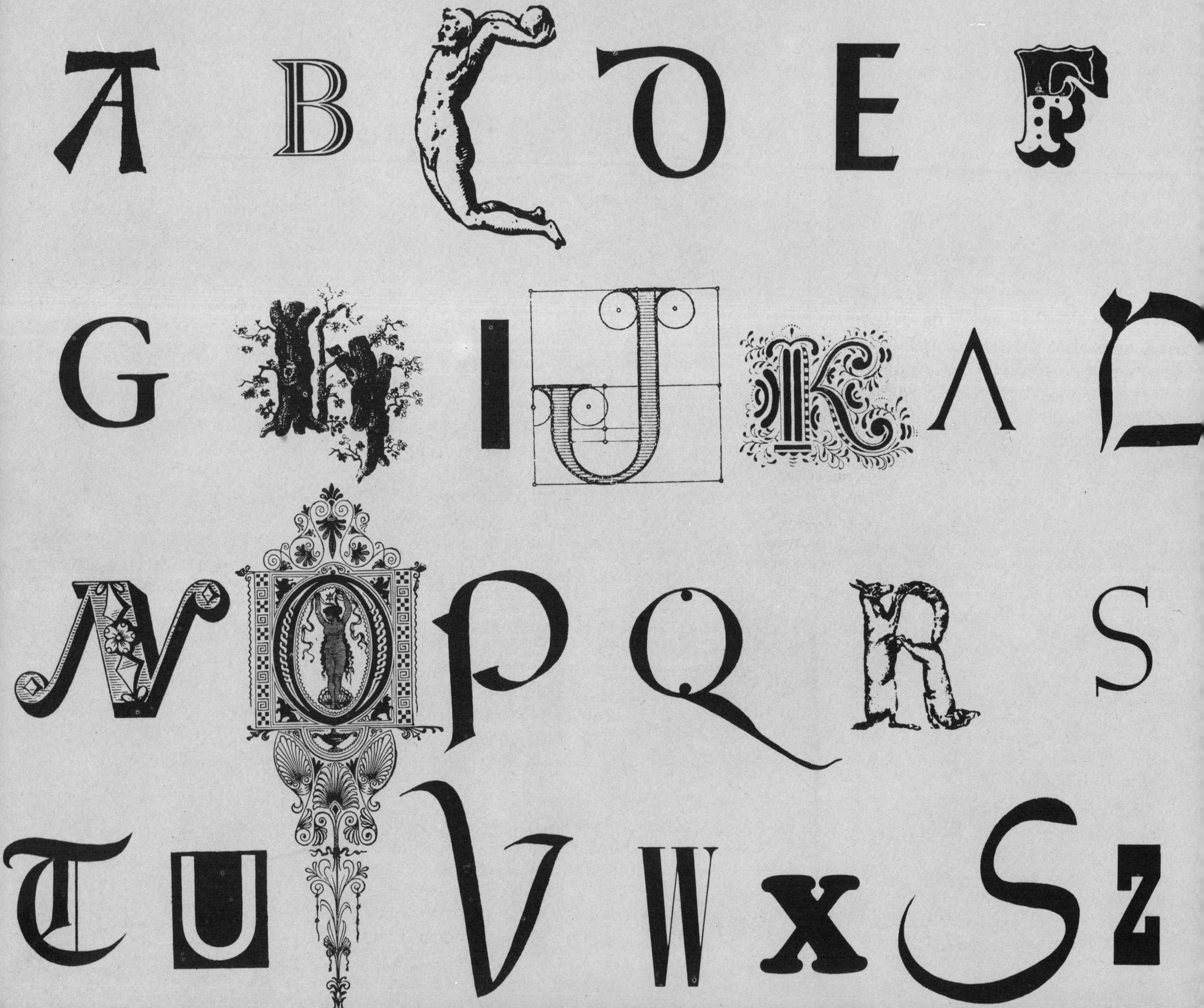

13 *expression in word form*

Any mark or series of marks placed on a surface has a communication value. Thus if a series of I-shaped marks are placed on a page next to a series of S-shaped marks, one can say that the curved forms are more active or more graceful than the other set. In letters of the alphabet the same holds true. Graphic content speaks. In an earlier section, it was noted that Chinese is essentially a pictographic language. Symbols describe objects, with meaning and form closely knit. In our alphabet, meaning and form are separated and it is possible for a word to convey one meaning through symbol and quite another in form, as we can see from the example in the margin to the right. It is the designer's job to get the symbol clothed in the appropriate graphic form. This, after all, is the task in any design enterprise. If we want the drawing of a man to be strong we find graphic means to convey this. The particular roman alphabet in which this book is set speaks firmly, clearly, with some grace. It could as well speak bluntly, shout, or whisper.

Our examination of the subject of letter forms will be based on larger letters than those on this page. While there are thousands of designers who routinely recognize 75 or 100 different type faces at sizes smaller than that seen here, it takes time to reach this level of skill. Careful classification of alphabets and the small sizes may be put off.

Word forms are seen unavoidably in daily life and we gain much of our information through them. The forms play a part in directing thought and action. An example is the case of a supermarket which replaced its heavy and crowded food ads with a thinner alphabet surrounded by lots of white space, only to discover that people stopped visiting the store, having received the impression that it was too expensive.

Some of the many different forms of the capital alphabet are seen in historical panorama in Figure 166.

Since a beginning designer has spent some years reading, it is time for him to begin developing an awareness of the role played by letter forms in directing his thought. Too, a tradition in graphic expression tells us that the well-rounded artist must be able to handle all the forms of the environment, a letter being no different from a leaf in this respect. Figure 122 (p. 108) shows words in natural play with the other elements. The designers of the great Byzantine mosaics included letters (*D* in Figure 166), as did those who executed tapestries. Dürer spent some time redesigning the Roman capitals (*J* in the panorama). Ben Shahn among contemporary artists handles all letter styles, an ability which stems from his apprenticeship on the lithograph stone, but he has especially inspired others through his revival of medieval forms (*A* in Figure 166). Those with thoughts of a career in advertising design should be aware that in this field design means correlation of word and picture, and control of both.

the dual function

Letter forms, then, are seen in dual function —symbol and form. We have seen an example of the letter in symbol and decoration in Figure 6 (p. 8). The Greeks, with their strong leaning toward economy, see basic structure in Figure 91 (p. 82). These letter forms inspired

Fig. 166 Composite capital alphabet of historical and contemporary letter styles. One letter each from the Greek, Hebrew, and Arabic alphabets are included. Most languages from India to our Pacific coast use alphabets which stem from a common prototype. Several letters from Alphabets and Ornaments, *op. cit.; several from* Handbook of Early American Advertising Art, *by Clarence P. Hornung, Dover Publications, Inc., New York, 1947; other letters from the author's collection.*

155

Fig. 167 Calligraphic signature in Arabic spells dove *in form and through symbol. The name of a tribal chief. From* Alphabets and Ornaments, op. cit.

Fig. 168 Mouse's tale and tail from Alice in Wonderland, *by Lewis Carroll. Rare cleverness in 19th-century letter manipulation.*

Fury said to
a mouse, That
       he met
        in the
        house,
       'Let us
       both go
       to law:
I will
prosecute
you.—
Come, I'll
   take no
   denial;
      We must
         have a
            trial:
                For
              really
               this
             morning
                  I've
              nothing
              to do.'
            Said the
             mouse to
            the cur,
             'Such a
                 trial,
              dear sir,
            With no
           jury or
          judge,
            would be
            wasting
             our breath.'
                'I'll be
                 judge,
               I'll be
              jury,'
             Said
              cunning
               old Fury;
                 'I'll try
                 the whole
                     cause,
                     and
                   condemn
                    you
                    to
                   death.' "

156

the lean Kabel alphabet designed in 1926 (*U*), throwing off 19th-century fussiness. A return to decoration through another culture is seen in Figure 167, a 17th-century Persian personal signature. Here Arabic letters are seen forming the contour of a dove. The letters also spell dove—triple meaning in symbol, image, and decoration. Some of the cultures of the Middle East have from early historic times to the present embroidered any forms with which they came in contact. Among alphabets interesting in form are the Chinese, many Indian, Hebrew (*M*) and Arabic (*Y* in the panorama). Cultures using the Arabic alphabet are especially fond of ornamental play in letter forms.

As might be expected, the Renaissance, with the image of man dominating the scene, saw the design of alphabets formed by human figures in strenuous calisthenics (*C*). As also might be expected, 18th-century alphabets were very fancy but demonstrate structure under the ornamentation (*K*). Popular romanticism in the 19th century spawned an odd assortment of alphabets, some exhibiting letters formed of mossy branches (*H*) while others featured animals (*R*). Other letters in the panorama of Figure 166 exhibiting 19th-century design ideas are F, N and Z. Many lettering forms of the 19th century compete with the derby hat in the contest for the ugliest forms known to man. Letter *O* in Figure 166 shows an example. These letter forms are so various in their ways of assaulting vision that they constitute a special area of typographical research.

One of the more clever utilizations found in the 19th century is that in Figure 168, in which words form the image of a mouse's tale and tail, a product of Charles Lutwidge Dodgson's imagination. As Lewis Carroll, Dodgson, a mathematician, wrote *Alice in Wonderland*, published in 1865. Nothing has been written concerning what the typographers said on receiving instructions for Figure 168 but it must have been colorful.

We begin to see in these examples and in the discussion that communication through letter form depends on basic form and placement. To this we can add color, value, texture, and culturally endowed symbolic content. In this latter category note the connotations of Black Letter (*T*), the alphabet of Gutenberg, perhaps better known to readers as Old English, which it is not. This alphabet is seen on wedding invitations, church hymnals, academic certificates, and labels attached to beer and liquor. A character in Walt Kelly's *Pogo* speaks in Black Letter, which makes it clear that he is an animal of the cloth.

studio work

Letters may be obtained in several ways. Plentiful in newspapers and magazines, they can be cut out and pasted on the working surface. Or letters may be cut out of either grayed or colored papers. An area may be painted with color and letter forms cut from it. Professionals use pens, brushes and mechanical drawing equipment to form various kinds of letters, and these tools may be used as skills permit.

We have seen letters used in decoration and texture, and Figure 134 (p. 118) is an example which also exhibits scenic qualities. In Figure 169 letters are used to build up a figurative shape. This kind of image stems from experimental work in the second and third decades of this century. As noted, the cubists put pieces of newspapers along with other environmental bric-a-brac into their pictures. During the 1920's experimentation centered more on the letters, with Tristan Tzara and others of the Dada group using unusual typography.

By selecting or creating letters of proper size we can express words like *elephant, tiny,*

ponderous, loud, and *bold.* It is possible to change sizes in the middle of a word to express words like *irregular, variation, disappear,* and *increase.* By spacing letters carefully we can give special emphasis to such words as *deliberate, crowded, impact,* and *acceleration.* We see the effect of close spacing in Figure 170a and in the example featuring the word *phobia.* This effect can be studied in advertising de-

Fig. 169 Figurative work with type collage. Designed by Mel Richman and Ray Heubner. Courtesy Holiday *Magazine.*

157

hiccup

sardine

flight

Fig. 170 a. Word expressing a quality through spacing. b. Communicating meaning through letter displacement. Both student projects from University of Wisconsin studios. c. Expression through letter form and spacing. Author's sketch.

sign, where letter spacing (spreading out letters) is used to communicate qualities of refinement, dignity, and sophistication. In placing letters out of vertical alignment we can communicate the essence of such words as *irregular, rhythmical,* and *corrugated.* We see such usage in Figure 170b. By placing letters with complete freedom, words such as *random, chaotic,* and *excited* can be given a particular impact. Figure 170c shows the result of such manipulation, using letters which fit the communicative need. Changing value within a word is also a fruitful graphic device. Words like *alternate, disappear,* and *revive* can be given a meaningful façade. With changes in color we can of course express *yellow, orange,* and so on. *Hot, cool, mourning, danger, fire, bloody,* and *sinful* can be clothed in their appropriate color. By cutting letters in pieces we can speak *hot, nervous, broken, jazz,* and *explode* with proper force. Different qualities can be obtained by using a different letter form for every letter in a word. Thus we can spell out *idiotic, confusion,* or *comical.*

Figure 171 demonstrates clearly what can be done with mature ingenuity. In this piece for a pharmaceutical house Herb Lubalin makes us feel to our roots the physical effects of a wracking cough.

Of course much can be learned from selecting the proper letter form. It is not necessary to know the names of the various styles to begin with. This knowledge is accumulated in due time. To practice selecting appropriate forms, one can choose styles from magazines and newspapers to fit phrases like the following: *First National Bank, a fragrance from the East, Stop, Road Ends, a little old lady in lace, a cool drink with a distinguished gentleman, watchmaker,* and so forth. It can be seen that in the first instance we need a style which expresses dignity possibly, and certainly stability, strength, and permanence. In this way styles are learned on graphic content alone. Type books offer too many suggestions through title of style. The type called Bank Script is no good for our initial phrase.

Script or cursive letter forms and writing are much the same. During the Renaissance when the italic slanted letter form was developed, (*V* in Figure 166), letters came to be tied together. These tied letters are called ligatures, and in the medieval half-uncial (*P* in Figure 166) whole words are so tied together. Ligatures are a device of expediency—the calligrapher doesn't want to lift his pen. When all letters are tied together we have a form that we call writing, or in the language of typography and calligraphy, script. With a pointed brush and black tempera pigment, we can begin practicing an informal script by writing the names of friends. The best way is to move right along. Good strokes depend on movement; slowing down means wobbly, uncertain strokes. After a time we can try expressing the meaning of a word through the form of the word. Try expressing the swift zigzag movements of *rabbit*. Other good words to try are *speed, rough, monotonous, elephant, violent, neurotic, graceful,* and *stupid*. The consistency of the pigment may be changed as well as the paper (smooth, rough, and so on), and the brush may move anywhere on the page. We see one of the descriptive words in Figure 172a. Here the pigment is quite fluid. In Figure 172b the meaning of the word is expressed by disconnecting the letters. Experimentation will reveal many of the qualities which can be communicated through the script letter.

By drawing the outline of a word on a linoleum block and carving away all excess material, the word will be left in relief. This relief image can then be rolled up with pigment and printed by hand pressure. To insure that the word is carved in reverse, it might be best to draw the word on a piece of thin paper first and then to turn the paper over before tracing it off on the linoleum. With this method of obtaining a word image, new ideas can be handled, mostly centering on repeating the image. By varying the value in repetition, a good page using the word *echo* can be designed. *Memory, harmonics,* and *maladjustment* are other words with meanings enhanced through repetition. *Motion* of course can be expressed quite well by this means. A sequence of images expresses the idea of action through time. We see this well done in Figure 173, where again we can almost feel the jar.

word and figurative image

When word and picture are used together, the idea is double impact. One does what the other cannot do. Thus one reinforces the other. Those images not tied to meaning through the device of coded symbol are ambiguous and open to many different interpretations. As we have seen, the coded symbol in its clearest state is not particularly interesting. If we want to obtain an image which is varied in graphic content we find that it becomes more ambiguous. Scarcely any two people interpret a painting in the same way, and sometimes two interpretations will be strongly variant. Words, too, carry ambiguous meanings, as we well know. If this is doubted one can try to define a word like *liberty*. However, since word and picture are two elements they act like a kind of range-finding device, pinpointing meaning. The two, in reducing each other's ambiguity, tie down the application. This is seen in Figure 174a, a simple idea of reinforcement. Without the word we are not absolutely sure what the girl is doing. Without the girl's image we would not be sure what skip applied to—school, a

Fig. 171 *The heart of an ad for Ciba Pharmaceutical by Herb Lubalin of Sudler and Hennessey. Courtesy the artist.*

Fig. 172 a. *Script form executed by brush and liquid pigment. Meaning of the word is expressed by the form of the word. Author's sketch.* b. *Meaning expressed by script letters disconnected. Student project from University of Wisconsin studios.*

159

Fig. 173 *Motion suggested by judicious placement and repetition. Designer: Ralph Coburn. Courtesy Massachusetts Institute of Technology.*

Fig. 174 a. *Word and image reinforce one another with meaning made precise, an action.* b. *Trait of character communicated through picture, letter style, and placement of letters.* c. *A state of mind on view through crowded white word and appropriate figurative image.* d. *Script word and found images join in a surrealist spatial arrangement. All from University of Wisconsin studio projects.*

beat, or a stone. Of course it will be noticed that the form of the word fixes meaning more precisely.

This kind of pictorial matter is readily available for collage purposes and can express whatever suits the designer's purpose: physical actions, textures, human emotion, human (or animal) utterance, odors, adjectives, traits of character, or states of mind. In Figure 174b we see an example which communicates a trait of character. Here the style of letter is well chosen, being somewhat thick, and the angled countenance of the letters adds to the impact. In Figure 174c a state of mind is put on view. The pictorial image is good—no doubt from a dance group—with the white crowded letters and spacious black ground contributing to the effect. Notice that the human figures look at the letter image. This too is important. Another collage by the same artist is seen in Figure 174d, here using a script. The frightening sense of space is created by the joint action of two found images, with a third needed to complete the whole.

It is natural that, given complete freedom in solving a problem, the ideas of some turn to humor ranging to the phantasmagoric. We also like a sense of punning. Well-received when good and deprecated when bad, the verbal play

on words has a graphic counterpart. In this, separate meanings of words converge, with the secondary meaning adding impact or absurdity. When we see an expression like "He fell through a window and suffered a pane of glass" we don't know how to spell pain. Most of us have at one time or another converted O O into a pair of spectacles. As we shall see, the surrealists sometimes arranged one image so that it could be read in two ways. This most intimate connection between word form and corroborating image is observed in Figure 175, with sans serif style O's serving as bicycle tires. A related kind of dual imagery can be achieved by cutting letters out of photographs.

calligraphy

Some of our great historic letter styles are executed with a wide nib pen. Such pens are wide across the tip and make thick vertical strokes and thin horizontal strokes. In Figure 166 the letters M, P, T and V have been executed with such a tool. Our lower-case alphabet was developed out of the Roman capital alphabet by calligraphers who used such pens. In the event that a student happens to be interested in this manner of letter formation, wide nib steel pens are available. Following the example

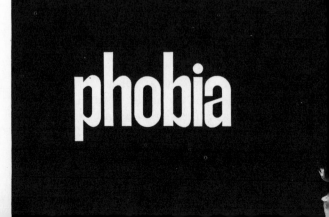

of great calligraphers, the student can make his own. Very good pens can be cut from small diameter bamboo stakes, the kind found in garden supply houses. Gardeners use these bamboo sticks to hold up plants. Bamboo has a tough, flexible surface and can be cut and honed to a very thin point. It can be fitted with a piece of coiled metal to hold ink. For full information see *Writing and Illuminating and Lettering* by Edward Johnston. First printed in 1906 and now again available, it is still the best book on this subject.

review

Letter forms possess dual content; symbolic and graphic form. It is the designer's task to correlate these two aspects of form so that the symbol is seen in a form appropriate to the communicative function.

For beginning exercises in letter form manipulation, letters may be cut from magazines and newspapers. From this source many dozens of different letter forms are available (see Figure 166), each designed to give the symbols a different shade of meaning. To gain specific ends through manipulation of words and letters, one can change graphic content by spacing, vertical alignment, axis, value, color, texture, size and style.

Some of the qualities which can be expressed are human utterance, physical actions, heat, sounds, motion, states of mind, and traits of character.

Found images and created words should be combined to fix the specific meaning of both. This principle should be kept in mind: the form of the word should describe its symbol meaning.

Fig. 175 *Advertising piece by Gene Federico of Doyle, Dane and Bernbach. Letter forms serve two purposes at the same time. Courtesy the artist.*

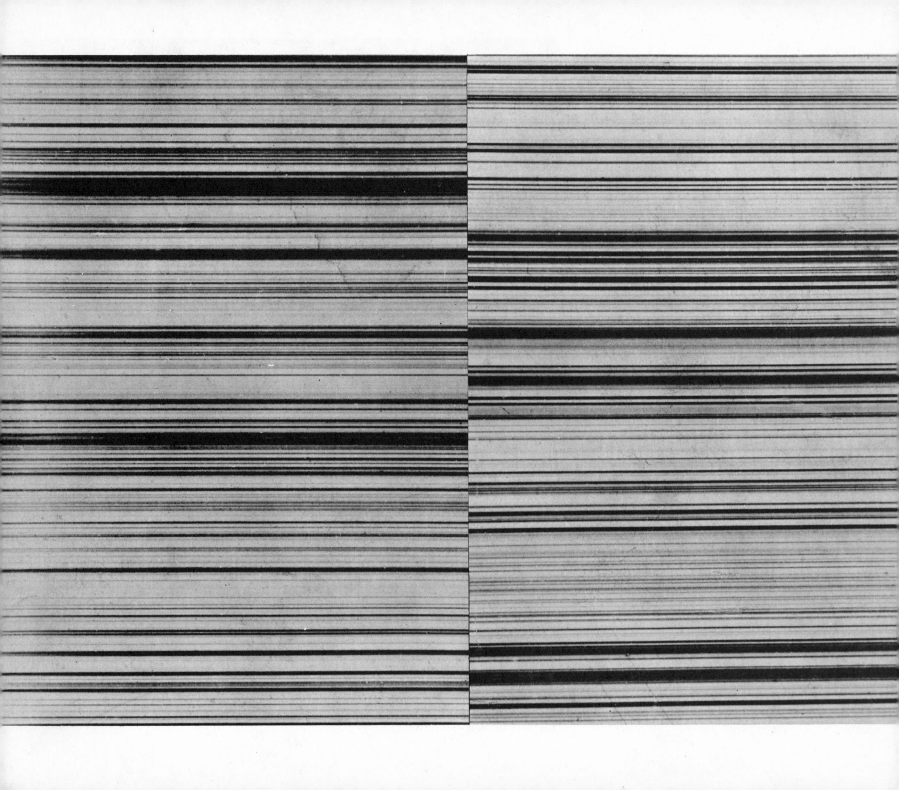

It seems strange indeed that artists have used color for upwards of 25,000 years without knowing much about how we happen to be able to perceive it. But the simple fact that color cannot be seen without light cannot have escaped early man—indeed, the cave artists used torches to get the necessary light to paint. The existence of widespread mythology centering on the sun (Fig. 155b, p. 140) and darkness gives support to the idea that early cultures knew that the sun was all important as a life source. The first word designations for color were undoubtedly those for darkness and light.

color theory

In about 1900 B.C. the Babylonians noted seven colored rings on a film of oil and water but failed to evolve any theory from their observation. First theories on color were put forth by scholars of classical Greece. Alcmaeon in the 6th century B.C. stressed black and white as being central to the phenomenon of color, and taught that color was a property of a substance. An all-important correction of this notion was provided by Empedocles (492-431 B.C.), who observed that color was a quality perceived by the eye and was not a resident property of objects. This hint on the subjective nature of the color phenomenon is fundamental to modern theory. Empedocles mentioned white, black, red, and yellow-green as the colors, with red corresponding to air. This latter notion persisted for a long time. Democritus (460-360 B.C.) stated that color is the judgment of men on various arrangements of atoms. He too saw white, black, red, and a vague yellowish-green, with red related to heat. Speculative theory and direct observation are strangely mixed here. Plato (428-347 B.C.) described black, white, red, and yellow, and Aristotle (384-322 B.C.) identified white, black, red, yellow, brown, violet, green, and blue—rare perception in his day. Even so, he saw the rainbow as tricolored (red, yellow and green) and believed that proper mixtures of black and white could form all the colors. There was not much to be found in color theory after this for another 1500 years. Vitello in the 13th century emphasized three colors particularly, red, green, and violet-blue. Thylesius in the latter part of the 15th century mentioned 12 shades of color. Maurolycus (1494-1577) saw red, orange, yellow, green, indigo, blue, and violet, which is modern in terminology. Marco Antonio de Dominis, in experiments performed around 1590 and published in 1611, discovered how raindrops refract the sun's rays to form a rainbow. He explained the additive principle of colored light, with a mixture of colors forming white light. Furthermore, Dominis demonstrated refraction with globes of glass filled with water.

Meanwhile artists were using many colors. With the aid of technicians and using the materials at hand, they worked in the wonderfully translucent encaustic, developed the tipped-tesserae mosaic with its light-scattering and additive color effects, discovered in pigment mixing the subtractive effect and secondary colors, worked with light and stained glass and discovered the difference between transparent and opaque color effects. This empirically derived knowledge has been rather neglected by scientific investigators who tend

Fig. 176 Normal solar spectrum made by a diffraction grating and recorded on a photographic plate. When materials absorb certain wavelengths from sunlight, the spectrograph patterns change and we see specific colors. Author's collage of spectrum records by Professor H. A. Rowland, Johns Hopkins University, 1888.

toward carefully controlled laboratory experiments. But there is perhaps good ground for believing that artists in the distant past have known more about color than many of their learned contemporaries.

Isaac Newton provided the first great breakthrough in color theory. In 1660 he passed a beam of sunlight through a prism and found it spread out in the rainbow colors. These, the so-called spectrum colors, are red, orange, yellow, green, blue, indigo and violet. With the aid of a second prism, Newton recombined the beam and the colors disappeared, white light resulting. He went on to combine two blocked-out parts of the spectrum, usually to find that a third, midway, color was formed by the combination.

This spread of color by a prism takes place because the molecular structure of the prism slows down colors as they pass through, in a selective manner. Red travels through glass faster, with orange next and so on, with violet slowest compared to the others. Thus it was discovered that light consists of a range of energy waves of different lengths. The energy we perceive as red is carried on a longer wavelength and is least affected by passage through a prism. The hues as lined up in a spectrum with their respective wavelengths in millimicrons are as follows:

400	450	520	580	650
violet	blue	green	yellow	red

Deeper reds continue to 760. Each color has a rather wide range of values. When violet, green, and red are added together, as in overlapping beams of light, the result is white light. These key colors are called primary colors. When violet and green are added together they form a color with an intermediate value in wavelength, blue; when green and red are added together they form the intermediate

yellow; violet and red form purple. This in brief is the classical theory concerning colored light.

When light comes in contact with various substances, certain wavelengths are absorbed, removed from the spectrum, and turned into another kind of energy. This kind of information can be recorded on a photographic negative. Figure 176 shows the photographed spectrum of sunlight made by a diffraction grating. In this way materials form an information potential. As sunlight strikes the various materials of our environment, various wavelengths in the spectrum are removed—for example, the green leaf absorbs all wavelengths except those around 520 millimicrons. Black absorbs nearly all of the light energy impinging upon it, while white reflects most of it. Thus most materials subtract something from white light. We are also able to read this information potential. Thomas Young in 1801 proposed that there were sensitive nerve fibers in the retina, that each fiber consisted of three parts, each one of which was excited by wavelengths of light corresponding to red, green, or violet. He held that the other color sensations were derived from the first three. Another theory is based upon the observed existence of rods and cones in the retina. Rods are held to be responsive to achromatic (colorless) vibrations, while the cones are held to be responsive to bright light and hues. Scientists have discovered in the rods chemical activity set off by light energy and in turn activating the electrochemical message system to the brain.

Precisely how color is perceived is not known and new theories are advanced from time to time. Whether there are one, two, three, or seven kinds of receptors has not been firmly established. Meantime, the image of the photosensitive electric cell provides a fair analogy of the initiating processes in the retina.

pigment

The designer's most frequent contact with color is through pigment and colored materials. Color in pigments of course have spectrum wavelength values. Here are a few typical values: cadmium red, 604.8; burnt sienna, 598.5; chrome yellow medium, 582.6; cobalt blue, 474.6. In performance, however, pigments do not act like light. The classical theory gave us a triangular system of pigment organization. This is seen in Figure 177a, with red, blue, and yellow making up the primary colors. Red mixed with yellow gives the secondary orange, blue and red give violet, and blue and yellow produce green.

Ewald Hering, a German scientist, developed a pigment theory based on four complementary colors: red/green and blue/yellow. According to Hering, all other hues and mixtures could be derived from these four coupled colors plus black and white.

Albert Munsell's color designation system, in use for half a century, starts with a basic five hues. These are shown in Figure 177b, with basic hues designated as red, yellow, green, blue, and purple. Munsell chose these five as basic for psychological reasons, believing that each was unique and distinct. The mixture of two adjacent hues results in an "intermediate" hue. But instead of calling the red-yellow mixture orange, Munsell calls it yellow-red. The other intermediate hues are blue-green, green-yellow, red-purple and purple-blue. When a basic hue is mixed with an intermediate, a "second intermediate" hue results. These are ten in number and are given such titles as purple red-purple, red purple-red, and so on. More subtle distinctions resulting from the mixture of two colors which are in adjacent positions on the color wheel are designated by numbers. Munsell recognized 20 gra-

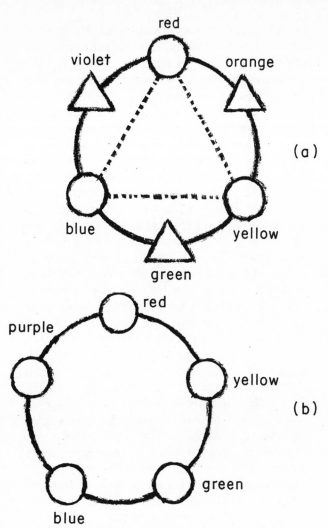

Fig. 177 a. *The classical practice of pigment mixtures. Red, yellow, and blue are the primary hues, with mixtures of any two producing a secondary hue. These secondary hues are orange, violet, and green.* b. *Albert Munsell's color designation system recognizes five basic hues. Mixtures of any two adjacent hues are termed "intermediate" in this system.* c. *Wilhelm Ostwald's color designation system assumes that there are six distinct color sensations. Besides black and white these are yellow, red, blue, and seagreen. This system pairs the complementary hues. Ostwald's full color wheel has 24 hues which may be mixed from the basic four. Yellow is numbered 2, red 8, blue 14, and seagreen 20. Readers are invited to fill in the appropriate hues in Figure 176 as a reminder of the ways in which the several systems vary.*

dations in hue between red and yellow, a total of 100 around the wheel.

The color system devised by Wilhelm Ostwald starts out in a different fashion. It assumes that there are six basic color sensations, four of which are chromatic and two achromatic. This system also assumes knowledge through psychological testing, since it holds that yellowness, redness, blueness, and greenness are sensations which do not resemble each other. According to this theory, in orange we discern yellow and red, and in purple both blue and red.

Ostwald's basic colors are arranged as in Figure 177c. Supporters of this system contend that each of the four basic colors is arranged in opposition to its true complement. To make a more complete wheel of colors in the Ostwald system, red is mixed with yellow to form orange, blue and red make purple, blue and green produce turquoise, and leaf green is the name given to the green and yellow cross. Ostwald, after having recognized 100 distinct hues around the color wheel, later reduced the number to 24.

It might be added that artists and others, while sensitive to different hues, cannot hold them in mental image very well, so that descriptions either in number or in Munsell language have little communicative value. Scientists use the word "hue" when describing pure color, artists use the word "color" not only for pure hues but for mixtures as well. In typical language one artist may say to another, "That piece of color works pretty well in there." The various systems suggest usable terminology which is not used. It is well to remember that in any color system mixing colors around the wheel, one color with the next adjacent, will yield as close to a pure hue as chemical mixtures permit. As he mixes colors across the color wheel, rather pronounced adulterations

occur. These he must learn to use or avoid to suit his needs.

Most design processes which manipulate pigments use both additive and subtractive phenomena. In cut-paper mosaic work a student may have tiny groups of yellow dots interspersed with blue. These tiny areas add their wavelengths together trying to make white. Of course between them they do not possess the entire gamut of wavelengths needed, but the effect is seen as a kind of gray. Both blue and yellow have wavelengths common to green, so when they are mixed they absorb or subtract all wavelengths except that of green, which we see. When we mix across the wheel, red and green for example, each subtracts the other's wavelength. As a result the two colors reflect very little and what is seen is a kind of dead, neutral tone. Theoretically, mixing all three primary colors results in black, with all wavelengths killed. Hence there is some risk in mixing across the wheel, but it is something every designer must learn to do, since few of those who use pigments use only pure hues at full power. If a color is adjudged too loud it can be grayed with a judicious amount of its complementary, eliminating the necessity of turning to black and white. It is essential that beginning designers have the color wheel well in mind.

The subtractive process is used in color printing, with tiny dots of superimposed primary colors subtracting and reflecting to make the secondary colors and dark mixtures. For technical reasons, some of the dots print next to each other and have the additive graying effect sometimes seen in the natural environment when many colors are seen together. The crowd seen across the field at a football game exhibits this phenomenon. Additive and subtractive effects can be seen in the tiny dots of Seurat's paintings. Additive effects are also

166

seen in the paintings of others using small broken passages of pure color. Monet and other impressionists feature this kind of play of color. When such paintings are seen at close range, purer tones are perceived, but at a distance these tones produce various derivative mixtures.

Another property of pure hues is the value intrinsic to them. This refers to how dark or light they naturally are, with black and white as the standards. One of the ways in which visual interest can be produced on a page is through contrast in light and dark, and if this effect is desired in working with color, the values of the several colors must be known. This knowledge is not automatically come by, because the greenness or blueness of a color can interfere with perception of its other properties. One can get a fairly clear idea of the value of a color by painting 2-inch squares of yellow, orange, red, green, blue, and violet and matching them with grays mixed from black and white. Thin paper should be used so that no intervening shadow prevents direct comparison. The eyes are squinted to lower illumination, and when a gray and a color fuse perfectly the coupling is made. This is an important consideration where the power of contrast is desired without loss of color content, since the addition of black to lower value will kill colors like yellow. Red, already low on the value scale, is harmed to a lesser extent by the addition of black. The use of value is such an important element in design that it should be learned from the outset.

adulterations of pure hues So far the pure hues have been discussed. We know that so far as pigment is concerned, red, yellow, and blue cannot be mixed from other colors, that orange, green, and violet can be, and that numerous versions of such color marriages as

red-yellow are recognized. Pure hues can be altered in three orderly ways, in addition to cross-wheel mixtures, as follows:

1. Colors may be altered by the addition of white.
2. Colors may be altered by the addition of black.
3. Colors may be altered by the addition of both black and white.

The Ostwald system presents a clear picture of these possibilities. It formulates an equilateral triangle with white at the top, black at the bottom, and pure hue off to the side. There are six steps between white and black, making eight in the entire scale. There are six steps between this vertical achromatic scale and the one square of pure color at the third apex of the triangle. Beginning with the black and white scale of eight, subsequent scales are seven, six, five, four, three, two and one, the pure hue. Of the 36 squares in the triangle, 28 will have some color. Those squares at the top of the triangle are progressive mixtures of color and white, those at the bottom of black and color, and all those inside are mixtures of all three. Letter numbers are used to designate the various squares. This in essence is the monochromatic triangle. Since the Ostwald system recognizes 24 hues, a total of 672 different gradations are designated. These 24 triangles are sometimes arranged in a sphere around the black and white vertical axis to form a color tree with all the 672 pigmented squares plus the eight achromatic squares on view.

Munsell uses a different system of notation and designates a comparable number of mixtures which are also arranged in a tree. These systems have particular advantage in the printing industry where standardization is desirable. Printing ink colors can now be designated by letter and number which carry information on the hue and additives. It is not foolproof, since different processes and different papers must be taken into consideration, absorption rate having an effect, as noted.

Of course when color is mixed with white its value becomes lighter. These mixtures are sometimes called tints, but artists do not use the term to any great extent. Rather, one may advise: "Try raising the value of that color," or "Take it down." A mixture of black and color is sometimes called a shade, but this may become confused with the light and shade of chiaroscuro, a term used in drawing where no color reference is intended.

When medium gray is mixed with a color, the intensity of the mixture varies with the proportion of each. This scale is from left to right down the middle of the triangle. Psychologists and physicists call this saturation, the amount of hue pigment in the mixture. Artists do not generally use the term saturation when talking about color. Strong, muddy, powerful, muted, subtle, weak, loud—these are some of the words, along with intensity, that are used to describe this aspect of color.

The psychologist's word *brightness* refers to the luminosity of color. In the mixing and application of pigments, several factors have a bearing on brightness: first, the way the pigments are ground; second, the manner in which they are applied; third, the surface used; and fourth, the strength of light playing on the pigment and surface. These factors determine whether light can get to surface and out again or whether the light is absorbed. Pigments are ground differently even in the same set of paints. Dye colors have the finest particles of pigment, permitting light to get to the surface and out again, carrying the hue content with maximum luminosity. Earth colors—the yel-

low-browns, red-browns and umbers—have coarser grains in most sets or lines of pigments. These grains quickly clog up the working surface, and light is absorbed by the pigment. An opaque matte surface results, with luminosity lost. In application, luminosity may be lost by piling one layer of paint on another until light is absorbed. Beginners will sometimes pile on earth colors, with mud resulting.

The surface varies luminosity by its value and absorptive power. Whether a paper soaks up large amounts of pigment, clogging the surface, or refuses to absorb pigment, leaving a thin layer of pigment on top, determines luminosity. Thus a blotter lowers luminosity and value, and even changes hue. The most luminous paint films are dyes put on white clay-coated papers, perhaps varnished slightly to stop absorption, or on very hard, high-finish illustration boards. As to the value of the surface, if one used a black paper and put yellow dye on it, the result would be essentially black. Here one would have to use opaque paints which absorb less light than black in order to make the color stand out. Thus to get the absolute maximum in power and visibility (relative to the field it is seen against), one would use a hue of high value (yellow), pigment ground fine (dye), color in full saturation (pigment particles covering the surface with no surface color mixing in), and a hard, smooth, nonabsorbing paper. In practice the designer is always seeking the best compromise available. When he needs the power of dark, he may sacrifice luminosity. Here the transparent glazing techniques developed by masters since the Renaissance are a genuine revelation. Rembrandt and others were able to keep shadows dark but with color and luminosity. These master painters should be studied in order to see how this is done. We also have new dye colors to broaden the range of the glazing technique.

studio practice

The reader may find it helpful to prepare a wheel with pigment or colored papers, or segments of a color tree. These color triangles are useful in observing the changes in a hue when it is altered with black, white, and gray.

As suggested, the value content of colors can be examined in the studio. These studies can prove helpful in the light and dark structure of color projects.

Mosaics can be made with small pieces of colored paper. These can test the effects of adjacent color relationships, the effect of small pieces of complementary hues in close juxtaposition, the effects produced by surrounding hues with black, and figure/field relationships using various color combinations.

Highly luminous bits of color can be used with duller surfaces for variety and comparison. Metallic papers and metal foils and bits of mirror can be used to test the effect of these highly reflective surfaces against pigmented parts.

review

Following the fragmentary contributions of Empedocles, Maurolycus, and Dominis and others, Sir Isaac Newton in the latter half of the 17th century began the investigations which led to the classical color theory. Hues were found to be carried on separate wavelengths of energy. Red, green, and violet light could in mixture form yellow, blue, and purple, and so were called primary colors. The classical theory led to a three-primary system in pigment, with mixtures of red, yellow, and blue forming the other important hues.

Early perception theory centered around three retinal perceptors, each supposedly excited by primary color wavelengths. Theory now presents a dual system of receptors of rods and cones, with the latter responsible for the reaction leading to the sensation of color. Knowledge of cone activity is still limited, and other theories are being studied.

Albert Munsell and Wilhelm Ostwald formed systems of pigment color in which hues were systematically altered with black or white or both. Munsell used five basic hues, Ostwald four.

Scientists and artists have produced these basic facts on color:

1. A basic property of color phenomena is hue —the ability of a material or pigment to absorb certain wavelengths of light energy and reflect others.
2. Each hue is inherently associated with a particular value in the light and dark scale.
3. A hue may vary in intensity or saturation, depending upon the amount of pigment on the surface.
4. A hue may be altered by the addition of black, white, or both, affecting value and intensity or saturation.
5. Brightness, or luminosity, is altered by structure of pigment, application of pigment, reflective power of the surface to which the pigment is applied, and strength of light used to perceive the effect.
6. Power is a product of amount of pigment times luminosity factors.
7. Low value hues are best perceived with maximum luminosity.

Some exercises to confirm these points will prove valuable in future enterprises.

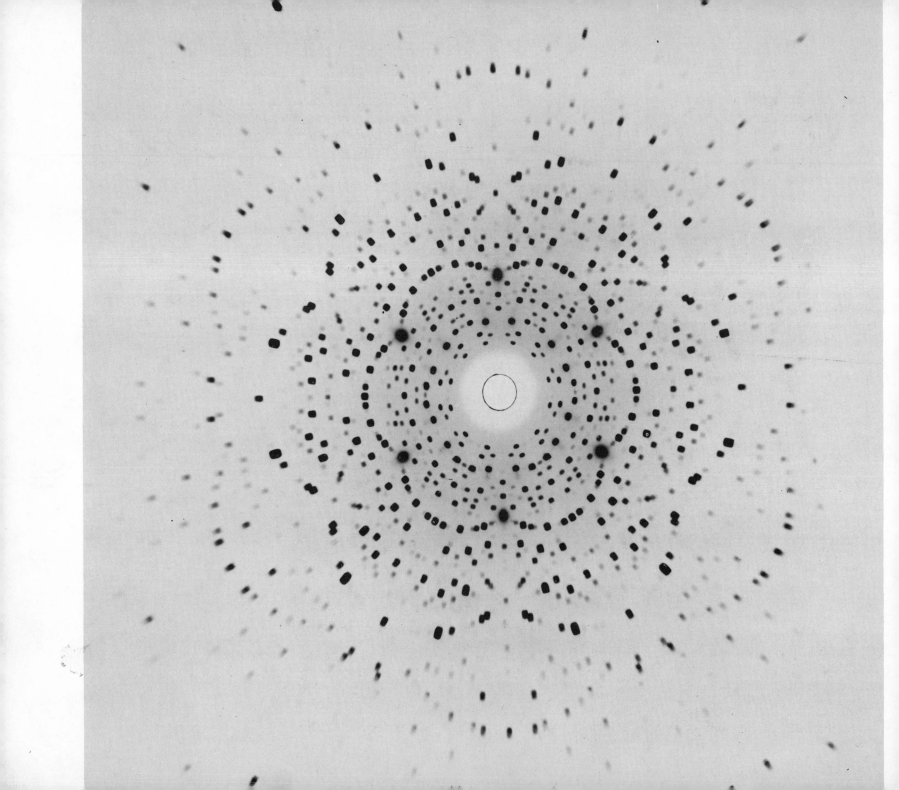

15 *transparency*

It will now be instructive to compare the image appearing on the opposite page (Fig. 178) with Figure 106e (p. 99), the painting by Courbet. The images show both 19th-century concepts of energy and matter and those of the present era. We see in Courbet the hard-rock external realism of the believable mechanical model, while in the X-ray diffraction pattern of a single crystal of the mineral beryl, we see the pattern of new nonmechanical concepts of universal structure. In many ways we are moving away from mechanistic conceptions and static form. The physicists are certainly done with 19th-century mechanical force concepts and now think of structure as in a continuous flux. The psychologist studies man in a continuum, with certain knowledge that he is a complex of cooperating structures in depth. Superficial appearance means little. Many scientists, as they delve ever deeper into the finer structure of the materials of their specialty, are finally confronted with a transparent universe with invisible essences exchanging invisible energy. And eventually we will all be drawn into this new realism.

The hard fixed image of permanent substance did not go, and has not gone, in a day. Wilhelm Roentgen discovered what he termed X-rays in 1895. Quickly following Roentgen's discovery that matter could be penetrated and recorded were discoveries by Becquerel, the Curies, and others concerning the phenomena of radioactivity. Certain elements were found to have the faculty of emitting, spontaneously, packets of energy which could penetrate material solid to the senses of sight and touch. These emissions were explained in terms of loss of atomic weight—almost understandable

in 19th-century terms—but since then many kinds of energy particles have been discovered, some of which penetrate apparently solid material as light passes through air. A present worry centers on the fact that the human being is in degree transparent to these radiations.

While these discoveries make us especially aware of the transparency of what we once supposed to be hard and fast substance, upon reflection we note the occurrence of transparency in the environment. The air we breath is transparent. In clear water, fish can be seen 30 feet down. Frozen water too is transparent. Many insect wings are transparent (Fig. 40a, p. 47), and the jellyfish and glass fish are examples of transparency in the aquatic environment. Natural gums and resins are transparent, as is the fossil resin amber. Gelatin, honey, and jellies exhibit the quality. Crystalline minerals are often transparent, and when colored are greatly admired; mica is one of these. Silk, rayon, and nylon are fabrics exhibiting transparent qualities. Of course glass and the various synthetic plastics are familiar materials which are at once hard and transparent.

The microscope, in use some 300 years, has repeatedly demonstrated the transparency of material. We see in Figure 179 one of these studies, showing elements of macerated wood. It is remarkable in its delicacy and continuity of form. Studies of this kind impress the artist with the expressive possibilities in the phenomenon of transparency.

Even in the 19th century the principle of transparency was familiar in graphic representation. The phantom view and other devices of engineering were in daily use. A device of necessity, transparency was used in communi-

Fig. 178 Laue photograph of an X-ray diffraction pattern of a single crystal of the mineral beryl. This shows solid material in recently available graphic terms. Courtesy Eastman Kodak Company.

171

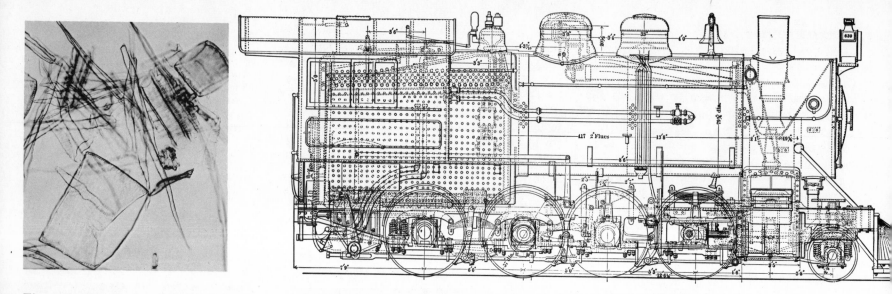

Fig. 179 *Microscope study of elements of macerated oak. A demonstration of transparency in the microcosm. Courtesy Professors William F. Millington and Emma L. Fisk and the Burgess Publishing Company, publishers of* Atlas of Plant Morphology, *1959.*

Fig. 180 *Mechanical drawing featuring the device of transparency. From January 1900 issue of* Locomotive Engineering.

cating information but was not to be seen in the art salon. The drawing in Figure 180 treats hard metal as if it were made of glass in order to show the relationship of parts in depth. Necessity sometimes forces the assumption of transparency, as in drawing a sphere with line (Fig. 58e, p. 59).

transparency in art

It turns out that the device of transparency is as old as art. In many paleolithic cave paintings one animal image merges into another. The French scholar Lucien Lévy-Bruhl investigated Font-de-Gaume and other caves very thoroughly, tracing the sometimes vague contours with infinite patience, and we are indebted to him for the analysis of these famous works both in line and in word. We see such a graphic analysis in Figure 181. This one is from the ceiling of the Pech-Merle "Hall of Hieroglyphics" and represents the patient work of Abbé Lemozi. The original was formed by fingers moving in wet clay and shows one form flowing through another with complete

freedom. Complete fluidity in point of view is found here, with mother goddess at lower right seen in one view and mammoth at upper right in another. One can hardly imagine a method of representation differing more from that of Courbet and his frozen image or his verbal expression of reality—that he "didn't paint angels because he never saw one." As Siegfried Giedeon has pointed out, Lévy-Bruhl stressed the idea of *participation* in cave art. The artist relives his experience in direct, physical contact with the material, removing the duality of experience/image and fusing them into one. Thought, memory, stimulus, and response are woven together as the artist acts out experience. The fixed concept of then and now disappears in a space-time flow as in life. There are no separate categories of (1) reality and (2) belief, and no grading system of (1) intellectual activity and (2) muscular pursuits.

There are some parallels between this kind of expression and that of the direct brush stroke seen in some Oriental painting (Figs. 35 and 101, pp. 43, 93). There are also parallels between Figure 181 and the contemporary action painters. That children use art as participation has been pointed out by Viktor Lowenfeld and others.

The idea of transparency is also basic to drawings and paintings showing invisible entities. Anthropologists find a good many of these examples. Pregnant animals are frequently shown with young visible inside, and at times internal structure is shown. We see this in Figure 182, an Eskimo painting. Dr. Hans Himmelheber, who collected this and other Eskimo paintings, identifies the artist as Maler Charles. In this work a hunter and two bears are shown. The bear in the lower part of the field has ribs, heart, stomach, intestine, and a mean look.

G. H. Luquet, the French savant, studied prehistoric art, the art of contemporary tribes, and the art of children, and drew certain shrewd comparisons in his book *Art Primitif* (Paris, 1930). One of his examples was the work of a child of seven showing a field with invisible potatoes drawn in. Luquet concluded that there were two kinds of realism in graphic representation. The use of transparency grew out of intellectual realism, with the painter using what he knew to be the truth rather than what superficial appearances told him. Luquet compared this kind of realism with the 19th-century concept of realism in the following way: "To the man of today, a picture is understandable when it reproduces that which his eye sees; to the primitive, when it expresses that which is mind knows."

One finds the feature of transparency in many parts of the world and in many cultures. Its persistence demonstrates that it is not a product of a particular style or local device but rather stems, as Luquet suggests, from a certain way of thinking. In Figure 183a, a Persian work, we see the human figure in a study featuring transparency. The outline of the figure, in terms of shape and proportion, is not the product of direct visual study but

Fig. 181 Paleolithic expression executed by fingers in wet clay, from the ceiling of Pech-Merle. Graphic analysis of Abbé Lemozi, 1952. Courtesy Art News.

Fig. 182 Eskimo painting on skin, featuring transparency. From Eskimokunstler, op. cit.

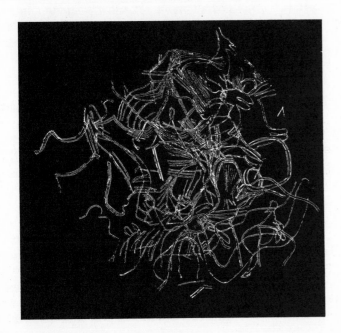

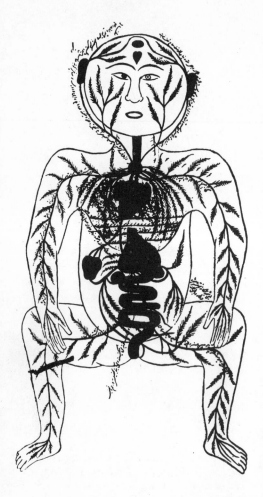

Fig. 183 a. *Transparency used in showing the arterial system of the human body.* From Sudhoff's Geschichte der Anatomie im Mittelalter, op. cit. *Original Persian manuscript in the India Office Library, London. Courtesy India Office Librarian. b. Noah's ark seen in a study featuring transparency. A copy of a 12th-century drawing.* From Astronomie Populaire, *Paris, 1883-1893.*

is rather an abstraction derived from the artist's mind—what Luquet calls "the internal image," consisting of "a spontaneous mental selection from among the visible attributes of the object." Again the artist paints what he knows to be true, selecting the method of abstraction for clarity. In Figure 183b we see the interior of Noah's ark, with compartments shown in abstraction. Myth and reality are strangely mixed.

Thus form conventions of modern art are not at all modern. They stem from older attitudes toward space, time, and form, attitudes less prevalent during the European period between 1500 and 1900 and in especial contrast to those of the 19th century.

It is not totally coincidental that the new work which broke away from the fixed position of external, static representations occurred at a time when theories of the structure of matter, space, time, and energy was undergoing drastic revision. Picasso's work of 1907 began the movement in art with a sudden jolt. Einstein's great studies began to be published in 1905. Startling changes in structural conceptions occurred in the next 15 years. Max Planck's revision of 19th-century ideas concerning the smooth flow of energy was published. Niels Bohr and others revised the static image of the atom. Electrons now changed orbits, giving off or receiving energy with each shift, in a constant state of excitement. Particles began to be tracked, and on dozens of fronts the static image disappeared. The work of Picasso, Gris, Braque, Klee, and many others revised the processes of image formation in a similar fashion. We have seen some of this work in another connection. Much of it centers on the idea of making the invisible visible—the exercise of intellectual realism. In Figure 184, Stanley William Hayter's "Composition," we see an intaglio which stems from the work done earlier in the century. Forms flow through each other freely and one form can be seen beneath another. In the vitality of the method of expression we see echoes of the Pech-Merle action reliefs.

With the assumption of transparency of form we may use the term *interpenetration*. This simply means that one form penetrates another and both are seen. Figure 97 (p. 89) illustrates this very well, and it can also be seen in the works of Picasso and Braque. *Simultaneity* is another term used in connection with transparent imagery. This means that two images can be seen at the same time, defeating overlap, which is a product of surface reality, and refuting the idea that two things cannot occupy the same space at the same time, an old mechanical notion outmoded by atomic physics. This idea may be tried out with a pencil, developing two images at the same time without removing the pencil from the surface. Later, forms may be differentiated with transparent values or color. The same idea can be tried using maskoid, a liquid rubber resist, or a wax crayon. Resists permit the combination of white and black line with value and color. In using pasted-in shapes, hidden forms can be completed with a line or change of value. This procedure permits the designer to *keep both shapes* instead of having one of the contours hidden as in the use of overlap.

new tools of imagery

The new concepts in science awaken within us a desire to make use of them in graphic enterprises. Science in this way has been inspirational. But science also interests us through tools of analysis. The scientists are engaged in forcing the environment to reveal its true image—no preconceived one will quite do. If

Fig. 184 "Composition," an intaglio print by Stanley William Hayter. One form flows through another in an assumption of transparent form. Courtesy the artist.

this information is collected in symbol form we are not much interested, since in all probability it is beyond our ability to read and interpret. However, some of the tools used by scientists show what things look like, and when this is the case we are interested. The X-ray is one of these pictorial devices. Used by a dozen branches of science but most popularly known as the physician's diagnostic tool, it re-

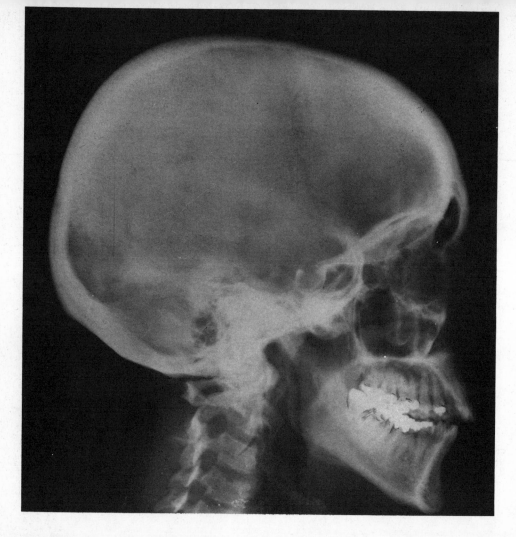

Fig. 185 Human head in an X-ray study. Energy waves of shorter wavelength than those of the visible range penetrate soft tissue but are absorbed by harder matter. Courtesy Dr. Erwin R. Schmidt.

ranged and recorded. These films are expensive, of course, but old ones are available.

Images from spectrographs and diffraction gratings (Fig. 176, p. 162) are also quite interesting. A physicist can show interested designers what these look like. Electron microscopes send energy into ever smaller areas of the microcosm and force ever smaller entities to reveal their images. The technique of Xeroradiography enables technicians to penetrate hard metallic solids and record their images as in a bas-relief.

With a strong light source (a slide projection machine will do), one can experiment with transparent imagery. Transparent materials are needed for this. Three-dimensional montages featuring glass bottles (clear or colored or containing colored liquids), colored film, painted acetate, photographic negatives, lace, X-ray negatives, silk stockings, and fishnets can be projected on to a white wall. Two light sources furnish the resource for double imagery. Black-and-white and colored slides may also be projected to enrich the effect.

A large part of life passes us by because of limitations in our vision. It is unfortunate that we are unable to see in our daily experience the elegantly ordered progression of forms exhibited in Figure 186. Reflection will no doubt reveal that it is just as well that we can see no better, although perhaps this is a needlessly conservative observation. At any rate it is clear that the knowledge of structure that we do possess is wasted as long as it is hidden. The only purpose of graphic convention is that of full expression.

We might initiate problems in transparency by obtaining a few rectangular blocks, rolling them up with ink, and printing them through and over one another.

Shapes can be cut out of stiff paper, covered with tempera paint, and printed on a blotter.

veals information of interest to artists. A physician is usually looking for a particular sign, but he along with artists can appreciate such subtle play of forms as shown in Figure 185. Here human tissue is rendered variably transparent through the action of energy waves shorter than those in the visible spectrum. X-rays are able to penetrate soft tissue but are stopped by harder material. Metal in the teeth of the patient pictured in Figure 185 absorbs energy, which fails to reach and expose the plate. A stencil in depth is thus ar-

Other shapes can thus be printed through and over the first.

Interpenetration of forms can be achieved rather easily with tools which leave linear tracks. Machines can be interpreted as if all parts were transparent.

review

Transparency in graphic expression is an idea based on intellectual rather than visual realism. It has been a factor in art from its inception and has only been interrupted by a close pursuit of monocular clues involving surface. First expressed in the keen anticipation of mastery in the Renaissance and then repeated in tired dogma into the 20th century, the absolute reign of surface conceptions in art was overthrown by the joined efforts of scientists undermining static mechanical conceptions of physical structure and by artists like Picasso who, rejecting surface appearances, returned to the imagery of life flux. At first the revived method underwent careful scrutiny in art (Fig. 112, p. 102) as did the revisions of structure in science; later it lent itself to more forceful expression, as in "Guernica."

In expressing life as a flux rather than as a frozen image, the old and new artists made use of abstraction and of transparency with its attendant effects: interpenetration, movement, and simultaneity.

Science has provided us with techniques which give a graphic analysis of structure in depth. Electron microscopes and a variety of X-ray techniques enable us to observe structure unavailable to common perception. These graphic forms from art and science are a forcible reminder that we are free to express our knowledge of forms to the limit of that knowledge with whatever devices seem most apt.

Fig. 186 Nautilus shell revealed through radiography. Courtesy Eastman Kodak Company.

177

16 *symbolism of color*

Some years back the owners of the Cincinnati baseball club advised radio commentators and newsmen that the club was to have a change in name. Instead of the Cincinnati Reds it was to be the Cincinnati Redlegs. This change was made because red has become associated with communism. Communists are called reds. In the minds of the owners, this consideration apparently took precedence over the several good connotations which red may have—virility for one. The change didn't stick very well and now again the team is the Cincinnati Reds. It is just as well because this sort of thing can lead to difficulty. Black is associated with death and mourning, yellow with cowardice, red with sin, white with surrender, green with jealousy, purple with pomp, blue with improper language, brown with a bad taste, and as for pink, it might well do in some connections but it wouldn't suit a ball club. The white we see in Figure 187 is that used in a wedding gown. Here white has a different meaning than that listed above. Red means danger to some people, while in another connection it means anger: to see red. Thus we see that color in design may have two meanings, one its plastic content—its pure hue, its wavelength—and the other a meaning derived from the culture in which we live. This meaning is shaped by the forces of history, plan, and accident, and has a bearing on the way we think about color, the way we react to it. In bad times paint companies reduce the number of hues produced, and the hues become more somber. In times of prosperity two-toned sports cars are seen and white sidewall tires attest to affluence—a symbol in the making. This then is the changing aspect of color, an aspect which we must study in order to gain a rounded view.

some historical notes

In earlier history there seem to be curious gaps in man's knowledge of color. Strange as it seems, early civilizations seem not to have perceived the number of colors that we perceive today. There is no way of knowing what they saw but identification and significance can be judged from references in literature. It is supposed that first references were to something vaguely colored. Black and red were probably the first colors recognized by a name, with yellow, blue, green, and purple coming later. The ancient Rig-veda Indian hymns feature black, red, and gold but make no mention of green, although there are references to nature, and fail to note blue, although the sky is mentioned often. There is no yellow but there is golden. Color in ancient Egypt centered around black, red, and gold.

Biblical Hebrew contained few words to express color. Only white, red, and green could be designated with a special word. Mention of yellow or blue is absent in early Hebrew literature. There are 430 passages in the Bible mentioning the sky, but there is no mention of its color. Other references are through likenesses to environmental color. Some of these are curious. Consider this from Revelation 4:3: ". . . and there was a rainbow around the throne in sight like unto an emerald." But perhaps this is poetic license. It may be that availability and familiarity have something to do with color consciousness and consequent recognition through nomenclature and sym-

Fig. 187 Symbolic meaning in white of bride's gown. Roman and Christian traditions were strong in the use of white. Author's collage.

bolic meaning. White was available to the ancient Hebrews in wool. They obtained scarlet from the insect coccus. The ancients got purple-red and purple-blues from shellfish. White, red, and purple all acquired early symbolic meanings. Green, blue, and true yellow were harder to come by in the natural environment.

The Greeks mentioned all the colors, but again red, black, and gold appear most often. Yellow, green, blue, and purple are often in vague reference. Some references are indeed hard to explain. Homer calls the sky black. An Egyptian song to Isis compares hair to turquoise. Homer describes the sea as wine-dark, black, or gray, never blue or green. Yellow is a pale ochre. Alcaeus over a hundred years later wrote: "Pure, sweetly smiling Sappho of the violet hair." Sappho herself uses the expression "greener than grass in spring." Surely this is a light yellowish green everywhere. Pindar speaks of the "violet-haired Muses" and "fire-red grapes." As noted previously, Greek scholars did discuss color but none seems to have made what we would consider to be a complete list.

The Romans, too, seemed to be in some confusion about color, confounding blue, violet, and gray. In Roman times brides wore yellow, but the garments are described as red. Vergil spoke of black hyacinths, and in the 6th century Cassiodorus compared green to spring, red to summer, white to autumn, and blue to winter. Roman writers stated that Greek painters used only those colors mentioned by Democritus: black, white, red, and (weak) yellow. Here one might ask, how did they know?

The Koran, sacred book of the Moslem religion, contains no reference to blue. A Persian writer mentions it in the 9th century. Moslems are fond of green, and our consciousness of that color may have been strengthened by

180

that cultural stream. Yellow may have come into our culture from the Orient.

We are indebted to Havelock Ellis for a significant contribution to our understanding of hue in the cultural stream. Ellis selected a list of important pieces of literature from several cultures and noted the number of references to color. It is possible that his list was not long enough to support a correct statistical approach but it included the Bible and works of Homer, Chaucer, Wordsworth, and Whitman, to mention a few of many. In the Ellis tabulation, black, white, and red are most frequently mentioned, with red retaining strength in all periods. Black runs well at all times, reaching a high point in Homer where it received 49 percent of all color references. Keats only mentioned it once. White was a popular color in many of the works, although Poe gave it a light treatment. Roman writers used white profusely (reflecting its status as the favorite color of the Romans). Green reached a high point in Wordsworth, not surprisingly, after a slow start in ancient times. In Wordsworth, Ellis noted 100 references to color, with 35 to green. Blue until recent times received small mention except in north European primitive works, giving rise to the thought that consciousness of blue may have reached our culture from north Europe. Blue comprises 14 percent of Coleridge's references to color. Yellow is completely absent only in Icelandic sagas and is mentioned most frequently by Poe.

Of the secondary colors, tints, and so on, brown is infrequently mentioned, except by Whitman. Coleridge and Shelley liked purple, although it is scarcely mentioned by the writers who preceded them. Gray is mentioned often by poets of northern climates but pink is scarcely noted. (One wonders how Ellis noted Homer's "rosy-fingered dawn.") There are so few references to orange that Ellis did not include a category for it. In ancient times anything resembling our version of orange would have been described as golden, since names were quickly found for the colors of important metals, gold, silver, and bronze. It is true that orange is a tough word for English poets but in some other languages it has a better ring, as in the Spanish *naranja*. But it may be that those psychological tests which indicate that there is a low preference for orange speak the truth.

When we look at paintings in a museum we are aware of relationships of color in a single painting, and if we are careful we may even make memory notes on these relationships. But museum study doesn't seem to reveal the color preferences of a whole culture, let alone those of individual artists. If it seems curious that the cultures of a few thousand years ago lacked nomenclature to deal with color phenomena, we can ask various of our friends to furnish the name for that color which is a combination of blue and green. Rarely will an answer be given. Color discrimination in our own culture is vague enough, as the following authenticated dialogue shows:

Policeman: Do you own a brown dog?
Observer: No, my dog is black, white, and tan.
Policeman: That's what I say, a brown dog.

assigned meanings in color

In Brahmanism yellow is a sacred color. In India, brides wear yellow, as they did in Roman times. In China yellow was connected with royalty and deity and the Chinese show a marked preference for it. It is conspicuously absent in Western religious symbolism. Here a sharp distinction must be made between yellow and gold leaf. Yellow is sometimes used in depicting the garments of St. Joseph and St. Peter, the latter association having to do with revealed truth. More often yellow is assigned to Judas. In the Middle Ages heretics were obliged to wear yellow. In Venice, Jews were singled out by it. According to George Ferguson, yellow crosses were used to identify plague in the Middle Ages. This led to the habit of relating contagion with yellow. Today we conjure with the myth of insanity connected with a preference for yellow, with Van Gogh offered as proof. In the theater yellow means bad luck. In our culture yellow is drowned in dire meaning.

The Mohammedan who has seen Mecca wears green. To this religious group green is the sign of ultimate achievement and is much admired in all appearances. Green was significant to the ancient Egyptians, who referred to time as the "ever-green one." In heraldry green stands for growth and hope. In the Christian tradition green means eternal life, spiritual initiation, and is used during the Epiphany season. Green is the color of the Irish national party. References to green in the sense of untrained go back to 1548. In academic vesture, green symbolizes medicine.

In ancient Egypt red was used to protect the dead. In China it is a sign of longevity and a favorite color. Red was the color of sovereign power in Rome, and has a similar meaning in the dress of church officials. It is the color of martyrdom and is seen in services commemorating the coming of the Holy Ghost. Red is the color of war and battle and, as noted, also signifies political radicalism. It is the color of sin and has a dozen other meanings.

The ancient Hebrews wore a fringe of purple-blue on every garment as a sign of the high dignity of membership. Purple-red has long been associated with royal power. It is also the color of penitence and mourning; in our culture many persons wear purple armbands as a sign that a loved one has departed. In literature a purple passage is one excessively ornate.

Besides Thomas Carlyle's "rose-pink hue of sentimentality," references to pink center on its effeminate quality. Girl babies are given pink garments. Those said to be tinged with radical belief are connected to this color, and it also has a cheerful connotation, as in "looking at the world through rose-colored glasses."

In the Jewish religion white is a symbol of man's mortality. White connotes death to a Japanese but in Roman times white was a joyous color. Candidates for office wore white as a sign of integrity, and vestal virgins wore white to signify innocence and purity, a custom which still prevails. All in all, white was the favorite color of Rome. White has long been a symbol of purity and holiness. Those without sin are associated with the color. In early Christian times white was worn by church officials. It is the color worn at baptism. Like green, which receives many meanings from its annual recurrence in nature, the meanings centering on white seem born of logic. If white gets dirty, it can be noticed.

Blue has some connections with the aristocracy. It also has meanings of faithfulness, quality, and innocence. References to blue may indicate sadness. In the church, blue symbolizes heaven and is the color of truth. Blue is always associated with the Virgin in paintings.

Black is the color of mourning, justice, formality, evil, magic, humility, the devil, death, and disaster. In the Jewish religion black is worn on solemn occasions. No doubt many of the sinister connotations of black stem from darkness and the real and imaginary dangers therein. As a sign of humility and solemnity it is simply the color without color—certainly an indication that colors denote gaiety and life. Gray, the color of ashes, also has a rather solemn countenance in symbolic meaning.

Thus we see that traditional meanings attached to colors vary from time to time and from place to place. In design there are times when these traditional values must be respected.

Colors are also given special meanings in coded systems used by various subgroups in the society. Here one must be in the group or acquainted with it in order to understand the meaning. This process is outlined in the discussion centering around Figure 14 (p. 20). Vestments worn in the Catholic church have special meanings, as do those worn in academic and royal processions. Doctors use color as a diagnostic tool. In many areas of science the presence of certain colors reveals information on structural content, with litmus paper the most familiar device of detection. In fraternal organizations colors carry special significance. In industry colors are used to identify certain kinds of electric wires, and color is similarly used to identify many other conduit systems. Many signal systems use color.

Nations have color signs through flags. States too list identifying colors, and universities follow suit, as can be noted at any football game. Here color is used as an instrument of group identity. It is comforting to belong to an order described as the Green Wave or the Crimson Tide. Political parties have been identified through color (orange and green in Irish history), as have fleets of ships, criminal syndicates, and cocktail rooms.

Color designation of race has been unfortunate from the outset. If only a single person had originated the idea, one could well wish him a black fate. The identification of Orientals with yellow has had unpleasant consequences in the United States. In the Orient, yellow has favorable connotations but in this country yellow is almost all bad. This enabled journalists (yellow) to refer to the presence of Oriental

Americans as the "yellow peril." The damage wrought by this particular coupling of color and human pigmentation is beyond estimation. Certainly it has meant suffering for countless individuals. By creating an unfavorable image in people's minds far from the area of economic interest, Congressional orators were able to block reasonable plans for immigration and citizenship. Eventually the image faded, but it undoubtedly did damage.

Nor is it likely that citizens whose ancestors came from Africa ever benefited from being associated with black, in most cultures the sinister color. In Spanish, for example, we find these meanings: *negro*—black, gloomy, dark. *Tiene una suerte negra*—He has very bad luck. Negro and black describe a physical appearance, although with poor accuracy, and also play a role in many a negative connection. It has thus been easier to create the mythical image of the Negro as something mysterious, dangerous, or different. The favorable connotations of red prevented its use in unfavorable comment on the American Indian. No doubt it would be better if everyone possessed an amber tint of pigmentation. Certainly it is unfortunate that color, an agreeable phenomenon, has played an unhappy role in human relationships.

color in popular reference

It will be noticed in the list of color references derived from daily experience that color usually occurs with some other factor of graphic potential. In embarrassment it is a red face, in green for the Irish it is a shamrock shape, and in penitence it is sackcloth and ashes. It is the handling of these two elements that establishes the connection and gives the impact. It may also be noted that a great many of the references are inconsistent. Our habits in using color are rather strange, too. Pink may be a proper color for a girl's room but it is seldom used in buildings. Yellow seems to be a good color for farm machinery and moving equipment but is not often to be found on automobiles. Red is worn by redcaps, Cardinals, baseball players, hunters, and clowns, but professors and jurists may not be seen in red. Young women may be garbed as the zebra but older women refrain from the use of exuberant apparel. Orange may not win a preference test but plenty of it is seen on circus day. Why must railroad conductors wear black like a badge? And why do some refuse to eat or drink from colored vessels? Is green correct for a go sign? Why is white fine for a house but not red? And why red for a barn but not purple? What does black lingerie mean? In short, does color make any sense at all?

Some of it does make sense. Nurses, doctors, and waitresses wear white because it shows dirt and thus is an immediate sign of cleanliness. Judges wear black to show that they are a dignified bunch and the conductor wears it to hide the dirt. Highway signs and hunters' clothing are yellow for high visibility, which makes sense. Red was used on barns because at one time red was a cheap pigment. A few such solid answers can be found. After that the whole subject is up in the air. Preference tests can be made but these merely reveal habitual ways of thinking about color. The truth is that to a large extent *color means exactly what a society says it means*. However, habit, this flywheel of society, is a ponderous weight and it is not easy to get people to change. Our ideas about color are very deeply embedded in the texture of our consciousness. For years manufacturers tried to get white into the kitchen and now they are trying to get it out. Refrigerators are now available in a variety of colors. Whether this

Red
- danger: signal flags, flares, gas containers
- stop: stop signs, railway signals
- fire: fire-fighting apparatus
- courage: *The Red Badge of Courage*
- sin: *The Scarlet Letter*
- anger: to see red, wave a red flag
- heat: red hot
- confusion and delay: red tape
- special day: red-letter day
- diversion: red herring
- prostitution: red-light district
- losses: red ink
- compassion: Red Cross
- virility: red-blooded
- liquor: red-eye
- intoxication: red-eyed; red-nosed
- embarrassment: red-faced
- guilt: caught red-handed
- war: Mars is red
- gay time: painting the town red
- sex: red-hot mamma

Green
- spring: freshness, newness, youth
- jealousy: green-eyed monster
- opportunity: give him the green light
- money: green stuff, greenbacks
- inexperience: greenhorn, green hand
- plant-growing ability: green thumb
- immaturity: green wood, green beer
- sickness: to turn green
- envy: green with envy

White
- cleanliness: uniforms for doctors, nurses
- truce: white flag
- heat: at white heat
- cover-up: whitewash
- the Presidency: White House
- uselessness: white elephant
- kind untruth: white lie
- cowardice: white feather, white-livered
- goodness: "That's mighty white of you."
- rage: white-lipped
- fright: white as a sheet
- Caucasian: white race
- death: pale as death

Orange
- **Halloween: orange (and black) decorations**
- Dutch royal family: House of Orange
- religious group: Protestant Irish

Black
- wickedness: blackguard, black-hearted
- disaster: Black Friday
- piracy: black flag
- political designation: black reactionary
- bad luck: black cat
- outcast: black sheep
- prosperity: in the black
- bleak outlook: future looks black
- poor mental outlook: black mood, black despair
- poor behavior: black record, black eye, black mark
- menacing glances: black scowl, black look
- exclusion: blackballed
- blasphemy: Black Mass
- police wagon: Black Maria
- extortion: blackmail
- weapon: blackjack
- secret society: Black Hand

Gray and silver
- experience: graybeard
- age: silver-haired
- terror or sickness: ashen-faced
- penitence: sackcloth and ashes
- intelligence: gray matter
- South in the Civil War: gray uniforms
- glib orators: silver-tongued
- optimistic view: silver lining
- clear tones in music: silver tones
- lack of discrimination: "At night all cats are gray."

Blue
- sadness: blue Monday, have the blues
- excess: talks or swears a blue streak
- surprise: out of the blue, a bolt from the blue
- quality: blue ribbon
- food: blue-plate special
- cruelty: Bluebeard
- repression: blue laws, blue nose
- rarity: once in a blue moon
- intensity: blue flame
- musical form: the blues
- boy babies: blue clothing
- pedantic woman: bluestocking
- brides: "something blue"

Pink and purple
- good condition: in the pink
- optimism: rosy future, looking through rose-colored glasses
- gathering of women: pink tea party
- anger: purple with rage
- fancy writing: purple prose
- royalty: royal purple, born to the purple
- mourning: purple arm bands

Brown
- after-effects: dark brown taste
- contemplation: in a brown study
- anger: to be browned off
- health: brown as a berry
- autumn: coloring of foliage

Golden
- auspicious times: Golden Age
- generous person: heart of gold
- superfluous action: gild the lily
- nostalgia: golden memories, golden days
- quiet: "Silence is golden."
- avarice: gold-digger

Yellow
- disapproval: a jaundiced eye
- cowardice: yellow streak down his back
- caution: yellow lights
- low newspaper morality: yellow journalism
- race fear: yellow peril (now in disuse)
- ill health: yellow complexion
- (Amber is more highly respected among poets

campaign will succeed is not yet certain. It may be that changing people's minds about color is not nearly so simple as creating a symbol through repetition and familiarity. It is a marvelous field for study because there are so many facets to it.

The immediate aim is to use color in communicating ideas. How shall we express heat, anger, jealousy, evil, or veneration? If traditional ideas can help, then they should be used. In some areas color symbolism is so fixed that we may not depart from traditional usage. Orange cannot be used to color the shamrock; green cannot be used for cupids and hearts. The designer should remember that clichés are made good through fresh handling.

review

Color acquires meanings in passing through the culture. These shape our attitudes and actions concerning color. Peoples have not always had full recognition of color. Black and red seem to have been the first colors named. Gold followed. Through Roman times, black, red, and white seem most stable in description, with blue, green, purple, and gray often confused.

In literature black, white, and red are most frequently mentioned. Green and blue are mentioned most often in northern countries.

Institutions of church and government are most influential in the development of the color symbol. All colors have acquired meanings from these sources. White, red, and green have acquired positive associations while yellow and black are usually seen in negative connections. Favorite colors vary from one social or religious order to another.

Color is used in daily expression to heighten and clarify meaning. This use has resulted in a large mass of traditional material at the designer's disposal.

The use of color symbol is often inconsistent, although red seems to denote action, white cleanliness, and black is rather consistently associated with misfortune. Outside of this, color seems to mean exactly what a culture says it means. The color symbol is rather strongly imbedded in the fabric of the culture, and the designer will not be able to change attitudes about color.

17 *motion*

When one picks up a piece of jasper and turns it around to see it from all angles, motion is involved. If a piece of sculpture in the round is to be seen as the artist intended, the viewer must walk around the piece. In examining a piano to see which view is most expressive, the viewer must move. Often a spectator examining a painting will move away from the picture and see the static image change subtly, with gross, meaningless patches of pigment soon falling into logical context. Participation in the visually interesting world requires that we move our eyes about so that we obtain the essence of three-dimensional experience. At times we move fast. Traveling in a fast-moving automobile, for example, we may pass through a forest with the sun in back of the trees; the effect for us is one of flashing off and on in stuttering jabs.

Or we may stand still with other forms of the environment providing the action. We may be standing at a window and see a flash or glitter of birds in pursuit. As a spectator at a dog fight we see a splash of kaleidoscopic action, a buzz of staccato jazz, raucous and blurred. Alongside a railroad track we see in the distance a tiny point which, slowly growing and growing, finally bursts on the scene in a tremendous blast of flashing façades. Or perhaps we observe the random and tireless zigzag of a housefly before it settles into its static black dot. These are experiences involving movement through space, experiences involving three dimensions. We work in two dimensions. Are we then completely at a loss when it comes to explaining three-dimensional experience in two dimensions? We cannot re-create such experiences but we can suggest

some of their dynamic quality. In so doing we will be combining static and dynamic imagery.

some notes on perception

The devices we shall use to suggest dynamic quality are in parallel with the processes of perception. When light strikes a receptor in the retina it reacts in an on-or-off manner—a static, not a dynamic concept. If this were represented with white representing excited receptors and black representing those unexcited, the image would be static. However, we cannot hold a static image for long. When optical arrangements are such that the same visual receptors are continuously stimulated, they cease to respond in a few seconds and the image disappears. To hold a static image, the eye oscillates back and forth in a scanning move-

ment, charging fresh receptors as it moves back and forth. When an object moves, successive groups of retinal receptors are excited. This occurs in a series of discrete steps like the "movement" in an electric sign. It will be noted that there is no actual motion in this sequence of static imprints. There is, however, a potential of motion. How this series of static images is translated into the sensation of continuous movement is not quite certain, but recently Jerome Y. Lettvin and colleagues at the Massachusetts Institute of Technology identified a "bug" receptor in the eye of a frog. Lower animals organize their environment largely in terms of movement.

That we do not need continuous movement in order to derive the sensation of it is proved through the motion picture. What we see on a motion-picture screen is a series of static im-

Fig. 188 Section of the Bayeux Tapestry, an 11th-century embroidery showing the Norman conquest of England in 1066. The work is 231 feet long. It is the only piece of narrative needlework surviving from the early Middle Ages. The action is seen in continuity, with the same set of characters appearing again and again. Courtesy Phaidon Press Ltd.

187

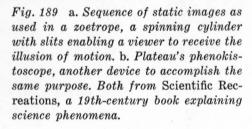

Fig. 189 a. Sequence of static images as used in a zoetrope, a spinning cylinder with slits enabling a viewer to receive the illusion of motion. b. Plateau's phenokistoscope, another device to accomplish the same purpose. Both from Scientific Recreations, *a 19th-century book explaining science phenomena.*

ages each separated by a brief interval of time. In the 19th century, before the invention of motion pictures, there were many gadgets which exploited the motion potential in static images. The simplest of these was the thaumatrope, a device which demonstrated the persistence of perceived static images. This gadget is a disk with strings attached to opposite edges. A bird cage is drawn on one side and bird on the other. When the disk is spun the bird is seen inside the cage. The thaumatrope is an interesting little device and easy to make.

A device to obtain the illusion of motion was the zoetrope. It consisted of a cylinder of cardboard with a stiff base, turned on a central axis. The cylinder was pierced with vertical slits at regular intervals. Opposite each slit was a static image, each part of an action sequence. When the cylinder was spun, the sequence of static pictures was seen as action. Some of these sequences are seen in Figure 189a. Another device based on the same principle was the phenokistoscope invented by J. A. F. Plateau (Fig. 189b). These examples

188

suggest that the static image has motion potential that we may be able to use. It will be noted that the pictorial materials used in these devices are two-dimensional.

motion in two dimensions

In order to communicate any sense of motion in two-dimensional work we must use graphic devices embodying the idea of *continuity*. And we must bring to the pictured work a little knowledge of physical forces, a little knowledge of the gross properties of the environment, because at times we supply, through knowledge and imagination, the idea of continuity. Take Figure 174d (p. 161), for example. The only parts of a sequence shown are the beginning and the end. We understand the gravitational forces involved and supply the implications of the predicament. Wind action is seen in the shape of branches, billowing of cloth, and the cant of an umbrella. We supply the knowledge which enables this kind of image to communicate motion. Thus in images of leaping, jumping, and walking the plastic content may be quite uneventful, yet we feel a movement. Perhaps we should call this motion through mental participation. An interesting project in flying figures is to cut found images completely free of their environment. This allows flexibility in the formation of space, with large and small figures creating the illusion.

When we supply part of the idea in the illusion of motion we get clues from the way objects point. In Figure 188, a section of the Bayeux Tapestry (really an embroidery), we get the idea that the action goes from left to right because the horses are facing to the right, and judging from the position of the sails, the boats are traveling in that direction also. The designers of this work were also cognizant of the fact that members of our culture read from left to right. The characters all make a number of appearances. This also accentuates the idea of a sequence in time, earlier on the left and later on the right. A fine mosaic in St. Mark's in Venice shows Christ making a journey. He is shown quite a number of times. This device is used, with a variation, in Muybridge's 19th-century studies of the human figure and in modern comic strips. Projects with pointing devices can be executed with the aid of arrows, hands, and other found material. See Figures 50 and 126 (pp. 55, 112) for excellent examples.

Continuity in line also suggests motion. The fact that nothing gets in the way to stop continuity in execution supplies the idea of flow. Transparency must be assumed here, for if overlap interrupts the line the suggestion is lost. Figures 64b, 181, and 184 (pp. 62, 173, 175) show line in action. The same idea is used in the light writing and the oscilloscope study at the end of this section. As noted previously, no more than pencil and paper are needed to give this idea a thorough tryout.

Motion can also be implied by drawing the path of a volume traveling from deep space toward the picture plane. Imagine you are putting a line around the space occupied by a baseball in a flight from pitcher to the plate. Your position of view is not head on but slightly to one side. If gravity curvature (or spin) is disregarded, the drawing will be round on the left and lines will meet on the right. Taken in itself, the drawing will express nothing but a kind of airplane shape, but in the proper connotation this idea combines the monocular clue of apparent size difference with a time sequence. This idea can be seen in dramatic instance in Picasso's "Guernica" (Fig. 121, p. 107). Here the head and arm enter the scene from a window removed in space. The same technique is often used in photography, with a fist close to the lens enormously enlarged and other parts of the body reduced in size. A linear expression of the same idea is seen in Figure 190, with small particles seen approaching the viewer. This is a representation of a meteor shower occurring November 27, 1872. We see this sort of phenomenon in motoring into a heavy snowstorm, with white particles seem-

Fig. 190 Particles in deep space come toward the observer with the path traced by line. In this representation of a meteor shower, motion is implied through a version of linear perspective. Author's collection.

189

Fig. 191 Figures in sequential image taken from a moving model. Transparency is assumed, insuring an uninterrupted flow in the line. From a University of Wisconsin classroom project.

Fig. 192 "Dog on Leash" by Giacomo Balla, 1912. Multiple imagery suggests movement through time. Photo courtesy the Museum of Modern Art. Collection of A. Conger Goodyear, New York.

ing to emerge from a common source and then suddenly shooting off in all directions. While in Figure 190 we see this phenomenon represented in straight lines, it is actually experienced as a curve. This perception is due to a breakdown in our tracking apparatus and accounts for the fact that in baseball any fast ball seems to shoot off to the side in a curve.

Combining different points of view in the same work also suggests a kind of action. When primitive artists combine the front view of the eye and the side view of the head they are crossing end views in a sequence. When these views are combined in a twisting action, a spiral motion is implied. This can be seen in dramatic image in Figure 150 (p. 134).

the multiple image An action pictured in a sequence of static images suggests motion on a two-dimensional surface, because of our knowledge of what the action ought to be.

Thus when a cave artist draws an animal with a double set of legs, we read the graphic information as an implication of motion. This device represents a moving object in a sequence of different points of view. Rather than showing the end views of a sequence, side and top or side and front, this method uses the sequential views. It is as if one took a cube and swept it slowly from front to side, after which motion various static positions were selected for combined imagery. In the 16th century, Michelangelo combined three such views of the human figure in a single two-dimensional work, a kind of experimentation typical of the Renaissance spirit of inquiry. This method has lately been revived by contemporary teachers. Sketches are taken from a model in a series of static movements and joined to represent a sequential action. Or the model is requested to remain active while class members draw. While moving, the model may occupy the same space

190

as in a previous position, so that transparency must be assumed. We see one of these studies in Figure 191. Action is completely established through plastic means and in two dimensions.

The intellectual stimulus which provided the spark for the modern exploration of motion in two dimensions was provided partly by a new look at primitive work but chiefly through notions sifting into the European cultural stream from scientific investigation. Active particles were seen to penetrate matter, and the X-ray (note title of mystery) created a stir in the newspapers. In the early part of the century Albert Einstein's general and special theories of relativity excited the imagination. Instead of mass, velocity, and time possessing separate and absolute values, they were seen to be inseparably connected. Velocity and time entered into considerations of appearance, and even now debate goes on concerning the visual aspect of a cube under conditions outlined in Einstein's theory. The group of artists most keenly interested in the graphic implications of speed and time were the Italian futurists. They were not interested in the devices of motion for their own sake but as an expression of a rather complex philosophy, part of which involved the rejection of Italy's past. The futurist manifesto written in 1909 declared: "We want to free our country from the fetid gangrene of professors, archaeologists, guides, and antique shops."

In Giacomo Balla's "Dog on Leash" (Fig. 192), executed in 1912, the various parts are seen in all positions of their movement through a brief period of time. An essentially static profile is given the appearance of life. One can see this method in limited use in the art of ancient Egypt and in the drawings of such respected artists as Ghirlandaio in the 15th century and Van Dyck in the 17th. The device of multiple representation is also seen in most

Fig. 193 Panel from Krazy Kat *by George Herriman, using the multiple image. Copyright by King Features Syndicate.*

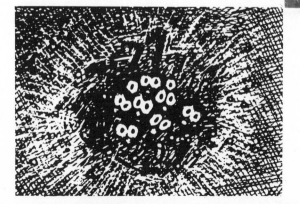

Fig. 194 "Nude Descending a Staircase (No. 2)" by Marcel Duchamp, executed in 1912. To cubist ideas on form analysis is added that of sequential development, suggesting a space-time continuum of four dimensions. Courtesy Philadelphia Museum of Art, Arensberg Collection.

Fig. 195 "States of Mind I: The Farewells" by Umberto Boccioni. The faceted form technique of the cubists and the multiple image method of futurism combined to communicate a mental image. Private collection, New York.

current comic strips. A rather famous example by Charles Dana Gibson showing a man shifting his gaze back and forth between two beautiful women was executed around 1900. We see another example of multiple imagery in Figure 193, a panel from the famous comic strip *Krazy Kat* by George Herriman. This panel illustrates Krazy Kat after a session with catnip tea. While he was an exceedingly clever artist, Herriman demonstrated that we do not necessarily have to possess fully matured skills in order to use graphic means of expressing motion. Herriman had a lot of interesting ideas and always seemed to use them simply and directly.

Perhaps the most famous picture to use composite views is Marcel Duchamp's "Nude Descending a Staircase (No. 2)" (Fig. 194). This work, executed in 1912, burst on the American art scene like a bomb. It was exhibited at the now famous Armory Show in 1913 and elicited a rich variety of unfavorable comment. The citizens who were so outraged had probably seen multiple imagery before but not in a salon. The picture was seen as unfaithful to nature, the kind of nature being of limited definition. It was known at that time that nature in microcosm is not static but in a perpetual state of energetic movement.

Here we see the form analysis of the cubists with structure reduced to planes, the assumption of transparency in the interpenetration of form, and the limitation of the spatial arena. Color was also very limited. Cubist works can often be likened to a screen, perpendicular to the line of vision, upon which planes are hung. However, in the Duchamp work there is a spatial continuum from front to back, with apparent size difference playing a part. It is essentially a cubist painting with a space-time countenance. The rhythm and change of pace in the structural development of this painting together with its monumentality, its inevitability, make this one of the very important paintings of the 20th century. A comparison with the Courbet work reveals some important differences between the centuries in which the works were done. More recently a stroboscopic photograph of a nude descending a staircase was made in order to illustrate Duchamp's approach. It does so in a way, but Duchamp's ideas embodied more than a graphic device. As in most fine art, the man transcends the means.

The futurists demonstrated a rather inordinate fondness for themes of force, strength, noise, action, violence, and revolution. They skillfully developed the means to identify these qualities, and although some examples contain more graphic bombast than is good for a work of art, their work should be studied very carefully to see how various kinds of action are communicated. One member of the futurist group, Umberto Boccioni, became interested in portraying states of mind. He executed a series of studies and finished paintings around 1911 in which mental images were given graphic form. One of these is seen in Figure 195. Using the devices of cubism together with the devices of motion illusion, Boccioni created an image typical of futurist tendencies. The fleeting, transitory forms merging and disappearing remind one of the flow of images in the stream of consciousness.

The pioneer work of Balla, Boccioni, and Duchamp excited others, and experiment in multiple imagery continues. Gyorgy Kepes and Herbert Bayer in creative work and teaching, along with Herbert Matter and Harold Edgerton in creative photography, are among those who have kept the idea alive in the United States.

the foggy outline When an object passes by the field of vision at high speed it registers

Fig. 196 a. Record album cover. Multiple forms in vague outline suggest swift movement. Courtesy Art Career School, New York City. b. Ad for an Italian gasoline. Forms are made to fade away by a gradual reduction in the value content. Courtesy AGIP Publicity Bureau, Rome.

193

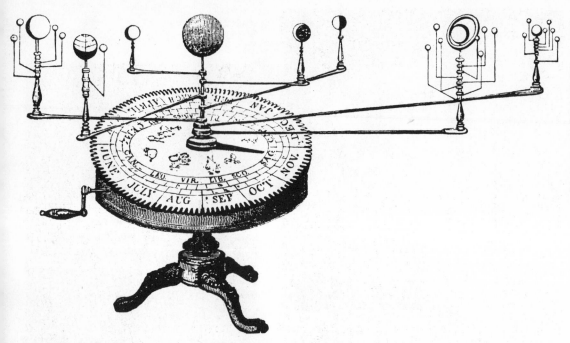

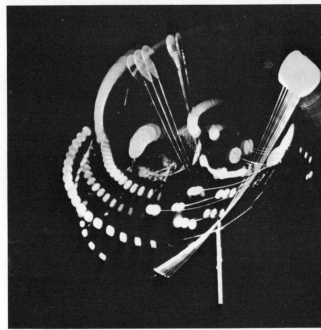

Fig. 197 a. *An orrery, a mechanism invented early in the 18th century to demonstrate the action of the solar system. From* Scientific Recreations. b. *Similar three-dimensional form, a mobile by Alexander Calder recorded in movement by stroboscope photograph. Courtesy Herbert Matter, Studio Associates, New York.*

as a kind of blur. At times this phenomenon is so marked that an individual is unable to identify the passing form. The graphic parallel to this visual phenomenon is an indistinct outline. Often this blur of contour is used on the back end of a moving form, a device seen so frequently that it has become a graphic cliché. This is no indication that the idea cannot be used well; we see the blurred contour used in a creative way in Figure 196a. This work makes use of multiple images in vague profile. In this kind of enterprise one can use a variety of tools: pencils, crayons, atomizers and spray paints. The photogram technique is also useful here.

The vague contour is used in a most appropriate context in Figure 196b, an ad for an Italian gasoline. A well-worn idea is given fresh meaning in this elegant expression of the quiet speed and precision of the modern

automobile. In marked contrast to much of the work of the futurists, the piece nevertheless exhibits its debt to them. Shapes fade away into the field through a gradual reduction of the value content.

new techniques in motion imagery

A stroboscope is an instrument designed to permit the observation of successive phases of an object in motion through periodic interruptions in the light source. The instrument, dating back to the end of the 19th century, allows a great number of photographic images to be recorded in a very short time. These sequential images reveal the structure of moving things. It is by now a quite familiar device in advertising. For a comparison between a static image and the dynamic quality of the sequential photograph, study Figures 197a and b. The mechanism pictured in 197a is an orrery, used in the 18th and 19th centuries to demonstrate the movements of the solar system. With 27 objects in ordered movement it must have provided a wonderful experience in motion. A similar kind of three-dimensional object, a mobile by Alexander Calder, is caught in the multiflash technique in 197b. Sometimes the light tracks the form in a continuous shape, while at other times the form is recorded in staccato images. It is clear that this technique is a valuable one to designers and scientists alike.

A cathode-ray oscilloscope may be used to obtain and record continuous patterns in an illusion of motion. Electric information fed into this instrument is translated into a continuous wave form. This gives the operator control over the patterns which will emerge. Figure 198a shows one of these moving forms in two dimensions. Ben F. Laposky has developed a method of converting these mathematically derived wave forms to color; a record combining several kinds of curves and three colors is quite impressive.

Long-exposure photographs permit the recording of light in movement. Light writing then becomes a creative technique. We have seen these long-exposure photographs which record the movement of automobile headlights and so on; now the light can be guided by a man's hand. Figure 198b shows one of these moving-light records. It will be noticed that the line varies in intensity, fading away when the light source is in the distance, accentuating the feeling of motion in depth.

Many devices have been developed to project moving light on a screen, some of them operated by a keyboard. These so-called color organs represent an extremely interesting area of further experimentation in color-motion phenomena.

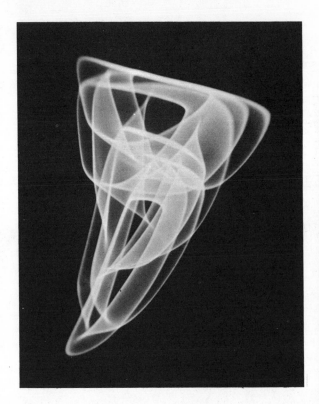

Fig. 198 a. Nonfigurative patterns derived from a cathode-ray oscilloscope. There is an illusion of continuous motion. Courtesy the artist, Ben F. Laposky. b. July 1953 ad for Gruen Lighting featuring the record of a moving light source. Less intense when farther away from the camera, the light source describes a pattern of motion in depth. Courtesy Gruen Lighting. Designer, Allen Porter; photographer, Marvin Rand.

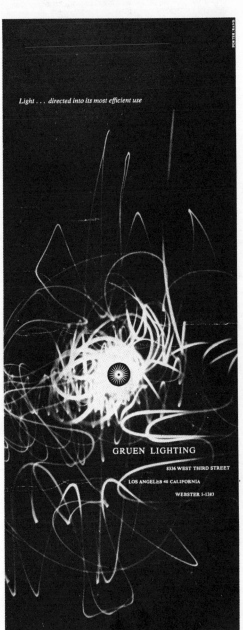

Light . . . directed into its most efficient use

GRUEN LIGHTING

8336 WEST THIRD STREET
LOS ANGELES 48 CALIFORNIA
WEBSTER 1-1383

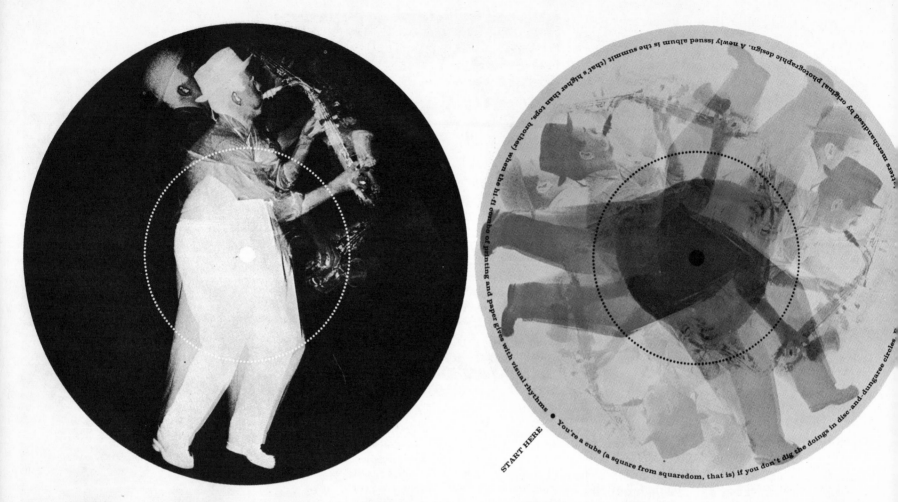

ROCK ROLL

Fig. 199 *Institutional advertising piece for the West Virginia Pulp and Paper Company. Superimposed sequential images arranged around an axis communicate a sense of spinning. Designed by Bradbury Thompson and photographed by Rollie Guild. Courtesy the designer and Westvaco.*

Photography of course permits the recording of either sequence images or the same image in repetition. We see the former usage in Figure 199, a piece designed by Bradbury Thompson. Here transparency is once again assumed. The cubist-futurist manifesto of simultaneity is expressed in a new way, with the superimposed images turning on an axis to communicate the idea of spin. We bring to the work a knowledge that records turn, which aids the illusion, but plastic means in this instance need little help.

suggestions for studio enterprise

A linoleum cut, simple in shape, can be printed by hand in sequential order. Color and value can be changed to augment the vitality of the total. A human figure in a dancing pose may be repeated. The environment will furnish the material for experiment—a frog, fish, falling leaf, or airplane are among the many organic or man-made forms which can serve as inspiration. Two linoleum cuts can express the notion of the flap of wings. Cut-out paper shapes, painted and printed, are an even simpler device. Or one may choose to express the function of a tool, as seen in Figure 200.

Found images can be laid out in spatial arrangements suggesting action, with drawn or printed forms assisting. Shifted stencil forms provide the means for sequential development and the idea of motion, or the example of the cave artist and Balla in endowing a static image with moving parts may be followed. Machine drawings can supply the basis for animation. The image of Charlie Chaplin caught in the production line may furnish an idea worth investigation.

When the cave artist printed his hand on the cave wall in multiple image, it was a symbol of his desire to maintain his identity in continued existence. A single print will not do; the continuity of life must be expressed, so he added more prints the next day. In this way the kinetic quality of life finds expression.

review

The idea of continuity has been expressed in two-dimensional graphic form from the time of the cave man to the present. Static views in two-dimensional work have been enforced from time to time. The idea of three-dimensional flux was to die out in 19th-century art and was expressed instead through science-inspired inventions which demonstrated perceptual phenomena. This kind of investigation led to the motion picture, which depends upon our ability to resolve static images into the sensation of continuous motion.

Scientific theories involving a space-time continuum laid the cultural ground work for the cubists and futurists. The latter, bound on the expression of motion, found the means to communicate it in a variety of ways but principally through sequential images. At the same time, in the early part of the century photographers were accomplishing the same ends through the stroboscope, an instrument which examines motion in sequence through the automatic control of interrupted light. Both techniques provide methods of exploring and recording the motion of life. Electronic equipment and long-exposure techniques are among the new methods used to express motion in two dimensions.

Techniques for the expression of motion center on the repeated image, which can be cut out of paper or carved in relief. A continuous line can also express movement, and silhouetted found images can create three-dimensional space through suggestion and size differential.

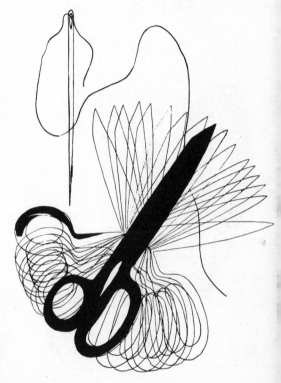

Fig. 200 A study explaining the function of a scissors. University of Wisconsin student project.

Georges Seurat: The Bridge at Courbevoie

Georges Seurat, the painter of "The Bridge at Courbevoie," was interested in the faithful interpretation of *local* color, the apparent color of surfaces. In his short life (1859-1891) he brought as much study and method to the problem of the interpretation of natural color phenomena through pigment as any painter in history. His palette was preserved, and revealed a row of hues in this order: yellow, orange, red, alizarin crimson, violet, blue, and green—an order which parallels the hues in the spectrum. Behind this was a row of the same hues mixed with white (to raise the *value* of the hue), and a third row consisted of pure whites. Seurat applied these hues in small dots of pigment, producing *optical mixtures* which rounded out a complete range of color effects. Thus his method approached the *additive* system of color arrangement in which two adjacent hues add their wavelengths to produce a third, often grayed, tone. In mixing red and green on the palette, each absorbs certain wavelengths from sunlight. Such mixtures are thus *subtractive*, and Seurat's method forbad such mixtures, as it also forbad the use of black (which is the absence of light and hue). In a method somewhat similar to Seurat's practices, the color effects in the full-color reproductions seen here are produced from tiny dots of three selected primary pigments: a red, a blue, and a yellow, with black added for form emphasis. Neither Seurat's method nor the method of color reproduction in printing is scientifically pure, but they may suggest studio projects in broken color for empirically-based learning.

Paul Gauguin, who created the work seen on the opposite page, is one of the modern pioneers in the use of arbitrary color—the departure from schemes based on natural appearances for the purposes of adding intensity to personal views. Van Gogh, Gauguin's contemporary and sometime companion, expressed the idea in this way: "Instead of trying to reproduce exactly what I have before my eyes, I use color more arbitrarily so as to express myself forcibly . . . " It is clear that in the Gauguin work reproduced here vestiges of *local* color remain. But the red represents Gauguin's method of obtaining a stronger reaction in the viewer. Gauguin's advice was, "If you like green, use a lot of it." With characteristic force he pushed the idea in canvases both brilliant and bizarre in color. In the Gauguin work echoes of *symbolic* color are seen in the blue and white garb of the spectators of and participants in the wrestling match. White has a long-established tradition of being symbolic of purity and innocence, while blue is also deeply embedded in the fabric of Christian symbolism.

In Picasso's work, local color has departed the scene to be replaced by a free play of striking complementaries, shielded and intensified by black. A Matisse influence in the checked patterns suggests Picasso's all-encompassing talent for the fusion and recreation of old and new ideas in color and form. This Picasso work is strong in terms of form, which indicates rather forcefully that the doctrine of arbitrary color is not a license for the undisciplined use of color in the name of art. While apparently achieving a greater freedom in the use of color than other contemporary artists, Picasso always attempts to communicate as well as to experiment.

Paul Gauguin: The Vision After the Sermon—Jacob Wrestling with the Angel

Pablo Picasso: Girl Before a Mirror

18 *color in action*

There have been many scientific studies on color, and a knowledge of them is necessary to our understanding of color phenomena. But most of what we need to know about color will come to us as we work. This empirically derived knowledge enables us to develop methods of using color suited to our personal needs. Figure 201 reminds us that it is on the working surface that color ideas are worked out.

There are many ways to represent a simple cube in color. Assuming that the cube has three facets, all that we are required to do is to make each different from the others. One hue will suffice, since the amount of pigment in each area can provide the differentiation. This would be called a monochromatic system of color modeling. In using light-valued colors, yellow, for example, very little contrast could be expected. A crimson would give more. The cube could also be pictured through the use of one color aided by black. This could give a maximum contrast in value, but would have less hue content. Furthermore, black actually alters hue content; black with yellow, for example, produces a drab green. One cannot expect to get a dark yellow by this means. Yet the darker-valued colors can be dropped in value with black and still keep considerable hue content. The cube could also be modeled with one color and white. In this case it is the darker-valued colors which may lose hue at lighter values. Low-valued hues made of dyes, however, retain considerable hue content when mixed with white. There are more of these colors available now, so that it is possible to paint at very high value and still retain color. Any modeling system using one color is a monochromatic system. Under ordinary conditions it tends to be dull, but in designing for machine reproduction a designer often has only black and one color to work with, in which case he must be especially ingenious in his design in terms of texture, boldness of shape, and sharp linear features. He would also have the white of the paper to work with but in order to make white a positive factor in the work, instead of acting as a passive field for the other elements, he must capture the white *inside* the shapes of black and color. In other words, the white of the paper has to be surrounded. This is a most important factor in designing for any print medium where the number of colors is limited. Studio practice should emphasize this. If black and a color are placed in a row there are only two colors active, but there are three if white is properly used.

complexity in local color

Now let us assume that the cube we are representing is made of smooth grainless wood and that we have all the hues available. It might be thought that one color could best represent a one-colored object, but this is not necessarily the case. Even if the designer is sticking faithfully to the *local* color of the cube (the color it appears to be) he still will employ a number of hues to represent it. He might use a basic mixture made up of red, yellow, black, and white but vary it, perhaps using some pigment on the red side. Others would go toward orange, while still others might tend toward a green or blue. This is not merely to obtain variety. It is in order, if we so wish, to be faithful in painting to the way objects look to us in the natural environment. Persons experienced in visual matters know that while a substance may appear a flat blue there

Fig. 201 (p. 198)   Rubbing from a painting showing the action patterns of the pigment. Author's sketch.

are probably other colors in it. Analysis through wavelength content reveals the truth of this. No substance outside a laboratory emanates a pure wavelength. To mix only one color for purposes of modeling our cube is to follow the technique of barn painters.

Then too, the local color of any object depends upon the hue quality of the light which falls upon it. A rather obvious example of this phenomenon occurs on winter evenings when there is snow on the ground. The light from the sun appears redder at evening because light travels through a thicker layer of atmosphere, which absorbs more of the nonred hues. When this light strikes one side of a snow ridge the snow will appear reddened, while the other side, receiving light from the blue sky, will look blue. This also happens in the home or studio where two light sources are contrasting. Ordinary light bulbs provide a light which is quite orange when contrasted to daylight, and designers try not to use the two lights in combination when they so conflict. Light from the sun changes color subtly through the day, and that is why designers prefer light from the northern blue sky. It is the most constant. Another interesting phenomenon is noticed when two different-colored light sources play on the same object and cast two shadows on a wall. Where the shadows do not overlap, they will be seen in two different colors.

local and arbitrary color

We can also represent the wooden cube by painting its facets with three entirely different hues—green, orange, and black, for instance. When we depart from *local* color we are using *arbitrary* color. The primary reason for this kind of departure is the increase in emotive power which these departures furnish without disturbing the illusion of form. To

quote Van Gogh: "Instead of trying to reproduce exactly what I have before my eyes, I use color more arbitrarily so as to express myself forcibly. . . ." The specific reasons for using arbitrary color vary with the personality and communicative intent of each artist and must be studied in the gallery. Few artists use monochromatic color arrangements except in informal wash drawings. The use of local color is seen in art chiefly from the Renaissance to the present. Pieter Brueghel's landscapes show this tendency, and of course it can be seen in the work of hundreds of other artists. There is no strict dividing line between those using local and those using arbitrary color. Gauguin is an example of a painter who combined the two. Arbitrary color is seen in the work from primitive cultures and in the modern art movement. Marc Chagall, for example, has painted a sky red, a man green, and a horse blue.

tonality

Supposing in addition to the cube we have a number of other objects to use in a design project. Let these include a purple cabbage, a vermilion hat, a green pepper, and a blue toy monkey. No doubt a fine picture could be made using the local color scheme. But there is no unity in the heterogeneous collection of objects and no unity in color either. It is possible to unify the illusion of such a group of objects through color. To do this it is necessary to depart from local color. We might build up a range of tones centering on blue and green, raising a few with white, shifting some toward green ochre, dropping one or two toward black, developing several grayed tones, and putting a touch of violet in a blue. These mixtures would give us enough value contrast to obtain strength in the modeling and yet keep the total color content unified. Color relation-

200

ships of this kind which are made up of a family group of hues are variously termed. "Harmonious" might be a good word, but it implies that there are certain color combinations which are satisfactory under all circumstances. We really mean that the colors are keyed together, and *tonality* is the best word for it. When we speak of the tonality of a painting we refer to the unity of its total color impact, and we can point out places where tonality is violated. In general it means that one color plays a major role in a work and that the various local colors are shifted toward this color. Sometimes when an artist chooses a limited number of colors for purposes of achieving unity, he is said to be using a limited palette. In the search for pure form (Figs. 112, 113, 114, pp. 102, 103) painters deliberately reduced color's exciting potential.

Another way of achieving tonality in a work is to depend on the transparency of the pigment. In this method our variegated set of forms can be roughly indicated with one transparent color, say a grayish brown. Then the modeling can be done with white. Various local colors can be suggested, and when the forms are built up sufficiently in dark and light, transparent washes or glazes can be brushed over the forms to give the whole a unifying tonality. The glazes sometimes center around one color. Words cannot adequately describe this method of achieving tonality. Besides furnishing a means to unity, transparent paint films have special optical qualities of luminosity and glow. For example, see the works of Rembrandt, El Greco, and other masters.

cool and warm colors

Colors are also said to be warm and cool. This quality is relative to the environment in which a color is found. Hues on the red-yellow side of the color wheel are designated hot or warm and those on the blue-green side of the wheel are said to be cool. Thus a purple which has a considerable quantity of red in it is a warm purple but if it is preponderately on the blue side it is cool. A green which is strongly yellow is also said to be warm, while a yellow which has blue in it is said to be cool, relative of course to a yellow which has red in its makeup. The communicative effect of warm and cool colors on the human creature is hard to evaluate. Cigarette manufacturers who wish to signify the cool quality of their product always use blues and greens, but perhaps this is in an associative context. Testing is difficult, because colors have to be presented in a shape and this is always a factor.

It is generally believed that in spatial illusion warm colors advance and cool colors recede. This means that if two objects of identical size are pictured as being equally distant from the viewer, the warm-colored one would seem to be in front of that in a cool color. The phenomenon can be tested by making a series of circles from left to right, identical in size. By attaching a stem to these forms they can be made into balloons. The field can be made a neutral gray. Various colors can then be placed on the balloons to see if some balloons seem to be in a forward position. The experiment can be varied with balloons of different sizes. There is certainly a difference in prominence, but whether it is caused by hue, cool content, or value is difficult to say. It is, however, a problem in designing with color. Sometimes a light blue will seem to leap off the surface. Keeping colors in their proper spatial plane is a concern. There are no rules to be written on it until we have more scientific data, so the designer must work on the problem as it occurs.

relationships in color

Color is a relative phenomenon. Absolute qualities in color can only be measured by machines under controlled conditions. Human beings cannot talk about absolute qualities in color because one color is never seen by itself —a color is always presented to us in association with at least one other. In speaking of color, then, we are in reality speaking of a relationship. Duality is the minimum. We have but to look about the room we are in to realize that this relationship is usually quite complex.

An orange-yellow combination is obviously different from one of orange-green or one of orange-black. This can be demonstrated by painting an orange square on each of five or six larger squares of different hues. The orange will be seen to change in hue and value, a phenomenon called color induction. A gray square will appear darker or lighter depending on whether its field is black or white. Visual acuity is dependent on hue combinations. Small print in green on a red ground is impossible to read and causes a disquieting dislocation in our perceptive processes. One color affects another in a dual relationship with a complexity which cannot be expressed in terms of one plus one.

In spite of accurate numbering systems, our terminology is incomplete and primitive in its capacity to refer to a single hue, let alone two in juxtaposition. This suggests that we humans are as creeping infants in our ability to discern, describe, and appreciate subtle relationships in color. We talk about colors one at a time. When an individual says "You look well in red," he is expressing a relationship good at the moment but subject to change. A number of environments can make a person look pretty bad in red. Because of the shifting properties of color, it is unlikely that any numbering system of colors will receive wide acceptance, since these systems are powerless to describe induction and other phenomena in color relationships. Suppose that a system were devised which designates a certain mixture as hue X, value 8. In one environment this combination may tend toward hue Y, value 7, while in another it may drift toward hue Z, value 9. Thus color systems designate colors one at a time, while the designer must learn to think in terms of color relationships. This he does as he progresses in his work, and books cannot teach it.

Artists become exceptionally sensitive to color relationships. The problem of getting colors to work together is the cause of much frustration. Ambroise Vollard, the man in Figure 110 (p. 101), told of the difficulties Cézanne had with the portrait. It required a hundred and fifteen sittings. "For one who has not seen him paint, it is difficult to imagine how slow and painful his progress was on certain days. In my portrait, there are two little spots of canvas on the hand which are not covered. I called Cézanne's attention to them. 'If the copy I'm making in the Louvre turns out well,' he replied, 'perhaps tomorrow I shall be able to find the exact tone to cover up those spots. Don't you see, Monsieur Vollard, that if I put something there by guesswork, I might have to paint the whole canvas over, starting from that point?' The prospect made me tremble."

Color relationships which please one person may not please another. Toward the end of his career Cézanne often found that raw canvas provided the proper tone for some passages. Max Weber, the distinguished American painter, relates that when Henri Rousseau, the primitive genius, saw such a passage in Cézanne's "The Bathers," he remarked, "Too bad he left so many places unfinished. I wish I had it in my studio, I could finish it nicely."

202

In order to understand color relationships as painters understand them, it is necessary to overcome a tendency to arrange colors according to the dictates of shape without regard to the external environments. To understand this, one might draw a sketch of a pitchfork in the margin of the book. The inexperienced painter will arrange colors so that they make logic in the interior of the shape, so that opposite ends match up in tone. But an experienced painter makes color adjustments between the pitchfork and the area adjacent to it. As this adjacent area changes in hue down the pitchfork, so may the tone on the pitchfork. The opposite ends may be represented by two quite different tones. This manner of color adjustment overcomes the false logic imposed by the shape. Unless a designer comes to think in these terms, his work may turn out to be a series of shapes which preserve their individual identity but which are unrelated in terms of color—in effect, a series of monochromatic studies in a single work. Since the design process involves color relationships it is best to establish tentative relationships all over the working surface at the very outset, unless, of course, white is to play a major role in the finished work, as it does in much advertising design. It does not matter so much what these original relationships are, but it is important that they be established. They suggest what is to be done next.

analysis of color use

As has been suggested, artists from less developed areas use the colors which the environment furnishes, and therefore their palettes are limited. Cave artists used earth colors and charcoal, primarily. It is interesting to surmise what some of these inventive artists would have done if they had had a full palette. We are indebted to Egbert Jacobson, the American scholar and designer, for some excellent studies on the color habits of painters who did have a full palette available. Jacobson's studies revealed that Giotto (1266-1366) used 9 adjacent colors on a 24-color wheel in one work. No colors from the opposite side of the wheel were used. El Greco (1541-1614) in the famous "View of Toledo" uses one half of the color wheel with the boundary colors a complementary pair. Many tones are grayed. In one work Rousseau also used half a color wheel from red around to green, a complementary pair. Gauguin, as might be expected, used almost all the colors in one of his works, with many complementaries emphasized. Here it should be noted that the complementary colors centering around red-green and blue-orange produce a clash when used in large areas and a neutralizing effect when used in areas the size of a brush stroke. In one still life Cézanne used adjacent colors from one third of the wheel and the complementaries from the opposite third. This suggests his grasp of the balancing and controlling action of complementaries. Van Gogh, too, considered the action of complementaries, saying, "There is no blue without yellow and orange." It is this kind of study which promises one day to answer some of the problems in communicating ideas through color. Jacobson's work already points to the possibility that artists are now able to handle more colors in a larger variety of ways than they once did. This does not mean, of course, that content is any better, for content depends on the man.

Certainly the modern movement has seen some fine colorists. Renoir's subtle color passages from one shape to another are masterful. Gauguin's color changes are often bizarre and exciting, while those of Braque are cool and elegant. Roualt reveals the somber power of black's role in color modulations, but Matisse often passes from one strong hue to another without an intervening neutral tone. Bonnard, Picasso, Munch, Soutine, and Kokoshka are a few of the artists who have contributed uniquely to ways of using color.

symbolic use of color

In the interest of providing a means of breaking down an exceedingly complex problem into smaller facets, it might be fruitful to think of the application of color as being directed toward three main ends: local color, arbitrary color, and symbolic color. We have discussed the first two. Very roughly speaking, arbitrary color was used widely before the Renaissance and is seen in the modern art movements. Symbolic color is important in religious art, and there is more of it before the Renaissance than after. In color symbolism, as we have noted, colors have assigned meanings. Thus the Virgin is always clothed in blue, and other colors have similar coded meanings in the Christian tradition.

After the Renaissance the church and the artists tended to go their separate ways for the most part, and symbolic use of color is not seen in secular works except where such meanings have become stable in the culture at large. In romantic paintings, death is a skeleton in a black hood. Courbet in "The Burial at Ornans" reflects color symbolism in the culture. Manet paints a wicked black cat in his "Olympia" which in that particular framework is powerfully suggestive. Rousseau in "War" paints the black horse of Revelation, and the rider's white shirt stems from the same source.

Symbolic color is rare in contemporary painting. It is rather more frequently used by designers who work for industry and business. It always signifies holidays where color plays a role—red and green for Christmas, and so on. In these cases the issue is forced, but a designer is glad to use an element which adds another layer of meaning to the work.

This section of the book has been designed to furnish a framework for long-range study of color. Such a study necessitates a good supply of color prints. Slides are unavoidably used, since the images they project are composed of colored light and differ greatly from pigment. Reproductions from magazines provide help, but they are usually distorted in color and size. The best way to study color is to see the real thing in a gallery; if this source is unavailable locally, plan trips to important galleries.

review

Since colors can never be presented singly, the designer is always concerned with relationships. Colors shift in hue and value relative to the hue and value of the surrounding color.

Local color is not the simple phenomenon it appears to be. Seemingly pure-colored objects reflect a variety of wavelengths, and many materials are minutely varied in color. Light sources vary, too. This necessitates the use of many tones in simple modeling.

Tonality in painting consists of unity through color selection, the limited palette, or glazing (a technique of applying thin transparent washes over light opaque paint).

In painting, adjacent areas are adjusted in color—a concept difficult to comprehend unless the tyranny of shape is overcome. Each color in a painting is part of a chain of events reaching all over the surface. Field shapes may not be neglected.

Complementary colors centering around red-green and blue-orange provide a way to powerful relationships when used in large areas and provide a neutralizing action when used in

brush-stroke sizes. The work of Egbert Jacobson suggests that artists have only recently become aware of the potential in these opposing sets of colors.

Color is primarily used in three ways: to pursue local color, arbitrarily, and symbolically. Artists use arbitrary color for personal reasons and symbolic color when a color has an assigned meaning. Symbolic color is rare in contemporary design and is chiefly found in advertising art. Arbitrary color is a mark of our own era.

205

Fig. 202   Beast of Revelation, from a 13th-century manuscript illumination. Mystically derived from contrasts with the world of sunlight and gravity to heighten sensation. From Il Libro delle Figure, *by Gioachino da Fiore, Torino, Italy, 1939.*

19   *images out of order*

"And I stood upon the sand of the sea, and saw a beast rise up out of the sea, having seven heads and ten horns, and upon his horns ten crowns, and upon his heads the name of blasphemy.

"And the beast which I saw was like unto a leopard, and his feet were as the feet of a bear, and his mouth as the mouth of a lion: and the dragon gave him his power, and his seat, and great authority.

"And I saw one of his heads as it were wounded to death; and his deadly wound was healed: and all the world wondered after the beast."

These lines from Revelation remind us that there is a world of the mind which assembles a kind of information different from that presented to us by our senses. Acting on a variety of other than visual stimuli, the mind formulates images in which the normal order of the environment is changed, with parts seen in new juxtaposition. When these visions are given graphic form, the comparison between them and the world of gravity and sunlight heightens sensations. In Figure 202, the beast of Revelation, environmental forms are reorganized to express meanings of mystical origin which pierce the logic of categories and produce new insight.

In a social order governed by logic, in which identical objects must have identical meanings, permeated with the statistical description of Newtonian physics and not yet struck by the random behavior of forces in microcosm, people have a tendency to hide experience which runs counter to the main trend.

Religion, the only activity which stems from a prelogical state of mind, is specifically exempted from the all-enveloping law which states that any experience which cannot be explained in logical terms is somehow corrupt. Superstition is admitted to by few. In general, in an area where scientific method has not yet prevailed, explanation goes back to prelogical terminology. Even the scientist may use the expression "It's in the lap of the gods" in regard to the progress of an experiment.

So there is an area of human experience untouched by categories of knowledge. In earlier history of the human race this area was much larger; it is currently much larger among primitive peoples than among those of older cultures. According to anthropologists, the reality in which primitive peoples move is itself mystical. Surface appearance means little to primitive peoples for they perceive objects according to their mystical properties. According to Lumholtz, the Huichol Indians believe that birds, especially eagles and hawks, hear everything. The same is true of their plumes, which the shaman uses in order to hear everything spoken to him from all points of the world and below it. A deer's tail is also plume, as is the deer itself. To the Huichol, the body of a deer, an eagle feather, corn, and the hikula plant possess the same mystical properties and are basically identical. Among primitive people, participation in this mystical world is complete. Tribal members insist that they *are* birds or aquatic animals. Thus an individual *is* a certain alive being, *is* a certain semihuman ancestor, *is* an animal closely identified with the tribe. In such a mystic world, art is born; and it is not surprising that graphic form is then concerned with meaning rather than with surface appearance. Writing on the Baining tribe, R. Parkinson remarks, "We find ourselves faced with a difficult problem. The Mitteilungen sees in these drawings serpents, and in fact there is something that recalls the head

and body of such; but the Baining affirm that they represent pigs. . . . The figure that follows might if necessary pass for a face, but according to the natives it represents a club, though it has not the remotest resemblance to such a thing. . . . We see how incorrect it is to interpret the ornamental decorations of a primitive people according to their resemblance to any object known to us. The Baining see in these conventional designs a shell, a leaf, a human form, etc. The idea is so firmly fixed in their minds that one can see the stupefied wonder on their faces when they are asked the meaning of these designs; they cannot conceive that anybody should fail to recognize at once the meaning of the decoration."

In Figure 203a we see an example of this private graphic language, a spirit configuration from the Iberian peninsula. Herbert Kuhn, authority on such rock paintings, thinks the image represents a rain spirit and forms his judgment on the probability that the comblike marks are rain in abstraction. In primitive works, forms are difficult to analyze for meaning because a single form does not always mean the same thing. From our background we assume that a symbol should have one meaning, but this assumption does not take into consideration the nature of the primitive mind. A certain form may mean absolutely nothing in one context, but seen in another, a sacred place, for example, may take on strong and definite meaning. Or a graphic form may have a number of meanings. Robert H. Lowie tested tribal motifs on Plains Indians and found as many as ten different interpretations within a tribe. Our esthetic standards are brought to bear on these works, and while the rock painting in Figure 203a is an excellent graphic statement, the earlier cave paintings receive more accolades because they are more like the Greek-Renaissance models.

Fig. 203 a. Rock painting of a spirit shape from the Iberian peninsula, first millennium B.C. An enigmatic form to us, clear in meaning to the people who made it. From Die Felsbilder Europas, by Herbert Kühn, Stuttgart, 1952. b. Paracas Indian embroidery from South America, circa 300 B.C.-A.D. 300. Supernatural beings, animal, and human life are in a connected plasm. Courtesy The Textile Museum, Washington, D.C.

In the Paracas mantle border, Figure 203b, we see only snatches of any kind of form which bears a resemblance to those of external, visual logic. In these mystic representations, however, we see in abstract graphic form the complex relationship among the deity, animals, and human existence. All are intimately connected.

It is this kind of reality, the reality of group belief, that shapes the imagery of the early periods in areas around the eastern Mediterranean. These are the areas which contribute most to our present state of civilization. During the period between 5000 B.C. and 500 B.C. the concept of reality changed. Man emerged from the mystic flux of his existence and gained a view of self as a distinct entity. Animals, vegetables, physical forces, and gods become more separated from each other. The concept of man as part of a group being waned, and man became important in his own right. Visual reality was recognized. These developments culminated in the savagely realistic Assyrian bas-reliefs and in the work of the Greek sculptors Phidias, Polyclitus, and Myron.

When the two concepts of reality meet in the same work, something curious happens. The work is neither fish nor fowl and is both believable and unbelievable. This is seen in the Egyptian deity Sekhmet, who has a man's body and a lion's head, an Assyrian deity with the body of a man and the head of an eagle, and the Greek centaur, half-man and half-horse. It can also be noted in surrealist painting.

The two kinds of reality existed side by side until the Renaissance, with the medieval period seeing a strong rejection of surface reality and a return to images of group belief. In an extreme form we have seen it in Figure 6 (p. 8), the enigmatic page from the Book of Kells, and much more of it can be found.

Roughly, the period between 1400 and 1900 saw the important artists interpreting their environment in terms of surface reality. Only occasional pieces defied the rule and exhibited the reality of irrationally derived images. Hieronymus Bosch (c. 1450-1516) was an exception and created great fantasies on the Last Judgment and other themes. His method combined surface realism with the images of humans, objects, and animals combined in a truly frightening way. The involvement and scale of his efforts prevent reproduction here, but he succeeded in creating a believable world of the damned, and no beginning artist should miss it.

When we are wholly involved in a world of mystic images there is no particular shock value to what we see. There is a kind of unity of treatment which makes smooth reading. Neither is there any particular shock in a unified work involving surface reality unless it treats events of horror. There is, however, impact in combining the two, as we see in Figure 204, a tree of affinity dating from 1490. Taken singly, the two images are quite innocent of emotion, but the combination communicates a wild sensation of horror. Whenever an object is ripped out of context and set in an environment foreign to it, our reaction is not complacent. It may result in a reaction of fear, surprise, amusement, or a combination of them.

One sees a tin can moving, and this unnatural phenomenon causes a sudden turn, hesitation, and perhaps apprehension until one observes a small creature moving about in the can. Or an ape is seen riding by in a Buick and a quick reaction of unbelief and wonder strikes suddenly. What is the meaning of it? Then this reaction turns to amusement on the thought that the animal is on his way to a television studio. A cat rips a doll and there is a sudden flash of emotion, a momentary tension in the real and imaginary image.

Francisco Goya (1746-1828) in Spain and William Blake (1757-1827) in England were two painters involved in mystic imagery. The former was often concerned with fantastic and sinister apparitions. His "Caprichos" is a powerful indictment of the society in which he lived. In his "Rain of Bulls" he shows the familiar object wrenched out of its natural environment. According to Elie Faure, when Goya's coffin was opened there were two skeletons in it.

We see one of Blake's works in Figure 205. Blake illustrated the Book of Job in 1825. The following lines from Chapter 14 reveal the kind of verbal image to which Blake responded.

8 And thou hast filled me with wrinkles, which is a witness against me: and my leanness rising up in me beareth witness to my face.
9 He teareth me in his wrath, who hateth me: he gnasheth upon me with his teeth; mine enemy sharpeneth his eyes upon me.
10 They have gaped upon me with their mouth; they have smitten me upon the cheek reproachfully; they have gathered themselves together against me.
11 God hath delivered me to the ungodly, and turned me over into the hands of the wicked.
12 I was at ease, but he hath broken me asunder: he hath also taken me by my neck, and shaken me to pieces, and set me up for his mark.
13 His archers compass me round about, he cleaveth my reins asunder, and doth not spare; he poureth out my gall upon the ground.

14 He breaketh me with breach upon breach; he runneth upon me like a giant.
15 I have sewed sackcloth upon my skin, and defiled my horn in the dust.

Essentially this is a return to the mystic image—certainly not a product of seen relationships. An intellectual mystic philosopher, Blake deliberately shocked and mystified those who sought close contact. He considered "copying nature" a waste of time. Nearly all of his work was related to literature. Often writers and graphic artists have a common interest in the imagery of insight. Blake himself was a man out of context, an inexplicable phenomenon in the polite circles of his time.

In the last several hundred years artists like Blake have been mutations in the art stream, cropping up for no apparent reason. Other artists who so appear are Odilon Redon (1842-1916) and Henri Rousseau (1844-1910), both unique. The former, knowing and subtle, created images shifting on the border of reality and mystery. Redon was at his best in the intaglio medium. Rousseau, a kind of gifted primitive, disregarded the spatial clue of aerial

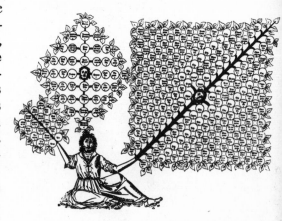

Fig. 204 "Tree of Affinity" by Crispus Joannes de Montibus, in the book Repetitio Tituli de Heredibus, *Venice, 1490. Shock created by two images joined out of context. From* Alphabets and Ornaments, *op. cit.*

Fig. 205 William Blake's illustration for Chapter 16 of the Book of Job, a temporary return to the truth of mystic imagery. Courtesy Ernest Benn, Ltd., London.

Fig. 206 "Washington Laying Down His Commission," Edwin H. Blashfield. Washington and Greek mythology are seen in strange mixture. From a mural in the Baltimore Courthouse, Maryland. Photo by the Hughes Company, Baltimore.

Fig. 207 March Hare and the Hatter stuff the Dormouse into a teapot. From Alice's Adventures in Wonderland by Lewis Carroll, illustrated by John Tenniel.

perspective and the painting technique of his day and made strange pictures of jungle life. His "Sleeping Gypsy" is a masterpiece.

The 19th century itself was strangely contradictory. It saw so many fine artists creating a plenty in the midst of the squalor of popular taste that the combined image is indeed surreal. At times, in reaching for symbolism, there was produced a work which unintentionally mixed images. We see such a work in Figure 206, a mural by Edwin H. Blashfield. Here George Washington is whisked out of the environment of command with its masculine texture and planted among a group of models acting the roles of Greek mythology as in a poor play. We can imagine Washington thinking, "Who am I? What am I doing here? What does it all mean?"

Another out-of-key event in the 19th century was the appearance of *Alice's Adventures in Wonderland*, in 1865, followed by *Through the Looking Glass* six years later. These were written by Charles Lutwidge Dodgson, who used the name Lewis Carroll. The imagery contained in these works makes use of the

210

deliberate juxtaposition of disconnected phenomena, the double meanings and elastic time concepts which are principal planks in the surrealist platform. And in Carroll's work we find passages which anticipate the ludicrous and destructive dada imagery. In the chapter entitled "A Mad Tea-Party" there is a conversation about a watch which would please any dada partisan:

"Two days wrong!" sighed the Hatter. "I told you butter wouldn't suit the works!" he added, looking angrily at the March Hare.

"It was the best butter," the March Hare meekly replied.

"Yes, but some crumbs must have got in as well," the Hatter grumbled. "You shouldn't have put it in with the bread knife."

The March Hare took the watch and looked at it gloomily; then he dipped it into his cup of tea. . . ."

Dodgson himself possessed a double identity. He not only wrote these memorable books but made his living as a lecturer in mathematics. As a mathematician he was good though not great, but he was thoroughly acquainted with the principles of logic and brought this knowledge to bear in the composition of logic's opposite.

Notice the strange juxtaposition of images in these excerpts from a poem in *Through the Looking Glass:*

But I was thinking of a plan
    To dye one's whiskers green
And always use so large a fan
    That they could not be seen.

His accents mild took up the tale:
    He said, "I go my ways,
And when I find a mountain-rill,
    I set it in a blaze;

He said, "I hunt for haddock's eyes
    Among the heather bright,
And work them into waistcoat buttons
    In the silent night.

Dodgson's books contain many phenomena pictured in modern surrealist imagery—the snapdragon-fly with burning head, for example. Figure 207 shows the March Hare and the Hatter stuffing the Dormouse into the teapot.

modern movements

The great forerunners of the formal movements in inverted imagery were Paul Klee, born in 1879; Marc Chagall, born in 1887; Marcel Duchamp, born in 1887; and Giorgio di Chirico, born in 1888. Klee had gained control of the mystical image by 1905, and thereafter for 35 years pursued the meaning behind surface appearances in every conceivable technique. We have seen several of his works in other connections. Chagall's dreamland, rich in arbitrary color, is intensely human. It is also intensely religious, partaking of the flavor of Gothic illumination. For Chagall, gravity is absent, as in a dream, and his space is peopled by gently floating animal and human forms. In an echo of folklore a cow plays a violin. The gentle quality of Chagall's Russian-Jewish poetic vision is touching.

Di Chirico in 1915 began a phase of work which he termed metaphysical. In this new world which he creates, sculptured figures are seen with pieces of solid geometry for heads. These are frozen in a framework of solemn architecture. In this world there is no sign of life except perhaps for the waving of tiny flags indicating the flow of a relentless wind. Often a train is seen in the far distance, emitting puffs of white smoke. The pictures which di Chirico painted during this short period are monumental.

Duchamp, having contributed much to our ability to grasp a dynamic environment in two dimensions, turned away from this conception and contemplated a complete overhaul of artistic methods of representation. This meant discarding all preconceived ideas and historical models of what art should be. It led to Duchamp's attack on art itself, which he implemented with satirical caricatures or brutal travesties on art tradition, finally culminating in his exhibition of a porcelain plumbing fixture.

The dada movement itself, which Duchamp's ideas helped to found, was started in Zurich by Tristan Tzara and other Russian refugees in 1916. Dada was a protest against the absurdity of a civilization then at war. Branches of dada sprang up in Germany, and there was one in New York, but the main center was Paris. The program of ridicule the dadaists set about to implement included the ridicule of all images, of all art. Our early freelance work in the dada idiom included "mustache painting." This term includes all forms of defacement of the human image, the addition of glasses, whiskers, and so on, in dada terminology.

The photography of Man Ray, the inventions of Francis Picabia, the collages of Kurt Schwitters, and the typography of Tzara attest to the inventive tendencies of the dada group, but in idea dada was self-defeating. As Tzara declared, "The true Dadaist is against Dada."

A group of dadaists with a program began surrealism. André Breton, a poet who had disagreed with Tzara, wrote the Surrealist Manifesto in 1924. Surrealism means the reality beyond surface. The surrealists were acquainted with the work of Sigmund Freud and set out to establish the validity of subconscious revelations. The movement in essence returned to the system of meaning formation found in primitive man, with the phenomena of coincidence given precedence over cause-and-effect logic. This mystic interpretation of life gave the surrealists new freedom of imagery, which

211

they proposed to use against man's oppressors: family, church, fatherland, and boss. It hardly turned out that way, however, as some of the surrealists became allies of industrial management and others exploited the method to become principal stockholders.

Max Ernst, German-born (1891), was the founder of the dada group in Cologne. A master of both collage and oil technique (he was self-taught in both), Ernst combined a fertile imagination with keen insight to create works of great power. We see one of his works in Figure 208. It is made of old engravings cut up and altered to suit his purposes. A parallel between this graphic work and literature is found in these lines from the Maori of New Zealand:

> Yes, from the Sky-God thou art,
> From the vast and lofty Rangi;
> From Tane, too, and Paia,
> Who raised on high the firmament
> At the separation of Heaven and Earth.
> From the very elements, the Winds
> The whistling, whirling Winds of Heaven,
> The bright flashing Lightning
> And the rumbling, loudly crashing Thunder.

The surrealists originally outraged society, but now we see their method used daily, broadening the avenues of communication. It is seen in the ballet, in stage settings, in store-window displays, at amusement parks, and in motion pictures, where the Marx brothers contributed notable footage in "A Day at the Races" and other films. Surrealist principles are also used in advertising, as can be seen in Figure 209, an institutional poster for the London subway, one of a series of posters in perhaps the longest unbroken line of advertising in the world. Here we see a shape which communicates a double meaning—the graphic pun employed by Giuseppe Arcimboldo in the 16th century, seen in the "transformation" playing cards of the

19th century, and reinvestigated by Salvador Dali in the 20th. The potential of the idea is readily discernible.

ideas for personal expression

With the primitive mentality suggesting that every environmental form is charged with meaning, with Freudian psychology suggesting the same thing, and with historical precedent suggesting graphic means, our ability to crack the boundaries between seen and unseen meanings is increased. Should a lady be likened to a flower, she can be so pictured. Is an enemy seen as a rat gnawing at the structure of society? What better than to put the idea in graphic form? Is a friend a talking machine? It's been done before, but it's still good. And if an acquaintance repeats himself like wallpaper, the graphic image is obvious.

Old engravings provide a source for experimentation in collage techniques, especially as

they provide the sensation of surface reality which, when intruded upon by or connected to disengaged forms from another environmental context, enhances emotional impact. Size and spatial texture can be carefully controlled to support the structure of belief, since the surrealist idiom does not depend on new methods of representation but on disguising the old. The effect of distortion in apparent relative size can be seen in Figure 210, a collage of old engravings. Similar effects may be obtained by a dislocation in other spatial clues.

Newspapers and magazines provide another ready source for the collage. These exhibit the face of society in a hundred and one facets, and combinations thereof can communicate order, chaos, tragedy, and humor in any order the designer requires. Two such collages can be observed in Figures 211a and b. In the former, grim reality enhanced by an empathic fear of falling is crossed with grisly humor as we see the sweet old ladies throw their secret

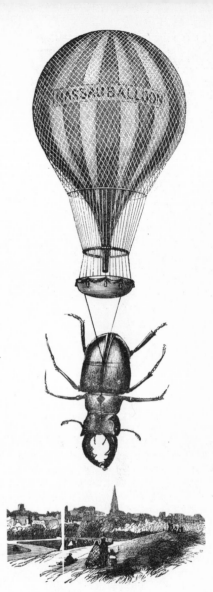

Fig. 210 Collage of old engravings in which normal size relationships are purposely distorted. Author's sketch.

Fig. 211 a. Found images tell a story with overlapping overtones of horror and humor. b. Human need, luxurious living, and indifference summarized in a collage of found images. Both from University of Wisconsin studios.

213

enemy over the balustrade. Hands clutch to catch. How did it turn out? See tomorrow's issue. In Figure 211b we see images of humanity in want juxtaposed with those signifying luxury, with the representations of indifferent officialdom surveying the scene in apprehension and contempt. Here one graphic image summarizes a tract.

As many an amateur photographer has found to his dismay, the doubly exposed negative may combine the forms of the environment in the manner of an hallucination. Ghostly dogs may haunt buildings, and human beings swim through fields of wheat. Combined negatives provide a means of exploring hidden meanings, as Figure 212 illustrates. Here the apprehensive eye of the young woman combined with the deep space provided by the arches in linear perspective which suggest memory, together with the persistent and everlasting qualities provided by the sea in motion, form a poetic image of one seeing into the dim recesses of past time.

review

Primitive peoples organize the environment in terms of meaning dictated by belief rather than in categories according to appearance. Thus to the Huichol Indians corn, deer, the hikula plant, and an eagle feather are basically the same. In a gradual development culminating in classical Greece, man separated the environment into discrete categories according to function and appearance. Art follows this mode of thinking.

At times in history the two manners of organizing the environment are combined in the same work, as in the sculptures of centaurs.

During medieval times the two modes of thinking lived side by side, but surface appearance was less important and images of belief were in the majority.

After 1400 the logic of visual truth was the main concern, but from time to time there cropped up artists less concerned with surface truth. Among these are Bosch, Goya, Blake, Redon, and Rousseau. After the turn of the century Klee, Chagall, and di Chirico continued the use of the illogical image and presaged organized movements. Such movements were organized originally by poets in 1916 and soon attracted graphic and plastic artists. Dada was nihilistic in idea and collapsed for lack of program. It was followed by surrealism. The manifesto for the surrealist movement was written by André Breton, a literary man, in 1924, and a host of talented artists were attracted to its imagery. Freud's work was an influence.

Surrealist imagery is now seen in ballet, in stage design, in window display, in moving pictures, and in advertising design.

Studio work centers on the collage, with old engravings and images from newspapers and magazines furnishing the raw material for expressing unseen meanings.

Fig. 212 Photographic montage made by combining different negatives. Courtesy Val Telberg, New York City.

glossary

arbitrary color Color not based on natural appearance

calligraphy Lettering style based on strokes from a distinctive instrument; painting style based on it

chiaroscuro Development of a form through use of light and shadow

coded symbol A mark carrying an agreed meaning for a group

collage Combination of pasted images

color induction Apparent change in hue or value caused by a changing environment

cubism Early 20th-century technique moving toward a planular simplification of form

cursive Tending toward writing, used of letter forms

dada A 1920 European art movement attacking society and art through destruction of held concepts

encaustic Painting with beeswax as a medium

field Background of any art work

fresco A method of painting on wet plaster

futurism Early 20th-century Italian art movement protesting social order and developing imagery of motion

glaze Pigment applied transparently

ground plane That part of an illusionistic work derived from the plane of the terrain

halftone Photomechanical reproduction of graduated values

hue One of a number of distinctive colors. Primary hues are red, yellow, blue; secondary hues are derived from combinations of primary ones

iconography Meanings and derivations of illusionistic material

ikon Image invested with special religious or magical significance

intensity (in color) Saturation $\times$ power of light source

interpenetration In illusionistic practice, two forms crossing and preserving identity

lithography Originally drawing on and printing from stone plates; now also photomechanical process using metal plates

local color In painting, color based on appearance

luminosity The appearance of pigmented surfaces as determined by the transparency of the paint film and strength of light source

marriage of contour Two forms using a common edge

modeling Creating an illusion of solid form by manipulating graded lights and darks

monocular clue A phenomenon of perception establishing space, size, and distance in the natural environment and in illusionistic practice

montage Combination of photographic, or other, images

multiple imagery Illusions centering on communicating motion

negative space Spaces or shapes between images of prime interest

overlap Monocular clue in illusion in which space is explained by the placement of one object or shape in front of another

perspective, aerial Monocular clue by which objects at a distance appear less sharp because of particles in the air and light scattering

perspective, linear A special case of the monocular clue of apparent size difference, used mainly in illusion in describing objects with straight edges

photogram Photographic process in which objects placed on a photographic plate leave their images after light exposure

pictograph Abstract depiction of environmental object

picture plane Physically, the working surface of a flat work; psychologically, the window of space illusion

printing, intaglio Printing process in which ink lies below the surface of the plate

printing, planographic Printing process in which ink lies on the surface of the plate: lithography, collotype, serigraphy

printing, relief Printing methods in which the ink lies on raised surfaces as in a fingerprint

resist A substance which repels a selected pigment medium

sans serif Lacking characteristic roman stroke endings, used of letter forms

saturation Quality of a hue depending on the amount of pigment in any sample

serigraphy Printing process using a stencil and silk screen

shade A hue as changed by black

surrealism Movement of painters and writers devoted to the juxtaposition of nonlogically connected images

texture In illusion, the composition of varied surfaces

tint A hue as changed by white

tonality In color illusion, a color scheme unified through the domination of one or two hues

transparency In illusion, the use of transparent materials or the assumption that objects or shapes are transparent

value A quality in illusion referring to the position in the scale from white to black

index